# THE FRIGHTFEST GUIDE TO GHOST MOVIES

First published by FAB Press, August 2018.

FAB Press Ltd.
2 Farleigh, Ramsden Road, Godalming
Surrey, GU7 1QE, England, U.K.

www.fabpress.com



Layout by Kevin Coward and Harvey Fenton.
FrightFest Guide original design by Harvey Fenton.
Film cast and crew credits, additional research and index by Francis Brewster.
Special thanks to Alan Jones and the FrightFest image archive.


Acknowledgement for visual material is due to the following organisations and individuals:
42/Fire Axe Pictures, 101 Films, A&E, Action 5, Admiral Pictures, After Dark Films, Alameda Films S.A., Alliance Films, Allied Artists, Almi Pictures, Amblin Entertainment, American International Pictures, American Zoetrope Productions, Amicus Productions, Anglo Amalgamated Film Distributors, AP International, Applause Pictures, Argyle Enterprises, ARTE, Astor Pictures, Avco Embassy Pictures, AVO Film, AXN, BBC, BEF, BFI, BH Productions, Black Rhino Productions, Bona Film Group, British National Films, BVG Films, Canal+, Castelao Productions, Catalyst Global Media, CBS Films, Chesterfield Motion Pictures, CIC, Cine2000, Cinema Group, Cinema Service, Cinematografica Emmeci Productions, Classic Film Industries, Columbia Pictures, Continental Distributing, Cross Creek Pictures, C.V. Kumar Productions, Dan Curtis Productions, DAR Motion Pictures, Dark Castle Entertainment, Dark Sky Films, Dimension Films, Dimension Home Video, Dimension Pictures, Discovery Films, Distant Horizon, Dongyang Hongjing Film & Television Culture Co., Dreamworks Pictures, The Dude Designs, Eagle Films, Eagle-Lion Film A/S, Ealing Studios, ECO Films S.A., Eden Ltd., Empire Pictures, Entertainment Discoveries Inc., Eureka!, Eurocine Films, Evergreen Media Group, Exclusive Media Group, Fetter Productions, Film4, Filmax Entertainment, Film Factory Entertainment, Five Star Productions, Fox International Productions, Futuramic Releasing Organization, Future Films, Gaia Film Distribution, Geneon, Genmaker Ltd., Ghost House Pictures, Glass Eye Pix, Golden Harvest, Golden Village, Grath H. Drabinksy Productions, Grenadier Films, Hammer Films, Hangzhou Herun Film Co., Harvey Entertainment Company, Haunter (Copperheart) Productions, Haut Et Court, Hemdale, Hispano Fox Film, Hollywood Pictures, Howard Mahler Films, ICAA, ICIC, ICO, IFC Midnight, Ikiru Films, Imagemovers, Invincible Pictures, J. Arthur Rank, Javelin Pictures, Just Films, Kudos Films, Lion International, Lionsgate, Loew's Inc., London Films, Magnolia Home Entertainment, Mandalay Pictures, MediaCorp Raintree Pictures, Mediafilm, Metro-Goldwyn-Mayer, Metro Pictures, Metro Tartan Entertainment, Midfield Films, Millennium Pictures, MOD Producciones, Monogram Releasing, MPI Media Group, New Century Entertainment, New Line Cinema, New Zealand Film Commission, Optimum Releasing, Orion Pictures, Palace Productions, Panik Professional Films Inc., Paragon Arts International, Paramount Pictures, Park Films, Pathe Pictures, P.E.A. Films, PolyGram Filmed Entertainment, Post-Art Design, Producciones Tauro Films S.A., The Producer Circle Co., Propaganda Films, Quartet/Films Incorporated, Raintree Pictures, Rank Film Distributors, Regia Films, RKO Radio Pictures, Safran Company, Satya Films Private Ltd., Screen Yorkshire, Selecta Vision, Semi-Professional Pictures, Shaw Brothers, SLM Entertainment Ltd., SODA, Spyglass Entertainment, Summit Entertainment, Think Studio, Thiru Kumaran Entertainments, Toho, Traveling Picture Show Company, Treasure Entertainment, Tri-Star Pictures, Turbo Productions, TVE, Twentieth Century-Fox, Two Cities Film, The UK Film Council, Union Films, United Artists, Universal City Studios Inc., Universal Pictures, U.T.A. Theatrical Accessories Distribution, Video Tape Center, Videovision Entertainment, Vision p.d.g., Walt Disney Pictures, Warner Bros., Warp Films, Well Go USA Entertainment, Western Edge Pictures, Wild Bunch, Wingnut Films, Woolner Brothers, Zentropa.

Front cover illustration:
Key art for The Fog (1980).
Frontispiece illustration:
Key art for Sleepy Hollow (1999).

Printed in the Czech Republic.

A CIP catalogue record for this book is available from the British Library.

hardcover: ISBN 978 1 903254 96 7

paperback: ISBN 978 1 903254 97 4

-THE DARK HEART OF CINEMA-

# FRIGHTFEST® GUIDE

# GHOST MOVIES

Axelle Carolyn

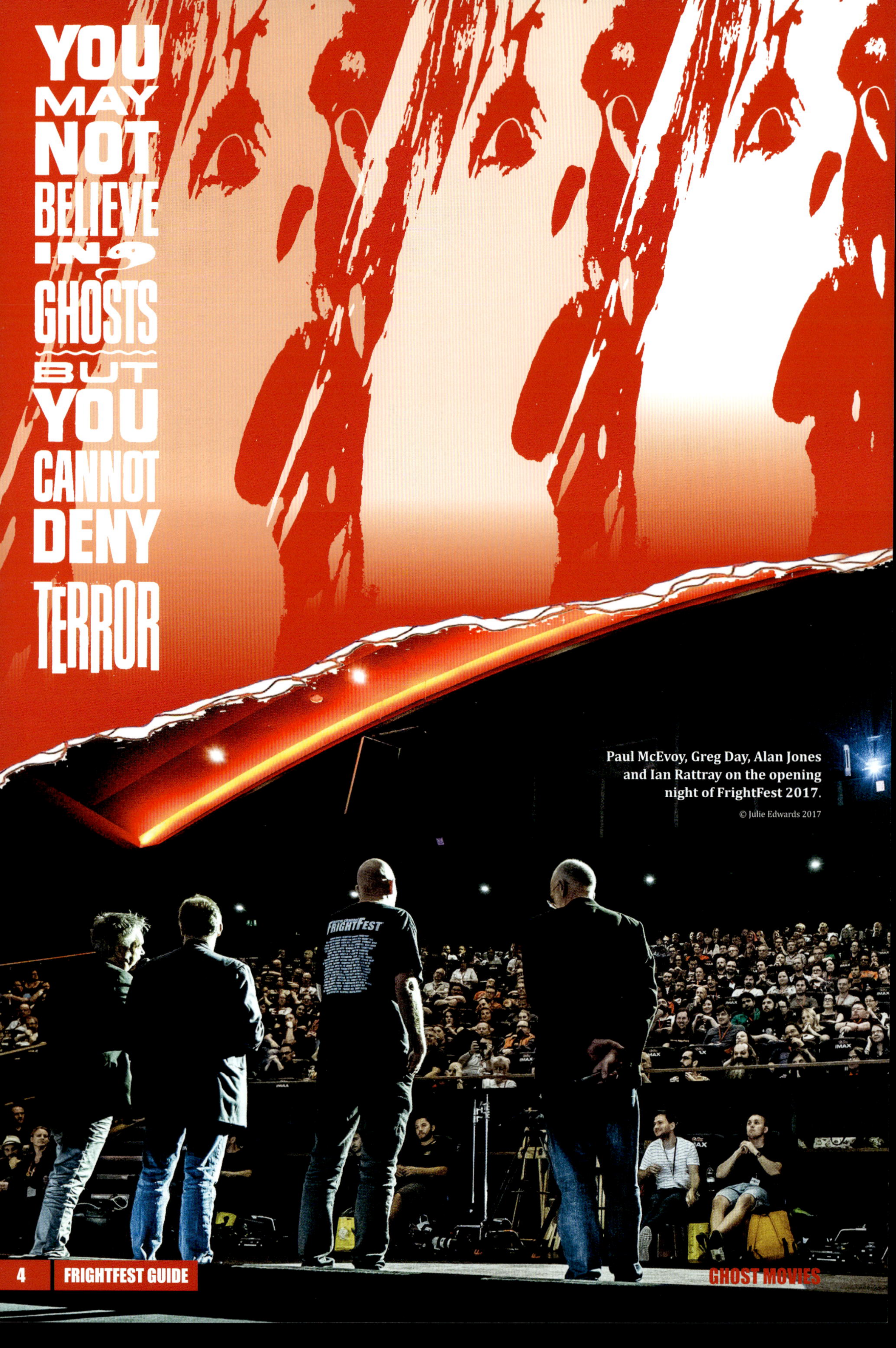


Paul McEvoy, Greg Day, Alan Jones and Ian Rattray on the opening night of FrightFest 2017.

## - THE DARK HEART OF CINEMA -

# FRIGHTFEST®

What would any horror film festival be without the staple ghost story? Throughout its nineteen years of programming the best the genre can offer at its three hugely anticipated yearly mega-events (as part of the Glasgow Film Festival in Scotland, in London every late August Bank Holiday and its Halloween Shocktoberfest) FrightFest, the United Kingdom's biggest, best and most prestigious all-round fantasy festival has featured a ton of creepy spooktaculars, nerve-jangling scare-fests, boo-tiful ghoul-aramas and myriad haunted houses of horror.

FrightFest being an eclectic festival, throughout our hair-raising, thrill-packed years, we've premiered everything from **Ghost of Mae Nak** (2005) and **The Disappeared** (2008) to **The Innkeepers** (2011), **Paranormal Activity** (2007) and **Insidious** (2010). We all, at sometime or another, question the possibility of an after-life and a good campfire tale can often answer both our hopes and fears. Ghosts appear in **The Innocents** (1961), **Poltergeist** (1982) and **Beetlejuice** (1988) but they're in completely different categories. And sometimes of course the best ghost stories aren't the scariest movies, just great family-friendly fun; watch **The Ghost and Mrs. Muir** (1947), **Ghostbusters** (1984, the good one!) and **ParaNorman** (2012) for proof. Which means the supernatural and things-that-go-bump-in-the-night have an even further range and longer reach into our lives than practically any other genre.

For the third FrightFest Guide, clearly needed following the wild success of *The FrightFest Guide to Exploitation Movies* by Alan Jones and *The FrightFest Guide to Monster Movies* by Michael Gingold, we wanted an author who knew the ghoulish genre inside out. And who better than writer/director Axelle Carolyn, who has helmed an atmospheric bone-chiller herself (**Soulmate**, a Halloween FrightFest 2013 attraction) and as you will read is well-versed in all things weird, wicked and witchy and knows what qualifies as a proper ghost movie.

Another must-have volume to add to your growing collection of a book series intended to build the knowledge of the curious spectator and cult connoisseur alike – the same maxim with which we meticulously produce our annual events that are globally famous and used by the international film industry as a litmus test for the future of the horror genre. And don't forget, FrightFest is not just a film festival or the friendliest community you could ever wish to join, it's an ever-increasing brand including our FrightFest Presents multi-platform entertainment label.

**~ Alan Jones, FrightFest co-director**

# AXELLE CAROLYN

A lifelong horror fan, Axelle Carolyn was brought up on a steady diet of ghost stories and Stephen King novels. She decided at a young age to embark in a career in film, but faced with the practical realities of having to move away from her native Belgium right after high school to pursue her dream, she followed her parents' advice instead, and went to Law School.

Soon after graduating however, she made the move to London and began contributing set reports and reviews to some of the most prestigious genre magazines and websites, including *Fangoria*, *SFX*, *IGN*, and *L'écran fantastique*. For the next few years, she covered festivals and shoots in locations as diverse as Prague for the first two **Hostel** films, Morocco for **The Hills Have Eyes** and its sequel, and Finland for the Lordi movie **Dark Floors**. Around the same time, she started penning screenplays, and sold her first script in 2005.

Axelle's first book, *It Lives Again! Horror Movies in the New Millennium* (Telos Publishing), a critical study of the early 2000s wave of horror, won the Silver Award in the Performing Arts category at *ForeWord* magazine's 2009 Book of the Year. Soon afterwards, her first fiction short stories started appearing in anthology books such as *Dark Delicacies III*, alongside tales by Clive Barker and Chuck Palahniuk, and the star-studded *Mammoth Book of Body Horror*.

After a brief stint in front of the cameras (most notably as a Pict archer alongside Michael Fassbender and Olga Kurylenko in Neil Marshall's 2010 release **Centurion**), Axelle directed her first short films in 2011. **The Last Post**, starring Jean Marsh, and **The Halloween Kid**, narrated by Derek Jacobi, both featured protagonists finding comfort in the supernatural and in the presence of ghosts. They screened at FrightFest, as well as dozens of other genre festivals, and can be found in the bonus features of the UK and U.S. DVD releases of **Soulmate**.

**Soulmate**, Axelle's first feature, was filmed in Wales in the fall of 2012. The story of a widow (Anna Walton, **Hellboy II: The Golden Army**) who moves to the countryside and encounters the spirit of her cottage's previous occupant (Tom Wisdom, **Dominion**), it opened FrightFest Halloween the following year before touring festivals around the world — including Sitges, the Leeds International Film Festival, SciFi London, and the Espoo International Film Festival. The movie collected a Best Director award from Rome's FantaFestival, as well as Best Screenplay at France's La Samain Fantastique, and a Best Actress accolade for Anna Walton at FantasPorto. This restrained Gothic romance is only available in the UK in a truncated version; the BBFC requiring 16 seconds of mandatory cuts to its opening sequence — a suicide attempt — in order to deliver a certificate. Of the movie, director James Watkins (**The Woman in Black**) was quoted saying: 'An intriguing ghost story that gave me tingles, chills and jolts. An auspicious debut.'

In 2015, after moving to the USA, Axelle created, co-produced and co-directed horror anthology **Tales of Halloween**, which included segments from directors Mike Mendez (**Big Ass Spider!** — also a producer), Lucky McKee (**May**, **The Woman**), Neil Marshall (**The Descent**, **Game of Thrones**), Adam Gierasch (**Night of the Demons**), Paul Solet (**Grace**), Dave Parker (**The Hills Run Red**), Ryan Schifrin (**Abominable**), Darren Lynn Bousman (**Saw II**) and Andrew Kasch and John Skipp. Axelle's own chapter, **Grim Grinning Ghost**, offers a tense supernatural chase building up to a jump scare. **Tales of Halloween** is Certified Fresh by Rotten Tomatoes, won Best Independent Film at the 2016 Rondo Awards and a 2017 Saturn Award. It was presented as the closing night movie of FrightFest 2015.

Axelle has served as an international jury member for several prestigious festivals, including Sitges (Spain), Neuchatel (Switzerland), Strasbourg (France) and Brussels (Belgium). As of 2018, she is a writer on Netflix and Warner Bros. series **Chilling Adventures of Sabrina**.

Axelle lives in Los Angeles with her best friend, canine movie star Anubis, who appeared in both her feature films.

Axelle Carolyn

© Jan-Michael Losada,

# INTRODUCTION BY ANDY NYMAN

We know how this starts.

You bought this book with the intention of reading it, not like all those other horror film books you have on your shelf. No, this one, this one you will actually read.

But before you do start at the beginning and properly read the whole book, you'll just check to see if your favourite film is listed. You'll find it, because the book is thorough. Then you'll read what Axelle has to say about it, and you'll mostly agree.

OK, *now* you'll start reading the book properl...... oh hang on, just before you do, you'll just check one other thing. Actually, now you've checked that, you'll have a look through all the pictures. Why not? You're alone, you can do what the hell you like and this is something to savour.

Aaah the pictures, we all secretly know that they're the best part of any book. That tingly excitement, wondering what the next page will have in store for you. A new book about a subject you love, the smell of the paper, so crisp and new. No one but you has ever seen this copy, your eyes will be the very first to gaze upon the images in this particular copy. Yes you like some of the trashy horrors, yes you like monsters and slashers and gore, but ghost stories, now that's special, that's different. Most of the pictures will be familiar, but maybe there's one that isn't. One that stirs something in you. Just one picture that has something about it that makes you go back to it and then stop for a second and stare at it. Really take it in. What film is that from? Why don't you know it, you're pretty scholarly with this stuff. So why don't I know this one? Why does the figure in the picture look so scared? Actually, why does he look so familiar and why does he seem to be pointing at you. No, not at you... behind you... ...almost as if he was trying to warn you. 'Behind you... don't turn around. Sssshhhhh, keep very still, it's still there.'

The first ghost story I can remember seeing was **The Fog**. It was also the first horror film I saw. I was 14 and it completely side-blinded me. I adore the film, but within its barnstorming pace were moments that I have now come to realise are, what make a ghost story really unique.

The words appearing on the driftwood in the film is a perfect example. In real terms it's a detail the narrative could do without, it doesn't hugely further the plot and yet... it is essential. For here is the point, a simple image and a moment that only exists to create discomfort. Within it is a sense that nature has a power. A power that we do not understand. It can control the weather, inanimate objects, and our very soul after we have departed. It is a super-nature, indeed the Supernatural.

Since my baptism with **The Fog**, I have adored ghost stories. That pure fear is why I watch horror films of all sorts, it is the feeling I most dread but most crave, it is why I return again and again to the genre. With the start of each new film that golden feeling... maybe this one!

When I think about the ghost stories I most love and the moments that have most affected me, it is a list I adore. The 'hand squeezing' in **The Haunting**, the face at the window in **The Innocents**, the dreaded climactic moments in the lift of **Dark Water**, the moment in bed during the TV version of **The Woman in Black**, pretty much every single frame of the BBC's **Ghost Stories for Christmas**. Then the moments that seem to have a foot in two camps, the ghost story and the traditional horror film, the girls finding **Mama** in their house, Hal Holbrook holding the cross in **The Fog**, that endless static shot of the bedroom in **Paranormal Activity**. Every moment one that chills, one that remains and one that haunts.

The Innocents

A ghost story cant just go 'BOO!', it has to really do something else, it has to make the hairs on the back of our necks stand up. They must reawaken arcane, long forgotten feelings that somehow can only be described by arcane, long forgotten words. They must disquiet & unnerve. Create foreboding, unease and fretfulness.

Dark Water

Axelle has a flair for horror. Her first beautiful book, *It Lives Again! Horror Movies in the New Millennium* became an essential look at how horror films had remained so popular and so important. Since then she has become a director in her own right, and a key player in the exciting LA independent horror scene. In this book, her expert gaze falls onto the history of ghost stories and a loving and critical look at the greatest ones ever made.

It will always be a personal journey, of course, after all we are all so different that the minutiae of what scares us is dependent on our life's experiences. But the broad strokes, the bedrock is universal: death of a loved one; unanswered questions; how and why life can be so unfair and so cruel. It's the same for all of us. Truly, one of the key ingredients of any great ghost story is vengeance. Like all great drama, for it to really hit home it has to be about something true, something that we can all connect to. After all, which of us hasn't wronged a fellow man, even in the tiniest of ways, without thinking of the consequences. The fallout from our actions can have consequences on our life and the lives of others, and everything can be changed in a heartbeat.

left: **The Woman in Black**

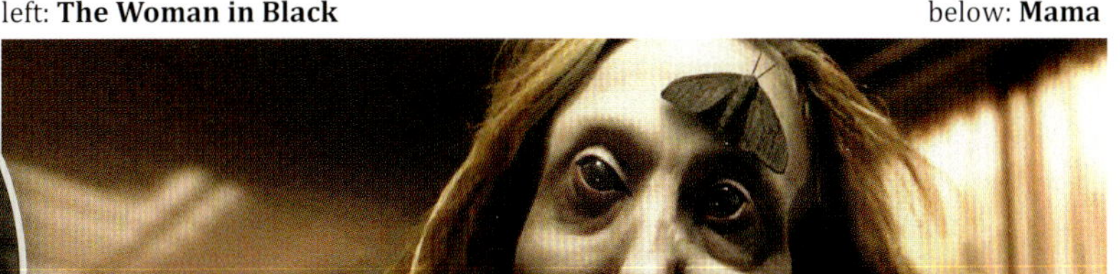

below: **Mama**

In this book Axelle deals with her own personal journey into the world of ghosts and what it is that strikes a chord with her. For myself and my writing/directing partner Jeremy Dyson, our fascination lead us to create **Ghost Stories**. It started life as a play that has now been performed all over the world and now, to use the language of my childhood, has become a 'major motion picture'. When writing and creating **Ghost Stories**, Jeremy and I explored our own lives, shone a light on our own histories and asked honestly and unflinchingly a dreaded question of ourselves '*what had we done wrong and what pain had that caused*'. It's the theme of our work and one that quickly leads down a path to deep regret and a sense of our own personal ghosts.

My quintessential ghost story moment is in Jonathan Miller's TV version of **Whistle and I'll Come to You**, for my money the scariest ghost story ever filmed, it never ceases to scare in the most sublime of ways. The suffocating cold sweat it creates is unmatchable. Indeed we pay homage to a couple of its moments within the **Ghost Stories** film. The moment in question is small, but is *everything*. Shortly after unwittingly invoking a spirit, our protagonist closes his eyes to attempt sleep. As he does an image comes to him, it is a horizon with the sun about to set. Silhouetted is a figure, it's tiny, almost too far away to see, but it is there, standing staring and still. The utter stillness tells you all you need to know, 'I am coming for you, I will not be diverted, we will meet and you will pay'. Therein lies the power of the ghost story, summed up to perfection by the tagline on the poster for **The Haunting** — 'You may not believe in ghosts, but you cannot deny terror'.

centre left: **Paranormal Activity**
centre right: **The Fog**
below: **Whistle and I'll Come to You**

Enjoy.

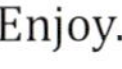

~ **Andy Nyman**

# FRIGHTFEST GUIDE

# GHOST MOVIES

# INTRODUCTION

## *What is a ghost?*

'In the dead of night, a noise [...] was often heard which, if you listened carefully, sounded like the rattling of chains. The noise would seem to be a distance away, but it would start moving closer... and closer... and closer. Immediately after this, a specter would appear in the form of an old man, emaciated and squalid, with bristling hair and a long beard, and rattling the chains on his hands and feet as he moved.' Interested in the house, yet weary of its low market price, visiting philosopher Athenodorus decided to spend a night in the building to figure out the mystery. Witnessing the apparition, he followed it to a part of the house where it disappeared without a trace. He then 'carefully marked the spot with a handful of leaves and grass. The following day, he asked a magistrate to have that spot dug up, and in that spot was found, intertwined with chains, the skeleton of a man. The bones were collected and buried [...] and after the ghost was thus duly laid, the house was haunted no more.'[1]

This story isn't the plot of the latest Hollywood remake, but the work of Roman lawyer and author Pliny the Younger (c.61—c.112 AD), in a letter to a wealthy and influential senator. Its similarities with modern tales, from the ghost appearing where its bones lay (most notably seen in **Poltergeist** and **The Legend of Hell House**), to the reduced price of the house (as in, say, **The Amityville Horror**), are striking. Arguably the longest-standing creatures in the horror pantheon, ghosts have haunted cultures worldwide throughout history, in shapes and ways that have remained remarkably consistent. Ancient Egyptians believed the dead could return if not properly buried and honoured; a story from the Ramessid Period (1186—1077 BCE), commonly known as 'Khonsemhab and the Ghost', speaks of the apparition of a man who no longer received offerings because his tomb had collapsed and no one remembered where he had been buried. Indian *bhoots* are restless souls wandering the earth due to a violent death, an unfinished task (remember **The Sixth Sense**?) or, again, improper funeral rites. Thai ghosts, or *phi*, are a fact of life, which few locals would dispute. The Chinese to this day celebrate the Ghost Festival on the fifteenth day of the seventh month of each year; a tradition originally created to honour and appease the dead. The Celtic belief that souls of the deceased roamed the earth and

*1.* Pliny The Younger, Letter to Licinius Sura, Book 7, Letter 27.

visited loved ones at the end of October, when the veil between this world and the next was at its thinnest, led to the celebration of Samhain, which eventually morphed into our modern-day Halloween. Harmful or benevolent, aimless or on a mission, ghosts, like death itself, have always been a part of life.

Closer to us, in the mid-nineteenth century, spiritism — the attempt to communicate with the spirits of the dead via mediums and séances — spread like wildfire through American and British high society in the wake of the American Civil War and the Crimean War. In a world obsessed with death, where so many grieved for loved ones lost in battle or from one of the many epidemics of the time, the thought of an afterlife and of the survival of the soul provided solace. This quest for comfort was often exploited by unscrupulous self-proclaimed psychics, who claimed to channel friends and family on the other side, or even to help them materialize before their sitters' eyes through ectoplasm, a substance exuding from the medium's body during séances, believed to be the very fabric of spirits. Some, such as the infamous Fox sisters of Hydesville, New York, rose to fame, often to be quickly exposed as frauds. Yet the popularity of spiritism kept growing, with various personalities publicly endorsing its practice. Sherlock Holmes author Arthur Conan Doyle, in his 1918 book *New Revelation*, wrote that spiritualism would soon be seen as a new religion: a revelation sent by God to bring solace to the bereaved. Doyle was also, along with fellow luminary Charles Dickens, a member of the Ghost Club, a London-based paranormal research organization that investigated hauntings; he later joined the Society for Psychical Research. Founded in 1882, the SPR described itself as 'the first scientific organization ever to examine claims of psychic and paranormal phenomena,'[2] and approached the matter through science-based methods, lending ghost hunting and séances a new legitimacy, while simultaneously exposing fraudulent mediums and psychics.

In the 1920s, after the death of his mother and subsequent failed attempts to contact her, Hungarian-American illusionist and escape artist Harry Houdini also turned his attentions to spiritualism. His avowed mission was to debunk the craze and reveal the most common methods used by phony mediums. 'Gladly would I embrace Spiritualism if it could prove its claims, but I am not willing to be deluded by the fraudulent impositions of so-called psychics, or accept as sacred reality any of the evidence that had been placed before me so far.'[3]

The Sixth Sense

*2.* https://www.spr.ac.uk/about-spr, retrieved April 2017.

*3.* A Magician Among The Spirits, Harry Houdini, preface, 1924.

Amongst the many purportedly paranormal phenomena he investigated was spirit photography, or the capture of ghosts in photographs. First engineered in the 1860s by Boston photographer William H. Mumler, who discovered its principle when accidentally double exposing a picture of his cousin onto a self portrait, creating the illusion of a phantom behind him, these efforts to create photographic ghosts mark the first time apparitions made their way onto film. Put on trial for fraud, Mumler was acquitted, as his accusers couldn't prove beyond doubt that his pictures were doctored. Decades later, Houdini demonstrated the technique, even manufacturing his own self-portrait next to the soul of the late Abraham Lincoln. Spirit photography remained a popular curiosity over the years and survives to this day, boosted by new technology, under the guise of ghost hunt recordings and alleged spirits caught on tape.

The spiritualist movement itself underwent another surge in the 1920s, spurred by the massive loss of lives from the First World War, then quickly faded away. Yet its indelible influence on the way ghosts are depicted in popular culture is undeniable, and it has directly inspired literature, then motion pictures, for the past 150 years.

Today's high society may no longer turn tables at tea parties, yet belief in the supernatural has hardly waned. A 2013 online study conducted by YouGov on behalf of the Association for Scientific Study of Anomalous Phenomena found that up to 52% of the British population believed 'some people [had] experienced ghosts (i.e. seen, heard, smelt or otherwise sensed the spirit of a deceased person or animal)'.[4] Polls regularly show that Americans are more likely to believe in ghosts than in man-made climate change. In a world where organized religion has lost its mass appeal, this intriguingly high percentage may be explained by the same urge which pushed spiritualists into the parlours of mediums: a need to believe in some form of afterlife, in a place where consciousness survives and loved ones can be reunited. There is comfort to be found in the existence of ghosts.

Given how long populations around the globe have believed in the supernatural, it is hardly surprising that storytelling, from folk tales to novels to motion pictures, have reflected this preoccupation. The United Kingdom and Japan in particular have shown strong dispositions towards ghost stories in literature.

In the UK, spirits notably appeared in the works of Shakespeare; the famous line from *Hamlet* — 'There are more things in heaven and earth, Horatio, than are dreamt of in your philosophy'[5] can be found quoted in movies from **Blithe Spirit** and **Dead of Night** to **Whistle and I'll Come to You**, evidencing its influence on the genre in every medium. Horace Walpole's *The Castle of Otranto* (1764), generally considered the world's first Gothic novel, also prominently features spooks.

But unsurprisingly, it is in the Victorian period that staples of the classic ghost story were established and that the genre flourished. Charles Dickens's *A Christmas Carol* has been adapted to the screen numerous times, while lesser-known short story *The Signal Man* is a subtler and more frightening tale of premonitory apparitions. Dickens's close friend Wilkie Collins contributed several stories to the genre, including his final novel *The Haunted Hotel*.

---

*4.* http://www.assap.ac.uk/newsite/Docs/Ghost%20UFO%20Survey%202013.pdf, retrieved April 2017.
*5.* Hamlet (1.5.167-8)

Ghost of Yotsuya (1959)

The Shining

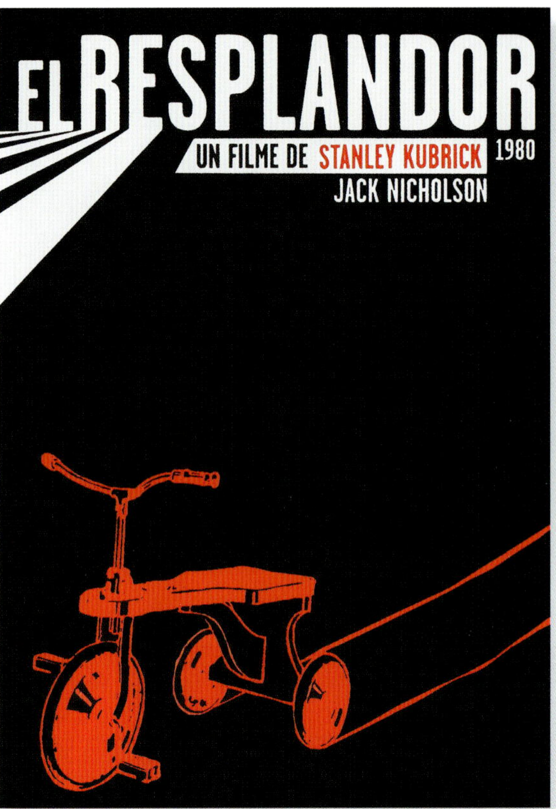


A laudanum addict, Collins believed in the paranormal, and often thought he was being followed by a doppelgänger he liked to refer to as Ghost Collins. Henry James's highly regarded 1898 novella *The Turn of the Screw* has been frequently adapted on film — most notably by Jack Clayton with **The Innocents** (1961) — as well as television, stage, and even as ballet. Oscar Wilde's delightfully comedic *The Canterville Ghost* (1887) has long been another popular source of inspiration for screenwriters. No overview of the period would be complete without mentioning M.R. James, whose short stories are so distinctive and influential, their style is known as 'Jamesian'.

In the 20th century, Susan Hill took up the mantle with novels such as *The Woman in Black* and *The Small Hand*; while in the U.S., Shirley Jackson (*The Haunting of Hill House*), Richard Matheson (*Hell House*) and Stephen King (*The Shining*) all saw their works turned into major motion pictures.

Outside the English-speaking world, the Japanese are the largest producers of ghosts on celluloid. It therefore comes as little surprise that they would have a rich history of apparitions in folklore and literature, dating back to some of Japan's earliest books, including 12th century *Genji Monogatari* ('Tale of Genji') and *Konjaku Monogatari* ('Tales of Times Now Past'). In the Edo period (1603—1868), the tradition of *Hyakumonogatari Kaidankai*, a game through which players invoked spirits through telling each other a hundred supernatural tales, popularized the genre. These *kwaidan* — or weird tales — involving ghosts, generally set in the past, and either frightening or comedic passed on from generation to generation, and were eventually collected into books such as Ogita Ansei's *Otogi Monogatari* ('Nursery Tales', 1660) or Ueda Akinari's *Ugetsu Monogatari* ('Tales of Moonlight and Rain', 1776).

Japanese ghosts, or *yurei*, are marked by symbolism: they are dressed in white, for the white funeral kimono of the Edo period; they have long, dishevelled hair covering their face, as corpses were buried with their hair hanging down. They are usually female, and often hell-bent on vengeance or on a mission to accomplish an unfinished task. *Yurei* are created through lack of proper burial rites, if they died in the throes of a strong emotion, generally when murdered or committing suicide. They can be repelled by *ofuda*, holy Shinto talismans which can be placed on their foreheads or on the doors of those one wishes to protect, or sometimes exorcized through proper rites or by helping them fulfil their purpose.

These hallmarks have carried over from folk tales onto film, making Japanese ghosts highly distinctive, from traditional *kwaidan* adaptations (such as the various versions of **Ghost of Yotsuya** and **Ghost of Kasane**) into the late 1990s and early 2000s Japanese horror craze, when white-clad, long-haired spirits took over the movie world.

This strong historical grounding in both genuine belief and literature goes a long way to explain why ghost stories on screen have benefitted from a respectability and mainstream appeal other horror sub-genres have rarely been granted. Indeed, few scary movies have been as universally lauded by critics and audiences as, say, **The Innocents**, **The Haunting** or **The Shining** — incidentally all adapted from best-selling novels. Some of the world's most revered filmmakers have acknowledged their influence: in his 2015 top ten of best scary movies for *The Daily Beast*, Martin Scorsese listed no less than seven ghost movies (**The Haunting**, **The Uninvited**, **The Entity**, **Dead of Night**, **The Changeling**, **The Shining**, **The Innocents**), while Steven Spielberg frequently cites **The Haunting** as the most terrifying film ever made.

Unlike most other types of horror, ghosts primarily rely on atmosphere and suggestion, rather than explicit gore and monsters. This makes them generally accessible to a wider target age group; a haunted house film with a family-friendly rating (12 in the UK or PG-13 in the U.S.) will likely feel less contrived and more satisfying to adult die-hard genre fans than a slasher

The Haunting

with a similar certificate. So, while in general independently financed horror movies tend to be scarier and more innovative (the **Paranormal Activity** franchise fits into this model), ghosts have also thrived in studio features, as seen in the past years with the commercial and critical success of glossy productions such as **The Conjuring**.

The history of cinema is generally thought to date back to 1895, with the Lumiere brothers' first screening of moving pictures at the Society for the Development of the National Industry in Paris. From these humble beginnings, it wouldn't take long to see the first ghosts pop up on celluloid, as they provided film pioneers the perfect opportunity to develop new cinematic tricks. Indeed the very next year, Georges Méliès premiered the world's first horror movie: **The Haunted Castle** (**Le manoir du diable**), which features a bat turning into a

The Shining

The Haunted Castle

In 1901, Booth released **Scrooge, or Marley's Ghost**. An ambitious piece comprising twelve scenes in different settings, and containing the first use of intertitles, this six-minute short marked the very first time Dickens's *A Christmas Carol* was adapted for the screen. The surviving footage shows Jacob Marley's ghost, replacing the three spirits of the original story, as a transparent apparition in white shrouds, as well as a striking use of superimposition for Marley's face on the door knocker. Booth's 1906 short **Is Spiritualism a Fraud?** featured a phony medium producing floating heads and disembodied hands for his sitters at a séance, and seeing his tricks exposed when the light comes on unexpectedly.

demon in a puff of smoke and conjuring up a witch, an imp, a skeleton, and ominous-looking ghosts in sheets. This three-minute short is remembered for its inventiveness, humour, and remarkable use of cuts to make characters appear and disappear out of thin air.

Influenced by Méliès, English filmmaker George Albert Smith, whose gifts as a stage hypnotist had warranted an invitation to join the Society for Psychical Research, employed similar tricks in his own short, **The Haunted Castle**, a year later; here also, a gentleman is surprised by the sudden appearance of a skeleton and a white-clad spectre. In 1898, Smith's **Photographing a Ghost** showcased double exposure, a technique he pioneered, to make spirits look transparent.

Also in England, magician Walter R. Booth directed a series of short trick films featuring ghosts, starting with **The Miser's Doom** (1899), where the titular penny-pincher is haunted by the spirit of a man whose death he precipitated, and **The Haunted Curiosity Shop** (1901), another Méliès-inspired piece in which various characters, including a see-through ghost and a skeleton, materialize and vanish under the incredulous eyes of a store owner.

Although narratively straightforward and, again, reminiscent of Méliès's groundbreaking work, **The House of Ghosts** (**La maison ensorcelée**, 1908), from Paris-based Spaniard Segundo de Chomón, features stunning stop-motion animation and truly novel ideas. At one point, a painting turns into a hole in the wall through which a creepy, long-fingered spectre looks down at unsuspecting visitors, before a ghost appears to shake its shroud at them. Objects on a table come to life and a knife slices through sausage and bread of its own accord, while an obliging teapot pours its content into cups.

In 1910, inventor Thomas Edison produced a 13-minute film adaptation of Dickens's classic, **A Christmas Carol**, directed by J. Searle Dawley. The short used the now familiar double exposure technique for its see-through ghosts, which this time eschewed white sheets in favour of rich period costumes.

GLUE
JOSEPH M. SCHENCK
PRESENTS
BUSTER KEATON
IN
THE HAUNTED HOUSE
Written and Directed By
BUSTER KEATON & EDDIE CLINE
Exclusive METRO Distributors
PICTURES CORPORATION
J.H. TOOKER

As the world moved away from trickery to develop storytelling skills, ghosts and other apparitions grew scarcer on the silver screen. Throughout the 1910s and 1920s, the only spooks of note were either comedic, dramatic, or a mixture of both, but never frightening, and generally revealed to be hoaxes.

American comedy **The Ghost Breaker** (1914), directed by Cecil B. De Mille, concerned a Spanish heiress who convinces a young man to cast away spirits haunting her newly inherited castle. Again, the ghosts turn out to be a con, made up by a neighbour to detract from his search for a treasure hidden within the building. Adapted from a play by Charles Goddard and Paul Dickey, the movie was remade by Paramount in 1922, but this version has sadly also vanished.

In **The Haunted House** (1921), Buster Keaton plays a bank clerk wrongfully accused, through a series of coincidences, of robbery. He hides from the police in an old abode where a troupe of actors from a local theatre also happen to be taking refuge from their audience, after a disastrous production. Keaton mistakes the thespians, still in stage attire, for ghosts, skeletons and devils. The sight of these sheet-clad, fully covered apparitions running disorderly around the house is rather funny, as are Keaton's exaggerated reactions to the various horrors he believes himself to be facing. Also worth noting are several clever tricks, such as a revolving plaque on the floor allowing him to run on the spot, a man assembled limb by limb who then comes to life, and some striking, spooky make-up on one of the supposed spectres.

Swedish silent classic **The Phantom Carriage** (**Körkarlen**, 1921), from director and star Victor Sjöström, is the first feature-length effort on this list. The last person to die before the clock strikes twelve on New Year's Eve is rumoured to be doomed to drive Death's carriage throughout the next year, and an abusive husband is forced to look back on his life and change his ways, when the conductor come to collect his soul turns out to be an old friend. Halfway between **A Christmas Carol** and **It's a Wonderful Life**, this touching tale of redemption makes great use of dissolves, flashbacks and special effects; the ghostly chariot itself, pictured through several layers of superimposition, is appropriately eerie.

top: **A Christmas Carol** (1910)
centre: **The Haunted House** (1921)
above: **The Phantom Carriage** (1921)

Finally, Paul Leni's **The Cat and the Canary** (1927), first in a series of adaptations of John Willard's popular play, set the standard for the old dark house sub-genre which would flourish in the following decade. A would-be heiress spends the night with her family in the mansion she is to inherit provided she is declared sound of mind by a doctor. Naturally, the house is reputedly haunted, and a killer known as the Cat is on the loose in the area. Ghosts are scarce and scares mostly played for laughs, yet this expressionistic gem, one of Universal's very first forays into spooky territory, contained plenty of striking imagery, with shadow play, darkened hallways and unusual angles.

The thirties were a golden age for horror. Boosted by the success of Tod Browning's 1931 **Dracula**, starring Bela Lugosi, Universal greenlit a version of Mary Shelley's *Frankenstein*, directed by James Whale, and quickly followed by **The Old Dark House** (1932), **The Mummy** (1932) and **The Invisible Man** (1933). Paramount and MGM followed suit with **Dr. Jekyll and Mr. Hyde** (1931), **Freaks** (1932) and **Island of Lost Souls** (1933) respectively. Interest in horror remained high for most of the decade, yet despite their customary appetite for literary adaptations, studios shunned the otherworldly for more earth-bound monstrosities. Vampires, mummies, werewolves, monsters, mad scientists and murderous apes all had their time in the limelight, but for the most part, ghosts remained conspicuously absent. In this age of monsters, what few spooks made it to the screen were again relegated to comedies, with a handful of exceptions (Mexican horrors **La Llorona**, 1933, based on a popular legend, and **The Phantom of the Convent/El fantasma del convento**, 1934; and American thriller **Supernatural**, 1933, in which a woman becomes possessed by the spirit of a murderer.)

In 1934, Laurel and Hardy starred in **The Live Ghost**, a characteristically goofy 20-minute short in which they enlist as crew of a rumoured ghost ship. The apparition, of course, turns out to be a sailor who had fallen in whitewash. The same year, some double exposed spirits appeared in **The Gold Ghost**, in which Buster Keaton appoints himself sheriff of a ghost town. British comedy **The Ghost Goes West** (1935) saw a Scottish spirit uprooted to America; hilarity ensued.

**The Ghost Walks** (1934) and a new adaptation of **The Cat and the Canary** (1939) further developed the old dark house genre, though again both chose a humorous approach. Henry Edwards' **Scrooge** (1935), another version of Dickens's story, elected to keep apparitions to a strict minimum: only the Ghost of Christmas Present is seen properly. **Topper** (1937) features its ghosts front and centre, but the tone is light, and the spirits charming.

Horror took a general hiatus in the second half of the decade, following a decision by the British Board of Film Censors to introduce an 'H' certificate to warn audiences of the content of genre films. This new rating made it in effect very difficult to sell scary movies in the United Kingdom, and deprived of its main secondary market, Hollywood all but ceased production for a few years.

The highlight of this meagre decade is undoubtedly **Lonesome Ghosts**, a Disney cartoon released through RKO in 1937. Mickey Mouse, Donald Duck and Goofy star as intrepid ghost hunters, called to a haunted house by playful spirits. What follows is Disney at its finest: fantastically fluid animation, lovable characters, a succession of hilarious gags, and all the spooky staples one might expect: a dusty old house, mysterious moans, creaky floorboards, and phosphorescent spooks. This enduring classic clearly inspired another set of bumbling trappers decades later in 1984's **Ghostbusters**.

By the forties, enthusiasm for monster pictures had waned, and with the notable exception of **The Wolf Man** (1941), the genre largely devolved into spoofs and sequels. Lugosi himself, once a world class star, was now relegated to the occasional cheapie. After the war, film noir took over as the go-to genre to express America's darkest impulses.

Ghosts, however, turned out in greater numbers than in the previous decade, although again, they were more likely to make audiences laugh than scream. Paul Dickey and Charles W. Goddard's play *The Ghost Breaker* was again adapted to the screen in **The Ghost Breakers** (1940). Comedic duo Abbott and Costello encountered spooks twice, in **Hold That Ghost** (1941) and **The Time of Their Lives** (1946). Music hall act turned movie star Old Mother Riley inherited a haunted castle in **Old Mother Riley's Ghosts**. The East Side Kids faced the 'monster killer' (and scared him off by pretending to be spirits) at their summer camp in **Spooks Run Wild**

top: Laurel and Hardy in **The Live Ghost** (1934)
above: **The Ghost Goes West** (1935)

(1941), featuring a cameo by Bela Lugosi. Charles Laughton played **The Canterville Ghost** (1944) in the first adaptation of Oscar Wilde's short story. And Universal produced **Ghost Catchers** (1944), with appearances by Lon Chaney Jr. and Tor Johnson, in which a couple of Manhattan nightclub owners attempt to drive a ghost out of the next door brownstone, only to realize the alleged spectres are a ploy by local gangsters to scare their neighbours out, in order to steal a stash of pre-Prohibition liquor hidden in the cellar.

Fake spooks also popped up in 1941 British thriller **The Ghost Train**, where the titular vehicle is said to appear periodically on an abandoned track and kill anyone who sees it. The train, naturally, turns out to be used by Nazis to transport weapons.

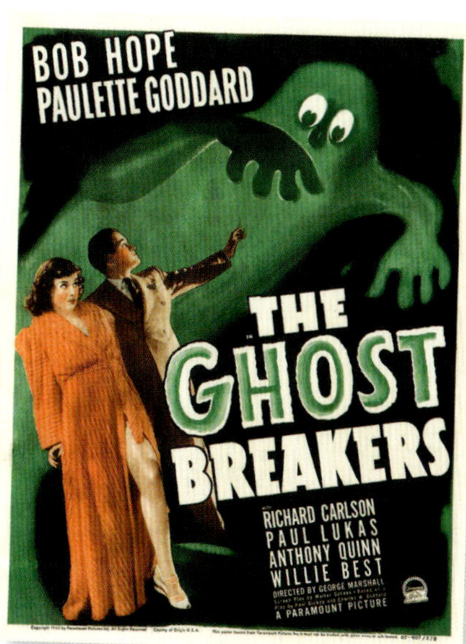


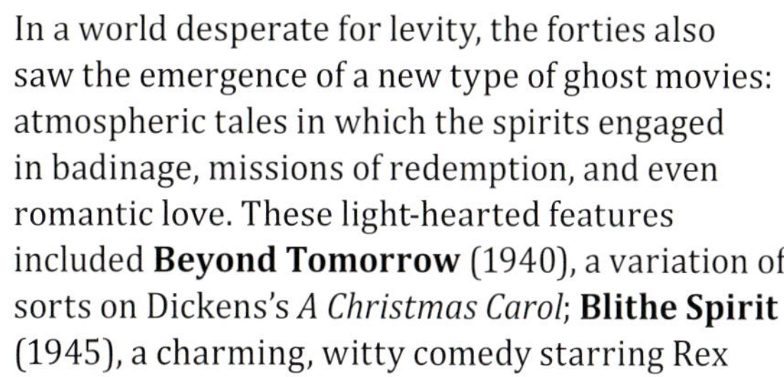

In a world desperate for levity, the forties also saw the emergence of a new type of ghost movies: atmospheric tales in which the spirits engaged in badinage, missions of redemption, and even romantic love. These light-hearted features included **Beyond Tomorrow** (1940), a variation of sorts on Dickens's *A Christmas Carol*; **Blithe Spirit** (1945), a charming, witty comedy starring Rex Harrison; British melodrama **A Place of One's Own** (1945); and David O. Selznick production **Portrait of Jennie** (1948). The sentimental ghost genre culminated in 1947 with Joseph L. Mankiewicz's masterpiece **The Ghost and Mrs. Muir**, a heart-warming piece on life choices and companionship, starring the delightful Gene Tierney and Rex Harrison.

Not all ghost stories, however, showed such high spirits.

experiences, targeting individuals or small groups; while these atomic age threats affected whole communities. By the start of the decade, romantic spectres had already gone out of style; comedies and foreign films, again, were a spirit's most likely haunts.

East Side Kids successors the Bowery Boys faced off a fake medium and a real haunting in **Ghost Chasers** (1951). AIP released two spooky farces in 1959: UK effort **The Headless Ghost**; and Hot Rod Gang sequel **Ghost of Dragstrip Hollow**.

The decade also offered a handful of otherworldly scary movies. Generally considered the first Hollywood production to centre around frightening, serious spooks, Paramount's **The Uninvited** (1944) establishes many of the staples and typical situations of the classic supernatural tale; while **Dead of Night** (1945), from Britain's Ealing Studios, offered five vignettes of varying intensity.

Also of note are foreign chillers **El espectro de la novia** (1943), featuring Fu Manchu, and *kwaidan* **Ghost of Yotsuya** (1949); Val Lewton-produced sequel **The Curse of the Cat People** (1944); and British horror **The Night Comes Too Soon**, aka **The Ghost of Rashmon Hall** (1948).

Post-war prosperity, combined with America's fear of the Cold War and the atomic threat, ushered in an age of creature features and drive-in movies. The public's appetite for giant insects, mutated monsters and mad scientists seemed insatiable in the fifties. Focused on technological improvements, major studios largely left genre films to independents such as James H. Nicholson and Samuel Z. Arkoff's American International Pictures. Horror now belonged to B-movies and to creeps from another world.

In this time of nuclear beasts, ghosts, by essence vestiges of the past, had a hard time fitting in. Hauntings are also personal

In Mexico, **The Living Coffin** (**El grito de la muerte**, 1959) presented a new version of the legend of La Llorona. Japan continued its exploration of classic *kwaidan* tales with **Ugetsu** (1953), **Ghost of Kasane** (1957), and a new **Ghost of Yotsuya** (1959).

The end of the decade, however, brought a wind of change. Benefitting from the now affordable use of Technicolor, British company Hammer Films brought the classic monsters back to the screen, rekindling an interest in Gothic, period scares. In the U.S., the search for new, clever ways to stand out in a crowded market pushed a couple of filmmakers to resort to marketing gimmicks, for which ghosts seemed admirably suited: for 1958's **The Screaming Skull**, Alex Nicol promised a free burial to whoever would die of fright watching his directorial debut; while the following year, William Castle added a flying skeleton to spice up screenings of **House on Haunted Hill**, and a ghost viewer — tinted glasses — for **13 Ghosts**.

Finally, Edward D. Wood Jr. — of **Plan 9 from Outer Space** fame — made **Night of the Ghouls**, a sequel to **Bride of the Monster**, in 1957. Starring Wood regulars Criswell and Tor Johnson, this haunted house investigation story was thought lost until its belated release on home video nearly thirty years later.

Between the JFK assassination, Vietnam, and the Manson family murders, the sixties were a time of anxiety on and off screen. Social unrest, upheaval and counterculture led to grittier, more realistic pictures where ordinary individuals were threatened in mundane settings (**Psycho**, **Peeping Tom**, **Rosemary's Baby**, **Night of the Living Dead**...) With the notable exceptions of **Carnival of Souls** (1962), set in contemporary rural America, and **The Haunting** (1963), which despite its old manor setting took place in present day, ghost stories seemed an ill fit for these new, bloodier, more grounded standards.

Yet the sub-genre blossomed in a concurrent trend of Gothic, period chillers spearheaded by American International Pictures in America, and Mario Bava in Italy, as well as in more mainstream literary adaptations. No more laughs, no more winks at the screen: this low-budget fare took their spectres dead seriously.

Having already found success with four movies based on the works of Edgar Allan Poe for AIP, prolific director/producer Roger Corman filmed **The Terror**, which Nicholson and Arkoff put out in 1963, in sets leftover from **The Raven**, which he had just finished filming. His last Poe picture, **The Tomb of Ligeia**, in which the titular woman's spirit haunts her old home, came out the following year. Also loosely Poe-related and released through AIP, Italian-French anthology **Spirits of the Dead** (**Histoires extraordinaires**/**Tre passi nel delirio**) brought together some of the most prestigious filmmakers and stars of its time.

Another omnibus, **Black Sabbath** (**I tre volti della paura**, 1963), gave us Mario Bava's first ghost story, quickly followed — the same month! — by **The Whip and the Body** (**La frusta e il corpo**), starring Christopher Lee, and three years later by **Kill, Baby... Kill!** (**Operazione paura**). All three are daring period pieces with lavish sets and beautiful, distinctive Technicolor cinematography.

In 1964, Italian filmmaker Antonio Margheriti helmed two eerie, underrated ghost stories featuring legendary actress Barbara Steele: **The Long Hair of Death** (**I lunghi capelli della morte**) and **Castle of Blood** (**Danza macabra**). Steele also appeared the next year in **Nightmare Castle** (**Amanti d'oltretomba**), from director Mario Caiano.

Meanwhile, Mexico and Japan continued their steady output of ghostly tales. From Mexico came two new versions of familiar legend La Llorona — **La Llorona** (1960), and **The Curse of the Crying Woman** (**La maldición de la llorona**, 1963) — and boarding school horror **Even the Wind Is Afraid** (**Hasta el viento tiene miedo**, 1968). Japan served more *kwaidan* movies with **Kuroneko** (1968), **The Snow Woman** (1968), and the quintessential, aptly titled **Kwaidan** (1964), as well as modern day story **House of Terrors** (aka **Ghost of the Hunchback**, 1965), which heavily borrowed from its Western contemporaries.

Black Sabbath

The Innocents

Last but not least, the decade saw some of the finest adaptations of literary ghost stories, which not only terrorized audiences of the time, but also influenced generations to come. Two of the genre's greatest masterpieces, **The Innocents** (1961), based on Henry James's story *The Turn of the Screw*, and **The Haunting** (1963), based on Shirley Jackson's *The Haunting of Hill House*, used the haunted house staples to explore the state of mind of their female protagonists. Both also heavily rely on atmosphere, elaborate production design, and stunning black-and-white photography. Less popular but no less accomplished, **Whistle and I'll Come to You**, a 1968 BBC production of an M.R. James short story, launched a tradition of Christmas ghost stories which lasted decades.

The turn of tide initiated in the previous decade reached its apex in the seventies. The faraway castles and misty graveyards of years past were by now long gone, replaced by the terrors of the nuclear family and its traditional habitats, whether they be children's bedrooms (**The Exorcist**, **The Omen**), prams (**It's Alive**), schools (**Carrie**, **Suspiria**), family vacations (**Jaws**, **The Hills Have Eyes**), or holiday celebrations (**Black Christmas**, **Halloween**). Filmmakers — and censors — no longer shied away from blood, and a sub-genre of ultra-graphic shockers developed, fronted by movies such as **The Texas Chain Saw Massacre** and **The Last House on the Left**.

In line with this new vision of horror, ghost movies finally deserted their Gothic settings and started haunting more familiar, contemporary environments. Continuing a trend initiated with **The Innocents** and **The Haunting**, this new generation turned their focus to the inner workings of their protagonists' minds. If horror in general posited that your stepfather or your next-door neighbour may be a serial killer, ghost stories raised the question, are we all going crazy?

**Let's Scare Jessica to Death** (1971), with its heroine on the brink of a nervous collapse, kicked off this low-key, slow-burn psychological trend. Two years later, British thriller **Voices** set off with the same premise: a woman released from a mental hospital starts feeling a presence in the country house where she is recovering with her husband. Lynn Redgrave starred in yet a new version of **The Turn of the Screw** (1974), this time for American TV. **Burnt Offerings** (1976) saw Karen Black possessed by a spirit inhabiting an old mansion. Another woman freshly out of the asylum is thought to suffer from delusions in **Shock** (aka **Beyond the Door II**, 1977), Mario Bava's last theatrical feature. Yet more psychologically fragile waifs appear in **Full Circle** (**The Haunting of Julia**) and **The Sentinel**, both 1977.

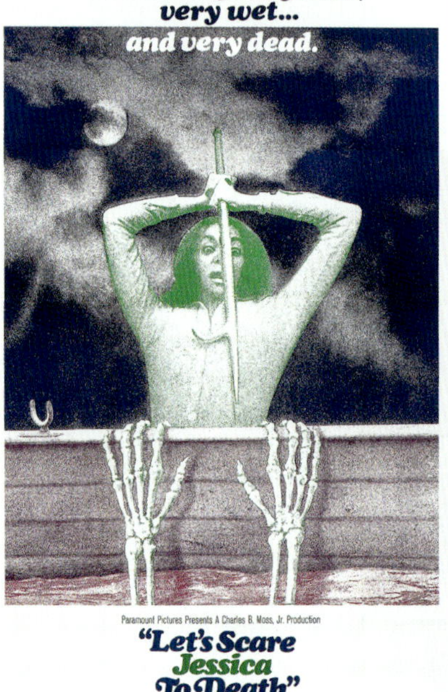


In 1979's **The Amityville Horror**, a family man is possessed by his new home's malevolent spirit, to his wife and children's dismay. Based on a best-selling book, itself relating highly controversial, supposedly real events, the movie was a massive commercial hit.

Taking a different approach to the genre, two British movies, Nigel Kneale's **The Stone Tape** (1972) and John Hough's **The Legend of Hell House** (1973), focused more on the clash between modern technology and ancient beliefs than on the psychological impact of the supernatural, though the latter subject is briefly broached too. This theme of science versus superstition, already touched upon in Kneale's popular **Quatermass** series, would recur in the following decades.

In the United Kingdom also, following the success of 1968's **Whistle and I'll Come to You**, the BBC launched a series of yearly adaptations which lasted from 1971 to 1978, **A Ghost Story for Christmas**, based on classic works from M.R. James and Charles Dickens. Undeniably the best of these simple, atmospheric shorts was moody Dickens tale **The Signalman** (1976), directed by Lawrence Gordon Clark, in which a mysterious man repeatedly appears to a signalman at a railway cutting to warn him of impending doom.

Thanks to a number of commercial home runs (**Jaws**, **The Exorcist**, **Alien**), horror re-entered the mainstream in the age of the blockbuster. Targeting ever wider crowds, the genre aimed to offer spectacles, making full use of elaborate special effect make-ups and visual wizardry. These groundbreaking techniques allowed moviemakers to film the unfilmable: ghouls, werewolves and shape-shifting aliens no longer had to be kept in the shadows, and from the early eighties, movies such as **The Thing**, **The Terminator** and **An American Werewolf in London** pioneered revolutionary effects from new masters Rob Bottin, Rick Baker and Stan Winston.

At the same time, the advent of home video allowed lower budget flicks to reach new audiences, and a straight-to-video market emerged. Slashers, sequels, and increasingly gory FX-laden shockers (**Re-Animator**, **Maniac**) thrived, ever upping the body count.

top: **Shock**
above: **The Amityville Horror**

Poltergeist

As a result of these technological improvements, horror cinema on the whole grew less prone to introspection and social analysis, and more geared towards teenagers and entertainment. Yet **The Amityville Horror** had rekindled the public's interest in serious, scary ghost stories, and the first half of the decade birthed a handful of bona fide classics.

Stanley Kubrick's **The Shining** (1980) took a cerebral approach to a bestseller from rising superstar Stephen King; John Carpenter, whose 1980 mystery **The Fog** centered on spectral sailors, also adapted a story by the author in 1983 with **Christine** (1983), about a haunted car slowly possessing its new owner.

**The Changeling** (1980) offered subtle yet incredibly effective scares. A cast of old timers starred in **Ghost Story** (1981), from a Peter Straub novel. Last but not least, **Poltergeist** (1982), a collaboration between director Tobe Hooper and producer Steven Spielberg, kicked off a profitable franchise, with cutting-edge visual effects and highly relatable protagonists. Inspired by real-life facts, **The Entity** presented an adult version of a similar phenomenon the same year.

Although smaller productions such as **Witchboard**, **The Wraith** (both 1986) or **Prison** (1987) continued to take hauntings to heart, bigger budgets once again took a goofy turn following the remarkable success of Ivan Reitman and Dan Aykroyd's classic comedy **Ghostbusters** (1984). If Gene Wilder's 1986 **Haunted Honeymoon** wasn't particularly well received, Tim Burton's **Beetlejuice** (1988), however, turned haunted house clichés upside down by adopting the point of view of the ghosts. The same year, Steve Guttenberg fell for a

Ghost Story

Beetlejuice

charming apparition in Neil Jordan's **High Spirits**, and Ghostbuster Bill Murray starred in **Scrooged**, a modernized version of Dickens's enduring Christmas tale.

The eighties also saw the explosion of Hong Kong movie production. Two movies quickly became genre cinema milestones locally and abroad: Sammo Hung's hilarious, imaginative **Encounters of the Spooky Kind** (1980), and Ching Siu-tung's fantasy romance **A Chinese Ghost Story** (1987).

Perhaps dulled by an excess of gore, scary movies made themselves scarce in the first half of the nineties, and were mostly dominated by psychos (**Misery**) and serial killers (**The Silence of the Lambs**). Horror had become unpopular, the word itself often replaced by the term 'psychological (or supernatural) thriller'.

The early part of the decade saw an unexpected resurgence of the romantic ghost, led by tragic love story **Ghost** (1990). British drama **Truly Madly Deeply**, in which a woman is haunted by her late boyfriend, came out the following year. Robert Downey Jr. becomes a better man through his interaction with spirits in **Heart and Souls** (1993); and Aidan Quinn falls under Kate Beckinsale's spell in **Haunted** (1995), which was adapted from a James Herbert novel.

With a few rare exceptions (**Sometimes They Come Back** in 1991, **Event Horizon** in 1997), the big screen offered few truly scary apparitions; and as ever, spooks turned into comedy fodder with movies such as **Casper** (1995), **The Canterville Ghost** (1996), or Peter Jackson's frenetically amusing 1996 offering **The Frighteners**.

On television however, a couple of shows provided genuine chills. On Halloween 1992, BBC 'live' broadcast **Ghostwatch** shocked the United Kingdom, with its team of well-known presenters investigating a haunted house where an apparition called 'Pipes' had been terrorizing the occupants. Actually a feature

film scripted by Stephen Volk and shot documentary style by Lesley Manning as part of BBC Drama's Screen One program, **Ghostwatch** led a surprisingly large amount of its audience to believe that what they were watching was real. Reports flooded in of viewers suffering from PTSD, soiling themselves or even committing suicide after the show, which drew in a record number of complaints. As a result, this groundbreaking work of fiction never aired again on UK television.

In Denmark, Lars von Trier's zany mini-series **The Kingdom** (**Riget**, 1994) mixed genres to depict supernatural occurrences in the neurosurgical ward of Copenhagen's main hospital. Highly idiosyncratic and filmed handheld in sepia tones, the show returned for a second season, but a planned third was sadly never shot. An American remake, **Kingdom Hospital**, created by Stephen King, followed ten years later.

If horror wasn't too popular in the first part of the nineties, the tables turned in the second half. After the unexpected success of Wes Craven's post-modern slasher **Scream** (1996), scary movies grew self-aware, and a slew of ironic slashers ensued.

Faced with a major economic crisis and its first large-scale terrorist incident (the 1995 sarin gas attack), Japan developed a new breed of scary ghost movies. J-horror, as the trend has been dubbed, finds its roots in Norio Tsuruta's 1991 video series **Scary True Stories** — as the title suggests, a collection of vignettes depicting reputedly actual events — and in Hideo Nakata's 1996 **Don't Look Up/Ghost Actress**; but it is Nakata's 1998 hit **Ring** (sometimes erroneously referred to as RINGU, a misunderstanding of the literal translation of the English word into Japanese) which launched the J-horror phenomenon worldwide. South Korea would soon follow suit, after its military dictatorship ended and censorship standards were relaxed, with films like the **Whispering Corridors** (1998) series. Entries in this Asian sub-genre had in common their slow pace, lack of explicit violence, and long-haired female ghosts, while also revolving around topical social issues such as the questioning of traditional gender roles, fractured families, child abuse, and a fear of modern technology.

The nineties saw the start of a wave of remakes which would plague horror for years to come. Although William Malone's 1999 reinvention of **House on Haunted Hill** turned out rather well, Jan de Bont's FX-fest **The Haunting**, with Liam Neeson and Catherine Zeta-Jones, underlines everything the 1963 original got right, by doing the exact opposite, replacing simple scares and a pervasive sense of dread with computer-generated images, loud noises, and clichés aplenty.

The decade ended on a high note for ghost stories, however, with a duo of excellent entries: mega hit **The Sixth Sense** (1999), which established M. Night Shyamalan as one of Hollywood's most respected filmmakers, and a month later, David Koepp's **Stir of Echoes**, based on a novel by Richard Matheson.

opposite lower: **Ring** (1988)

below: **The Others**

The combined effect of **The Sixth Sense** and **Ring** brought upon an avalanche of supernatural flicks in the new millennium. In America, **What Lies Beneath** (2000) was a remainder of a time when studios considered horror a dirty word, a thriller tinged with a hint of paranormal.

A year later, Nicole Kidman starred in **The Others**, a masterpiece with genuine chills, from Spanish director Alejandro Amenábar. Gore Verbinski's **The Ring** (2002), a remake of Nakata's movie, not only launched two sequels, but also an onslaught of Hollywood re-imaginings of J-horror hits, including **The Grudge** (2004), **Dark Water** (2005), **Pulse** (2006), **The Eye** (2008), **One Missed Call** (2008), and **Mirrors** (2008).

Long-haired ghosts continued to flood Asian productions with hits such as **Ju-on**, **The Eye** and **Dark Water** in 2002, **Into The Mirror** and **One Missed Call** in 2003, **Shutter** and **R-Point** in 2004, **Reincarnation** in 2005; then later, **Epitaph** (2007) and **Phobia 2** (2009).

Thailand brought its own twist to the ghost craze, with **The Unborn** (2003), British director Paul Spurrier's **P** (2005), **The Unseeable** (2006), and **Alone** (2007). China, however, enforced a ban on supernatural content as part of a 'clean-up' campaign in preparation for the 2008 Beijing Olympics. 'Wronged spirits and violent ghosts, monsters, demons, and other inhuman portrayals, strange and supernatural storytelling for the sole purpose of seeking terror and horror'[6] were now forbidden to appear on screen.

---

*6.* http://www.reuters.com/article/us-ghosts-idUSN1442888920080214, Retrieved May 2017.

right: **The Devil's Backbone**
below: **Lake Mungo**

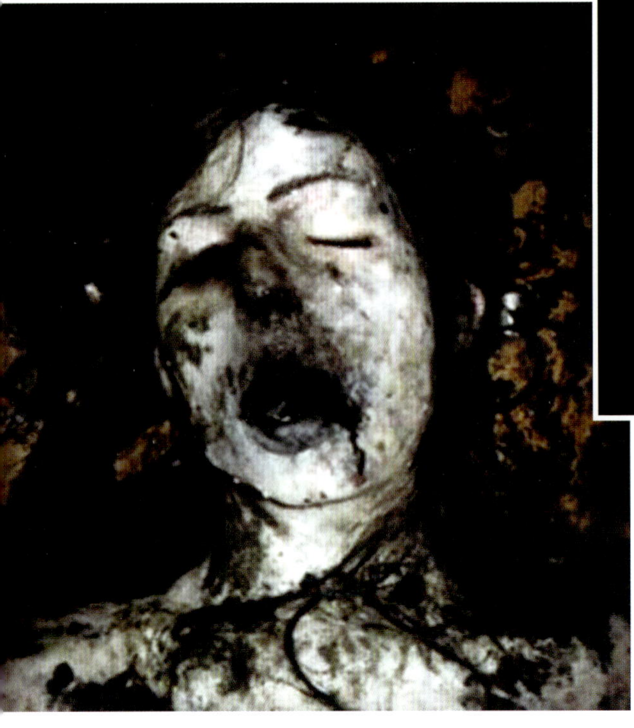

In 2007, on-screen apparitions had been galvanized when Paramount acquired and released micro-budget effort **Paranormal Activity**, whose commercial success took pundits by surprise. Often imitated but never equalled, the movie, directed by Oren Peli, also helped popularize the found footage format. Of its direct successors, only **Lake Mungo** (2008) is truly worth singling out.

The international expansion spread to countries which had so far shown little interest in the genre. Spanish-Mexican co-production **The Devil's Backbone** (**El espinazo del diablo**, 2001) is arguably one of Guillermo del Toro's best movies to date. The filmmaker also executive produced **The Orphanage** (**El orfanato**, 2007) for Spanish first-timer J.A Bayona. France gave us **House of Voices** (**Saint Ange**, 2004). From India came fantasy-comedy **Chandramukhi** in 2005, the same year as Singaporean horror **The Maid**.

Finally on television, British reality show **Most Haunted**, a spiritual heir to **Ghostwatch**, has investigated paranormal happenings across the United Kingdom and abroad since 2002, first on LivingTV, then online. Setting up cameras for 24 hours in each location, the team documents hauntings and hopes to find evidence of life after death while entertaining viewers with various noises, ouija boards, and dimly lit close-ups on frightened faces. And from 2005 to 2010, Jennifer Love Hewitt starred as a woman helping the dead accomplish unfinished tasks in American drama series **Ghost Whisperer** on CBS.

The first half of the 2010s was marked by the rise of independent movies, fronted by **Paranormal Activity** producer Jason Blum and his company Blumhouse, and **Saw** director James Wan.

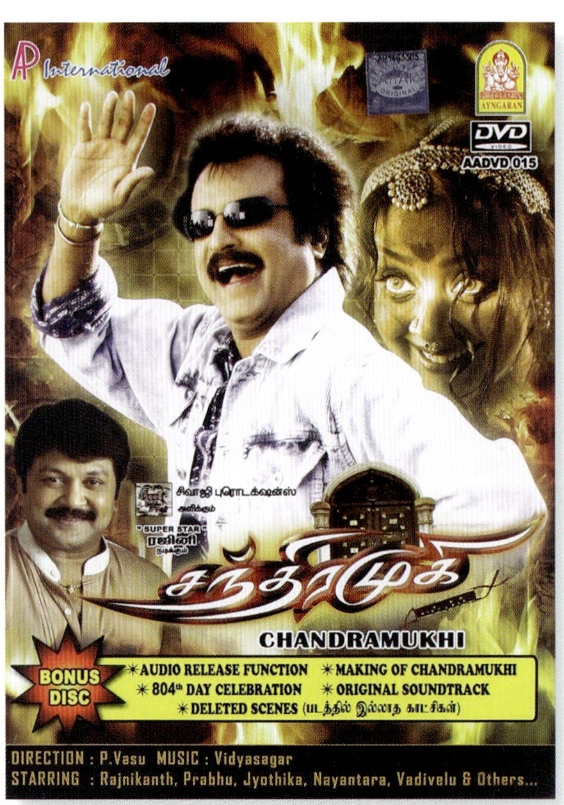


opposite top: **Insidious**
opposite bottom: **The Conjuring**

In 2010, Blum and Wan decided to collaborate on **Insidious**, the micro-budget story of a boy haunted by demons. The gamble paid off: the movie was a huge hit which started a franchise, put Wan back at the top of the horror ladder, and sealed Blumhouse's position as a leading force in the genre. Blum would go on to produce, amongst others, ghost stories **Oculus** (2013) and **Ouija: Origin of Evil** (2016), both of which were directed by Mike Flanagan, as well as **Sinister** (2012) and its sequel (2015); Wan would find huge success with another franchise, this time for Warner Brothers: **The Conjuring** (2013), based on the exploits of real-life paranormal investigators Ed and Lorraine Warren. In 2014, Wan launched his own company, Atomic Monster, which gave us **The Conjuring** spin-off **Annabelle** (2014), about a haunted doll, and its follow-up **Annabelle: Creation** (2017), as well as **The Conjuring 2** and **Lights Out** (both 2016).

Other indie ghost stories of note include Ti West's **The Innkeepers** (2011), Vincenzo Natali's **Haunter** (2012), and Ted Geoghegan's **We Are Still Here** (2015). And on the studio front, auteur Guillermo del Toro executive produced Andrés Muschietti's **Mama** (2013) before going on to direct his own haunted house story with **Crimson Peak** (2015).

International interest in ghosts persisted into the new decade. India's **Haunted 3D** (2011) and **Pizza** (2012), Bengali comedy **Bhooter Bhabishyat** (2012), Hong Kong horror **Rigor Mortis** (2013), Thai comedy horror **Pee Mak** (2013), and Laos's **Dearest Sister** (2016), continued Asia's strike. Spain contributed **Ghost Graduation** (2012), New Zealand hinted at the genre with **Housebound** (2014), and Ireland gave us **The Lodgers** (2017).

In the UK, **The Awakening** (2011), with Rebecca Hall and Dominic West, was promptly followed by another period chiller: **The Woman in Black** (2012), from the revived Hammer Films, starring Daniel Radcliffe. Massively popular, the Susan Hill adaptation prompted Hammer to give it a sequel, **The Woman in Black 2: Angel of Death**, as well as produce another ghost tale, **The Quiet Ones**, both in 2014. The same year saw the release of this author's own haunted house, **Soulmate**, filmed in Wales. On stage, Andy Nyman and Jeremy Dyson's terrifying play *Ghost Stories* premiered in Liverpool in 2010 ahead of its triumphant year-long run in London, and was later turned into a feature film with Martin Freeman.

From vaporous entities to full-body apparitions, vengeful souls to benevolent love interests, haunted inanimate objects to recurring phenomena, movies have portrayed spectres in all their possible shapes and forms.

The Woman in Black (2012)

This book relies on the traditional definition of a ghost as the disembodied spirit of a dead person, to decide what movies qualify for inclusion. This excludes, for example, **It Follows** (2014), because the entity isn't a dead person, or **A Nightmare on Elm Street** (1984), since Freddy Krueger is a flesh-and-blood murderer in the dream world. It does include poltergeists: situations where souls don't manifest themselves visibly, but through physical disturbances (biting, hitting, rapping, levitation, etc.), as in **The Haunting**, **The Entity**, or, naturally, **Poltergeist**.

In an effort to present the most complete picture of ghost movies across time, cultures, and sub-genres, however, some adjustments have been made.

China's *jiangshi*, an undetermined hybrid between spirit and vampire, is considered a spectre for the purpose of this overview. Also in cases such as **Insidious**, where hauntings are said to be caused by demons, or, as in **The Cat and the Canary**, are found out to be bogus, they have been included whenever the movie functioned according to the mechanisms and classic scares of a haunted house picture.

Arguably the most frightening sub-genre of horror, ghost stories tap into our most primal fears and challenge our beliefs in life after death. They have captivated and terrified audiences since the dawn of time, and now, it is your turn to witness the horror.

Can your heart stand the shocks of…

***...spooks running wild around New York City?***

***...snowbound hotels whose dark pasts drive their caretakers to murderous insanity?***

***...villages terrorized by their deceased residents returning to their former abodes?***

***...grieving widows confiding in ghoulish undead lovers?***

***...leprous pirates hiding in banks of unnatural mist?***

***...skeletons flying over screaming, delighted audiences?***

***...paranormal investigators trapped in cursed properties?***

***...high school students unleashing vengeful souls of the dead through Hasbro board games?***

***...the blood-curdling wails of Mexican phantoms crying over the loss of their murdered children?***

If so, welcome to our review of the 200 most memorable ghost movies: a collection of the most shocking, harrowing, romantic, puzzling, haunting tales ever committed to celluloid.

Some may delight you, some may appall you… Some may even horrify you!

SELMA LAGERLÖFS

KÖRKARLEN

BERÄTTAD I LEVANDE BILDER AV

VICTOR SJÖSTRÖM

OFFICIN: SVENSK FILMINDUSTRI

ENSAMRÄTT: A.B. SVENSKA BIOGRAFTEATERNS FILMBYRÅ STHLM

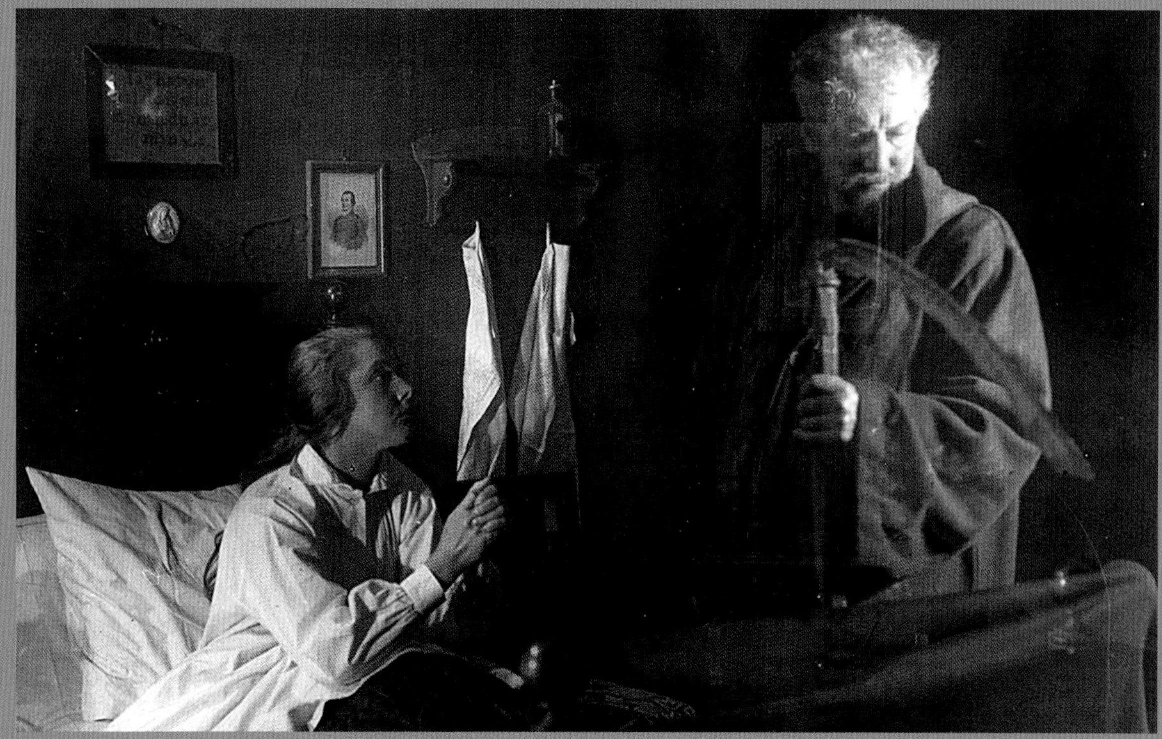

## THE PHANTOM CARRIAGE

Sweden, 1921
Director: Victor Sjöström. Producer: Charles Magnusson [uncredited].
Screenplay: Victor Sjöström. Cinematography: Julius Jaenzon.
Cast: Victor Sjöström, Hilda Borgström, Tore Svennberg, Astrid Holm,
Concordia Selander, Lisa Lundholm.

According to Swedish legend, the last person to die before the clock strikes twelve on New Year's Eve is rumoured to be doomed to drive Death's carriage throughout the next year. In this silent classic, and the first feature-length effort on this list, an abusive husband is forced to look back on his life and change his ways, when the conductor come to collect his soul turns out to be an old friend. Halfway between **A Christmas Carol** and **It's a Wonderful Life**, **The Phantom Carriage**, from director and star Victor Sjöström, is a touching tale of redemption which involves very little spookiness, yet makes revolutionary use of dissolves, flashbacks and special effects. The ghostly chariot itself, pictured through several layers of superimposition, is appropriately eerie. Based on the 1912 novel *Thy Soul Shall Bear Witness!* (incidentally the movie's UK release title, while the U.S. also knows it as **The Stroke of Midnight**) by Nobel prize winner Selma Lagerlöf, **The Phantom Carriage** was filmed entirely on soundstages, against the wishes of the famed author, who hoped to see it shot on location. The success of the picture, whose influence on Ingmar Bergman is such that he paid it homage in **The Seventh Seal** (1957), and spurred MGM co-founder Louis B. Mayer to invite Sjöström to Hollywood, where he directed a series of films under the name Victor Seastrom, before returning to Sweden.

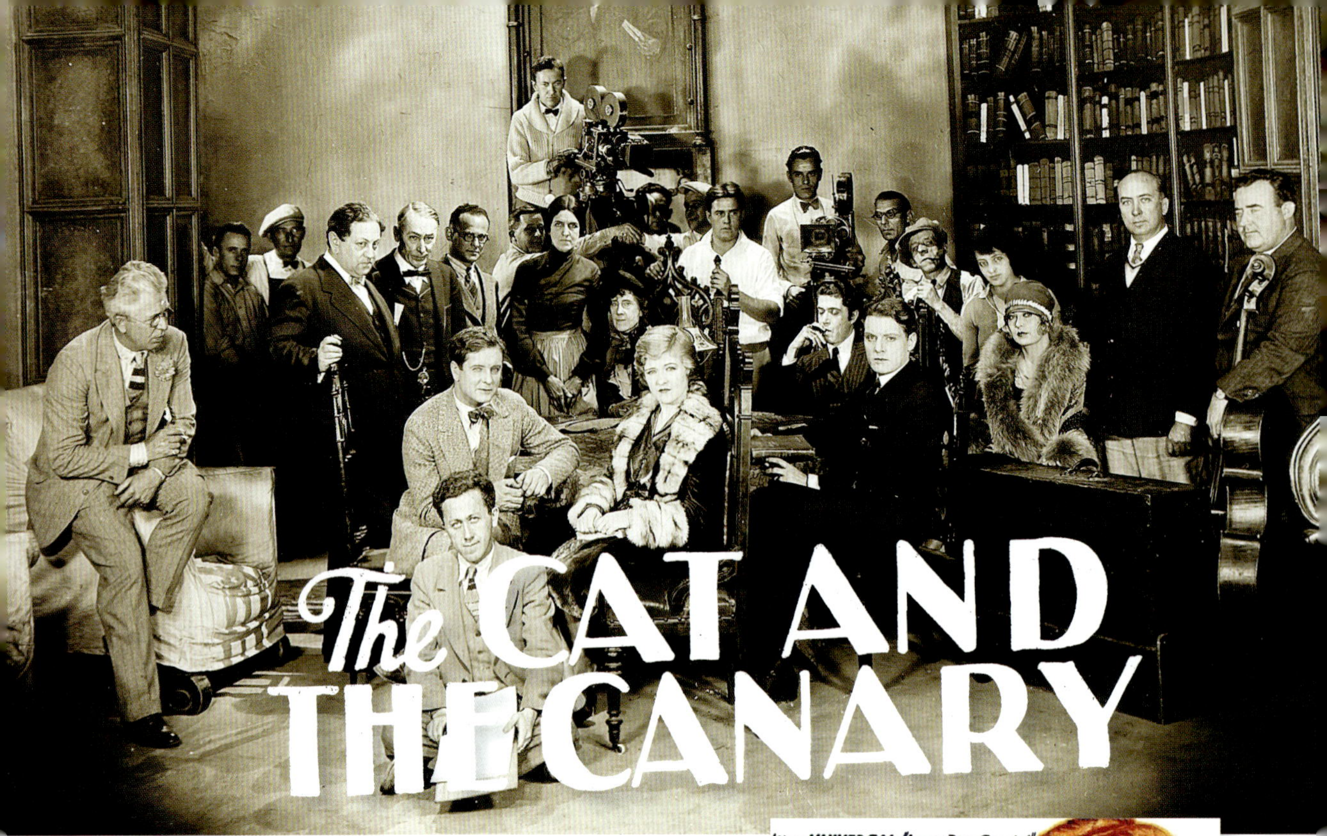
The CAT AND
THE CANARY

## THE CAT AND THE CANARY

*Various adaptations*

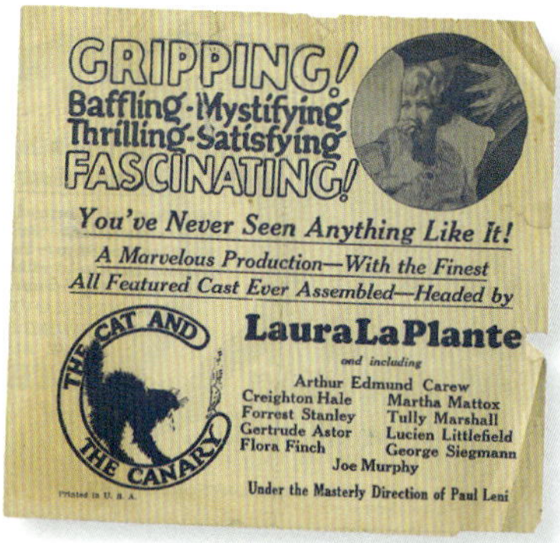
GRIPPING!
Baffling-Mystifying
Thrilling-Satisfying
FASCINATING!
You've Never Seen Anything Like It!
A Marvelous Production—With the Finest
All Featured Cast Ever Assembled—Headed by
Laura La Plante
and including
Arthur Edmund Carew
Creighton Hale
Martha Mattox
Forrest Stanley
Tully Marshall
Gertrude Astor
Lucien Littlefield
Flora Finch
George Siegmann
Joe Murphy
THE CAT AND THE CANARY
Under the Masterly Direction of Paul Leni

'It was a dark and stormy night...' Twenty years after the death of eccentric millionaire Cyrus West, his potential heirs assemble in his creepy old home to read his will. Distant relative Annabelle inherits his fortune, provided she is declared legally sane. As the family endeavour to drive her crazy over the rest of the night, an escaped lunatic known as the Cat sneaks into the house...

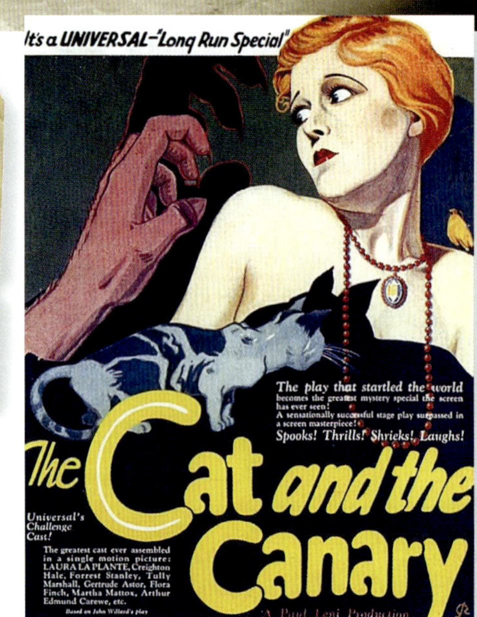

John Willard's 1922 play *The Cat and the Canary* was a massive hit on Broadway. It wouldn't be long until Universal Pictures, then at the start of their love affair with dark thrillers and horror (**The Hunchback of Notre Dame**, 1923, and **The Phantom of the Opera**, 1925, both starring Lon Chaney, had been box-office hits), bought screen rights. Willard had reservations, fearing that audiences would no longer flock to the stage once the twist ending became widely known, but eventually relented.

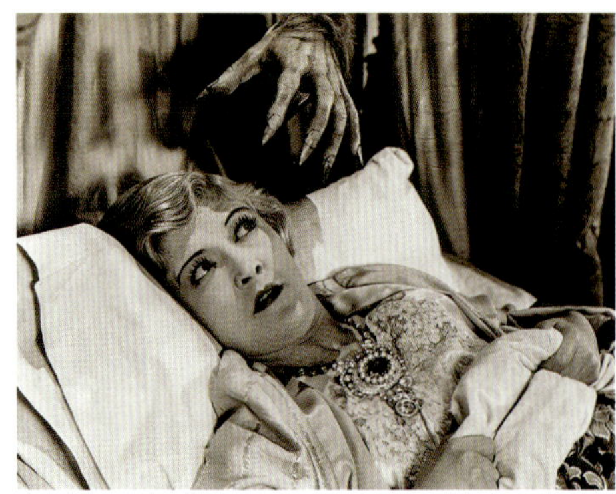

Impressed by German Expressionist Paul Leni's **Waxworks** (1924), Universal's Carl Laemmle hired the director, who also designed the striking sets, to head its first adaptation in 1927. Leni's **The Cat and the Canary** opens with a surreal scene of giant superimposed cats assembling

It's a UNIVERSAL-"Long Run Special"
The play that startled the world becomes the greatest mystery special the screen has ever seen!
A sensationally successful stage play surpassed in a screen masterpiece!
Spooks! Thrills! Shrieks! Laughs!
The Cat and the Canary
Universal's Challenge Cast!
The greatest cast ever assembled in a single motion picture: LAURA LA PLANTE, Creighton Hale, Forrest Stanley, Tully Marshall, Gertrude Astor, Flora Finch, Martha Mattox, Arthur Edmund Carewe, etc.
Based on John Willard's play
A Paul Leni Production

over the dying man, and includes all the staples of the old dark house genre, from billowing curtains, exaggerated make-up, hidden trapdoors and frightening shadows, to the camera gliding through the deserted halls of the spooky mansion. Although not *per se* a ghost story — the only spirits alluded to turn out to be rather less than supernatural — the movie establishes many of the haunted house conventions, and had an enormous influence on Universal's subsequent horror output. It is reported that Leni liked to use a gong to startle his cast at the appropriate times. He would go on to direct three more pictures for Universal, including 1928 classic **The Man Who Laughs**.

Directed by Kiwi filmmaker Rupert Julian (**The Phantom of the Opera**, 1925), 1930's **The Cat Creeps**, a pre-code talkie remake from Universal, was, like Tod Browning's **Dracula** would later be, filmed both in English and in Spanish (as **La voluntad del muerto**). Little survives of the film today.

By the late thirties, the plot had grown so familiar that the only way to tell the story again was to play it for laughs. Paramount's 1939 version sees comedian Bob Hope lead the cast with puns and quips, and trades expressionist chills for spooky fun ('more harebrained than hair-raising', said the New York Times review), enhanced by moody camerawork from Charles Lang (**The Ghost and Mrs. Muir**, **Charade**). Elizabeth Patterson, who had starred in **The Cat Creeps**, reprises her role. This version, directed by playwright and filmmaker Elliot Nugent (who would go on to helm 1949's **The Great Gatsby**, starring Alan Ladd), is often listed as one of Walt Disney's inspirations for Disneyland's Haunted Mansion ride.

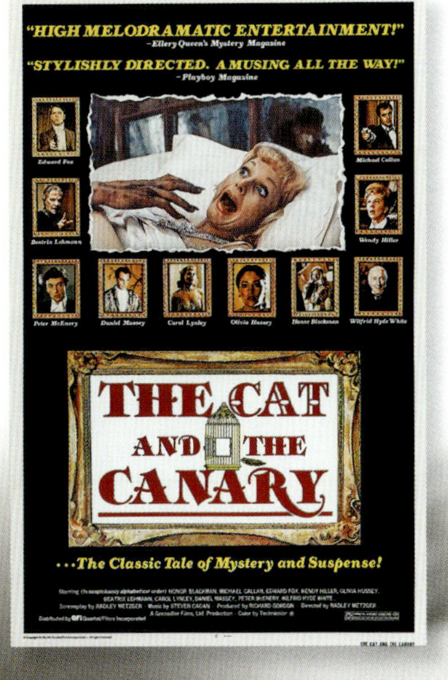


One more **The Cat and the Canary**, this time an Agatha Christie-style thriller from erotica director Radley Metzger and starring Honor Blackman and Olivia Hussey, came out in 1978. It brought little new to the proceedings, and by then the plot had become much too well known to thrill audiences.

## LA LLORONA

Mexico, 1933
Director: Ramón Peón.
Screenplay: Carlos Noriega Hope.
Cinematography: Guillermo Baqueriza.
Cast: Ramón Pereda, Virginia Zurí, Carlos Orellana, Adriana Lamar, María Luisa Zea, Antonio R. Frausto.

One of Mexico's most beloved folk tales, the story of La Llorona — the Weeping Woman — has been adapted to the screen an extraordinary number of times, starting with this 1933 effort from Cuban actor, writer and director Ramón Peón. Various versions of the legend exist, but all follow a woman betrayed by the man she loves (often a 16th century Nahua and a conquistador), who drowns the couple's children out of spite after being left for a younger woman. Realizing what she's done, she drowns herself in the same river. But she is refused access to heaven, and is condemned to roam the earth, a cursed soul forever in search of the children she murdered. Peón's **La Llorona** starts at a little boy's birthday party, where in the midst of the festivities, his mother starts worrying about an old curse affecting the first borns of her family. Until the arrival of talkies (with 1932's **Santa**, directed by Antonio Moreno), and Universal's version of **Dracula** targeting the latino market (George Melford, 1931), horror hadn't been a popular genre in Mexico. But **La Llorona**, the country's first scary movie and a major hit, would change it all, launching a series of popular supernatural pictures in the rest of the decade, including **El fantasma del convento** and **Dos monjes** (1934).

## SUPERNATURAL

USA, 1933
Director: Victor Hugo Halperin. Producer: Edward Halperin.
Screenplay: Harvey Thew, Brian Marlow, Garnett Weston.
Cinematography: Arthur Martinelli.
Cast: Carole Lombard, Randolph Scott, Vivienne Osborne, H.B. Warner, Beryl Mercer, William Farnum.

Known until then for her comedic parts, Paramount leading lady Carole Lombard stars in **Supernatural** in the dramatic role of Roma Courtney, who attends a séance and is possessed by the spirit of vengeful murderess Ruth Rogen, who 'killed her lovers after a riotous orgy in her sensuous apartment'. Released in a time when turning tables and communicating with the dead wasn't entirely uncommon, despite spiritualism being thoroughly debunked, the picture clearly paints its medium as a fraud and exposes some of his tricks. Yet unusually for the period, which largely saw ghosts as comedy devices, this pre-code mystery deals with possession and the supernatural with absolute earnestness. It also daringly features a female serial killer, to this day still a rare phenomenon in movies. Lombard famously clashed with director Victor Halperin (**White Zombie**), who unintentionally kept filming the side of her face, which bore a scar she preferred to hide. Particularly torturous were her facial transformation scenes, achieved through stop-frame photography, as Lombard, who hated to sit still, had to remain perfectly motionless while various stages of make-up were applied. She was also dissatisfied with the part, which she felt didn't play to her strengths. Yet her admirably nuanced performance in the dual role is the movie's highlight.

"SUPERNATURAL"
WITH
CAROLE LOMBARD
RANDOLPH SCOTT
VIVIENNE OSBORNE
H.B. WARNER
a Paramount Picture
Story by
GARNETT WESTON

## THE GHOST WALKS

USA, 1934
Director: Frank R. Strayer. Producer: Maury M. Cohen.
Screenplay: Charles Belden. Cinematography: M.A. Anderson.
Cast: John Miljan, June Collyer, Richard Carle, Henry Kolker, Spencer Charters, Johnny Arthur.

Stop me if you've heard this one: a group of strangers find themselves stuck in an old mansion on a stormy night, where a murder is perpetrated and things go bump in the night. A typical entry into the then-popular old dark house sub-genre — spooky whodunnit mysteries in which ghosts typically turn out to be elaborate hoaxes — **The Ghost Walks** sets itself apart, however, by presenting its main twist at the end of the first act: the spirit summoned by psychic Beatrice (Eve Southern) in the mansion where a playwright (John Miljan), a theatre producer (Richard Carle) and his secretary have found refuge, is revealed to be part of a live play rehearsal. Yet moments later, Beatrice is found murdered, her body disappears, and the plot picks up again, spiralling into a series of improbable surprises. Stage direction and performances are fairly theatrical, and hints of screwball comedy rather dated, but there are just enough claps of thunder, escaped lunatics, and candlelit apparitions for this quickie to be remembered. With no less than 84 directing credits to his name over the course of his career, Frank R. Strayer, a World War I veteran under contract with Columbia Pictures, had previously found moderate success in the genre with **The Monster Walks** (1932), and **The Vampire Bat** (1933), starring Lionel Atwill and Fay Wray.

## THE GHOST GOES WEST

UK, 1935
Director: René Clair. Producer: Alexander Korda.
Screenplay: Geoffrey Kerr, Robert E. Sherwood.
Music: Mischa Spoliansky. Cinematography: Harold Rosson.
Cast: Robert Donat, Jean Parker, Eugene Pallette, Elsa Lanchester, Ralph Bunker, Patricia Hilliard.

Offered a two-year, three-films contract with British producer Alexander Korda's London Films, esteemed French writer-director René Clair collaborated with U.S. playwright Robert E. Sherwood for his first English-language film, a witty satire of the clash of cultures between America and the Old World. Adapted from Eric Keown's 1932 short story *Sir Tristam Goes West* (itself likely inspired by Oscar Wilde's *The Canterville Ghost*), **The Ghost Goes West** pits a Scottish 18th century spirit doomed to haunt the dark halls of Glourie Castle, against an American businessman who buys the building, ships it brick by brick to Florida, and uses its spook as a publicity stunt. So hands-on was his producer that Clair reportedly considered removing his name from the picture, and although he completed a second movie for the company (**Break the News**, 1938), he returned to France before filming the last feature of his deal. **The Ghost Goes West** stars English actor Robert Donat (**The 39 Steps**) — against Clair's wish, who had hoped to cast Laurence Olivier — in the dual role of the ghost and his descendant, as well as **Bride of Frankenstein**'s Elsa Lanchester in a small part. One of the year's biggest hits, it was voted Best Film by *Film Weekly* in 1936.

## A CHRISTMAS CAROL

*Various film adaptations*

One of the best-known and oft-adapted tales ever written, Charles Dickens' *A Christmas Carol* was first published in 1843. Inspired, as many of his works, by the author's childhood experiences in a shoe-blacking factory, the redemption story of Ebenezer Scrooge, an avaricious man visited by the ghosts of Christmas Past, Present, and Yet To Come, was an instant success and had a profound influence on both literature and Christmas celebrations themselves.

It is therefore little surprise that screen adaptations would appear as early as 1901, with British short subject **Scrooge, or, Marley's Ghost**, which presented elaborate trick effects in its six-minute runtime. After a number of short films, the first feature-length version, **The Right to Be Happy**, would come out in 1916.

Directed by Henry Edwards, **Scrooge** (1935), with acclaimed actor Sir Seymour Hicks in the titular role, is the first to be held as a genuine classic. Seymour had already played the part in a number of stage versions as well as a 1913 short of the same name. Filmed in atmospheric low lights, the movie does not, however, show the spirits (besides the Ghost of Christmas Present), beyond silhouettes and shadows.

The success of **Scrooge** was promptly followed by MGM production **A Christmas Carol** (1938), a glossier picture directed by Edwin L. Marin and produced by Joseph L. Mankiewicz, and which would benefit from frequent subsequent re-releases and television runs. Originally intended for Lionel Barrymore, the part of Scrooge eventually devolved to Reginald Owen (**Mary Poppins**) when Barrymore's health forced him to decline. Rushed into production after various delays, this family-oriented version devotes more screen time to the secondary

characters, including the Cratchits (Gene and Kathleen Lockhart and their daughter June).

Directed and produced by Brian Desmond Hurst, British feature **Scrooge** (1951) was an instant hit in its homeland, but released on Halloween (as **A Christmas Carol**) in the U.S., it initially struggled to find its transatlantic audience. Television re-runs eventually cemented the film's reputation as the ultimate take on the tale, and Alastair Sim as the true face of the delightfully ruthless miser.

**Scrooge** was also the title of Ronald Neame's 1970 musical, starring Albert Finney. Nominated for a BAFTA, four Oscars and five Golden Globes, it was adapted into a UK stage production, *Scrooge: The Musical*, from 1992.

Mickey Mouse, in his first theatrical appearance in over thirty years, cameos as Bob Cratchit alongside — who else? — Scrooge McDuck as Ebenezer in **Mickey's Christmas Carol** (1983), an animated short released with re-issues of **The Jungle Book** (in the UK) and **The Rescuers** (in the U.S.)

Less traditional, but perhaps all the more relevant today, is Frank Oz's 1988 comedy **Scrooged**, in which cynical television executive Frank Cross (Bill Murray) is visited by the spirits while producing a sexed-up, violent version of the story. At first turned down by Murray, the script was then reworked extensively by comedy writers Michael O'Donoghue and Mitch Glazer, and offered the **Ghostbusters** star his first leading role without the support of an ensemble.

Brian Henson's all-singing, all-dancing **The Muppet Christmas Carol** (1992) sees Michael Caine star with Kermit, the Great Gonzo and Rizzo. Familiar muppet faces were originally cast as the ghosts, then replaced by brand new characters to better underline the ominous aspect of the apparitions.

Patrick Stewart reprised the part he played on Broadway and the West End for 1999 television movie **A Christmas Carol**, a much darker version made for TNT.

Robert Zemeckis' uncanny 3D motion capture animated picture **A Christmas Carol** (2009) introduced the story to a new medium. Jim Carrey leads an all-star cast and not only plays Scrooge, but also the three Christmas ghosts.

Finally, **The Man Who Invented Christmas** (2017), by Bharat Nalluri, tells the origins of the story, with Dan Stevens as Charles Dickens.

## TOPPER

USA, 1937
Director: Norman Z. McLeod.
Producer: Hal Roach.
Screenplay: Jack Jevne, Eric Hatch, Eddie Moran.
Cinematography: Norbert Brodine.
Cast: Constance Bennett, Cary Grant, Roland Young, Billie Burke, Alan Mowbray, Eugene Pallette.

Based on a 1926 novel by Thorne Smith, **Topper**, from director Norman Z. McLeod and Laurel and Hardy producer Hal Roach, stars Cary Grant and Constance Bennett as rich and carefree George and Marion, who crash their sports car after a night on the town and awaken as spirits. Understanding they must perform a good deed before they're allowed into heaven, they set out to brighten the life of stuffy, tame banker Cosmo Topper (Roland Young), encouraging him to live it up, with unexpected consequences. Light, entertaining and energetic any time its charming ghostly duo is on screen, this screwball comedy is also notable for its visual effects, likely inspired by Universal's 1933 **The Invisible Man**. Objects fly through the air, car tires change magically, and George and Marion appear, disappear or remain see-through ('We only have a certain amount of ectoplasm to use to get visible', Marion explains.) Yet it's for its supporting actor (Young) and sound recording that **Topper** garnered its two Academy Award nominations. A big box office hit, it generated two sequels and a TV series, as well as a 1979 made-for-TV remake; and was also the first black-and-white movie to be digitally colourized and re-released, in 1985.

## BEYOND TOMORROW

USA, 1940
Director: A. Edward Sutherland.
Producer: Lee Garmes.
Screenplay: Adele Comandini.
Music: Frank Tours.
Cinematography: Lester White.
Cast: Richard Carlson, Jean Parker,
Harry Carey, C. Aubrey Smith,
Charles Winninger, Maria Ouspenskaya.

When guests cancel on their Christmas eve dinner at the last minute, three elderly engineers (Charles Winninger, C. Aubrey Smith, Harry Carey) decide to throw out their wallets with ten dollars and their business cards inside, and invite whoever finds them and is honest enough to return them. Their two impromptu guests quickly fall for each other, and when the three gentlemen tragically die in a plane crash, their spirits watch over the young couple. Former actor A. Edward Sutherland directs **Beyond Tomorrow** (also known as **And So Goodbye**), a sentimental, bittersweet Christmas movie produced by acclaimed cinematographer-turned-producer Lee Garmes (**The Secret Life of Walter Mitty**), along with Academy Award-nominated screenwriter Adele Comandini, who adapts her own story. The cast is peppered with faces which were or would soon become familiar to B-movie buffs: Maria Ouspenskaya (the gypsy woman from Universal's **The Wolf Man**, 1941), Jean Parker (**The Ghost Goes West**), and Richard Carlson (**Creature from the Black Lagoon**, 1954) playing a character so dopey, it's almost hard to sympathize when things go south by his own doing. As with most holiday movies, **Beyond Tomorrow** carries a message of selflessness and altruism, and gained popularity with yearly seasonal viewings.

## THE GHOST BREAKERS

USA, 1940
Director: George Marshall.
Screenplay: Walter Deleon.
Music: Ernst Toch.
Cinematography: Charles Lang Jr.
Cast: Bob Hope, Paulette Goddard, Richard Carlson, Paul Lukas, Anthony Quinn, Willie Best.

The funny spookshow sub-genre flourished in the forties following the success of **The Ghost Breakers**, starring no less than legendary vaudevillian Bob Hope. Based on a 1909 stage play (*The Ghost Breaker*, by Paul Dickey and Charles W. Goddard), already adapted into (now lost) silent films in 1914 and 1922, this goofy comedy follows the customary plot pitting unwitting heroes against gangsters in a haunted mansion — this time mixing real and fake ghosts, and throwing in a voodoo zombie for good measure. Set in a beautiful candlelit plantation estate in Cuba, **The Ghost Breakers** succeeds in atmosphere as well as laughs, despite insensitive racial quips, and a tendency to reveal as much of the leading lady (Paulette Goddard, re-teaming with Hope after 1939's **The Cat and the Canary**) as censorship laws will allow. A box office hit, it helped popularize the supernatural comedy, with everyone from Old Mother Riley and the Bowery Boys to Abbott and Costello soon cast against spooks of various kinds. Director George Marshall, who also worked with W.C. Fields and Laurel and Hardy over the course of a career spanning fifty years, remade the movie as **Scared Stiff**, with Jerry Lewis and Dean Martin, in 1953.

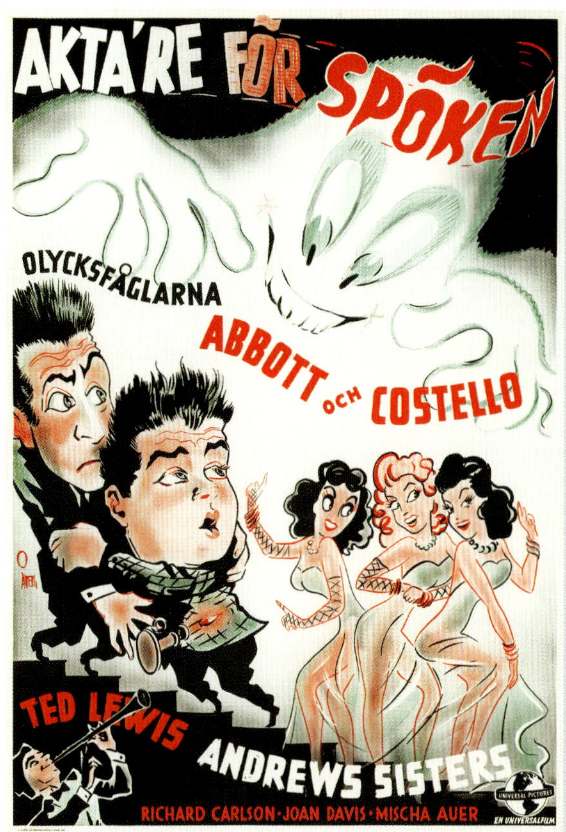


## HOLD THAT GHOST

USA, 1941
Director: Arthur Lubin. Screenplay: Robert Lees, Frederic I. Rinaldo, John Grant.
Cinematography: Woody Bredell.
Cast: Bud Abbott, Lou Costello, Richard Carlson, Evelyn Ankers, Joan Davis, Marc Lawrence.

**Hold That Ghost** marks vaudeville duo Bud Abbott and Lou Costello's first foray into horror spoof territory, a genre they would soon be renowned for. One of their earliest features, this slapstick classic takes on the old dark house tropes as two gas station attendants are stranded with a bunch of gangsters in an apparently haunted tavern. As would become typical of the stars' output, the thin plot is a mere excuse for their theatrics, and the mix of physical comedy and witty dialogue which had by then become their trademark. Originally titled **Oh, Charlie**, the movie, which contains several night club musical numbers by The Andrews Sisters and Ted Lewis and His Orchestra, is one of the double act's biggest successes, and would go on to be re-released in theatres twice then several times on home video, in addition to being performed by the stars as a radio play on Louella Parsons' popular program *Hollywood Hotel*. **Hold That Ghost** was the third of four pictures featuring Abbott and Costello and released by Universal that year (unsurprisingly for the era, the others — **Buck Privates**, **In the Navy**, and **Keep 'Em Flying** — were military-themed); all were directed by Arthur Lubin, who would go on to helm the studio's 1943 **Phantom of the Opera** adaptation starring Claude Rains.

## OLD MOTHER RILEY'S GHOSTS

UK, 1941
Director: John Baxter. Producer: John Baxter.
Screenplay: Con West, Geoffrey Orme, Arthur Lucan.
Music: Kennedy Russell. Cinematography: James Wilson.
Cast: Arthur Lucan, Kitty McShane, John Stuart,
A. Bromley Davenport, Dennis Wyndham, John Laurie.

The eighth of fifteen pictures starring British music hall drag act Arthur Lucan as Irish washerwoman Old Mother Riley, **Old Mother Riley's Ghosts** sees said lady inherit a haunted castle in Scotland. Naturally, the presumed spooks are nothing but a front for an industrial espionage plot, and the no-nonsense dame ends up giving the bad guys a fright of their own. Co-starring Lucan's comedy partner and real-life wife Kitty McShane as Mother Riley's headstrong daughter Kitty, this micro-budget farce features spooky sounds, projected apparitions, talking skeletons, and ceaseless pantomime humour. As with most British wartime movies, whose mandate was to entertain, the emphasis is squarely on farce, leaving no room whatsoever for actual frights. Old Mother Riley would again square off against the seemingly supernatural — in the shape of Bela Lugosi — in her final film **Mother Riley Meets the Vampire** in 1952. This time Kitty would not appear, as her off-screen relationship with Lucan had grown as strained as their constantly bickering characters. Lucan would die a couple of years later and McShane would attempt to continue the double act with his stage understudy, Roy Rolland, as Old Mother; but the new duo was short-lived, as they never captured the success of the original.

## THE CURSE OF THE CAT PEOPLE

USA, 1944
Directors: Robert Wise, Gunther V. Fritsch. Producer: Val Lewton.
Screenplay: Dewitt Bodeen, Val Lewton. Music: Roy Webb.
Cinematography: Nick Musuraca.
Cast: Simone Simon, Ann Carter, Jane Randolph, Kent Smith,
Elizabeth Russell, Eve March.

'The Beast-Woman haunts the night anew!' Picking up a few years after where Jacques Tourneur's **Cat People** (1942) left off, **The Curse of the Cat People**, despite its misleading advertising campaign, has very little to do with the felines, zoos, and sexual undertones of the first film. Yet RKO executives were keen to maintain the link to the previous success, against producer Val Lewton's wishes. Instead of panthers, **Curse** gives us an early example of the haunted child staple as six-year-old Amy (Ann Carter), daughter of Oliver and Alice Reed befriends the ghost of her father's first wife, cat woman Irena, whom no one else is able to see. Simone Simon, Kent Smith and Jane Randolph reprise their parts from the Tourneur movie; and the character of Amy isn't unlike Irena in the original: an imaginative loner who doesn't fit in, surrounded by men who force her to conform. Carter gives a convincing performance, despite losing a front tooth in the middle of the shoot and being instructed from that point to act with her mouth shut. **The Curse of the Cat People** gave their first directing credits to Gunther von Fritsch, and to his replacement when he fell behind his eighteen-day schedule: then-editor Robert Wise, who would go on to direct one of the greatest ghost movies of all time, 1963's **The Haunting**. Production was further complicated by RKO's demands to reshoot and add scenes, in the hopes to turn this poetic, dreamlike ode to childhood into a supernatural thriller.

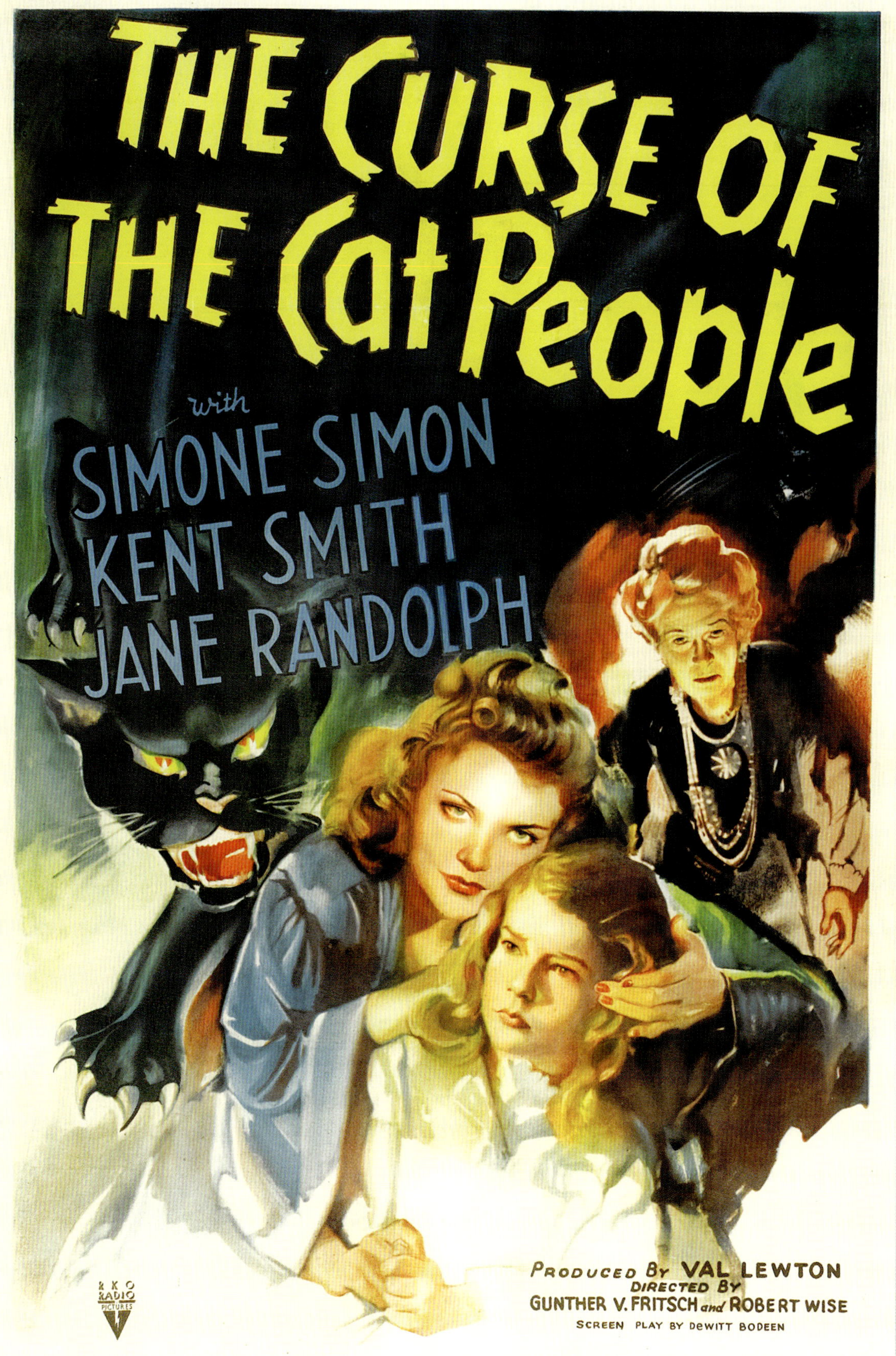
THE CURSE OF THE CAT PEOPLE
with
SIMONE SIMON
KENT SMITH
JANE RANDOLPH
RKO RADIO PICTURES
PRODUCED BY VAL LEWTON
DIRECTED BY
GUNTHER V. FRITSCH and ROBERT WISE
SCREEN PLAY BY DEWITT BODEEN

## THE CANTERVILLE GHOST

*Various film adaptations*

Published in two parts in February and March of 1887 in the Court and Society Review, Oscar Wilde's light-hearted *The Canterville Ghost* charmed both sides of the Atlantic with its parody of Gothic horror, a then-popular literary genre, and its satire of cultural differences between the old continent and the New World.

Mixing comedy with mild macabre thrills, the novella recounts the tribulations of Sir Simon Canterville, the centuries-old ghost haunting Canterville Chase, when an American family moves into his home and refuses to be frightened by the apparition. As their New World pragmatism turns to bluntness, lack of manners and excessive consumerism, the old British spirit fusses, stuck in its ways, until the family's fifteen-year-old daughter takes the time to listen to him and treat him with dignity.

It naturally wouldn't be long before such popular, classic entertainment made its way onto the screen. The first adaptation on record came out in 1944 from director Jules Dassin, a former assistant to Alfred Hitchcock, who had started his filmmaking career three years earlier with a twenty-minute adaptation of Poe's *The Tell-Tale Heart*.

With Charles Laughton as the titular spook, and cameos from Universal character actress Una O'Connor and future Ed Wood regular Tor Johnson, this version strays the farthest from its source material, replacing the family with a U.S platoon during World War II, and kicking off with an introduction set in the seventeenth century, when Sir Canterville was still alive.

Dassin reportedly replaced **Topper** director Norman Z. McLeod at the helm when McLeod failed to gain the trust of Laughton, at that point already a massive star. He would be blacklisted in 1950, but thereafter pursued a successful career in France.

A series of television adaptations followed this initial effort, including outings for the BBC (1962), ABC (1966, as a musical starring Douglas Fairbanks Jr.), as well as a Soviet cartoon (1970) and a CBS Radio Mystery Theater play (1974).

1986 American-British made-for-television co-production **The Canterville Ghost** offers the rather strange pairing of Sir John Gielgud with Alyssa Milano in a story heavily centered on the American family and in particular the daughter, here named Jennifer, who sets out to solve the mystery of the haunting and release the ghost from his curse.

**The Canterville Ghost** (1986)

The 1996 Hallmark version directed by Sydney Macartney sees Neve Campbell's plucky Virginia team up with Sir Patrick Stewart's Canterville ghost to convince her family of the wraith's existence. Although still decidedly family-friendly, this adaptation has a slightly darker tone, as the spirit broods over life and death and the meaning of being a ghost.

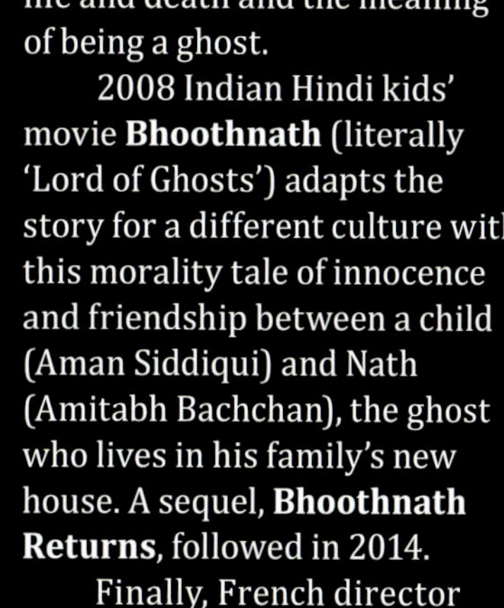


2008 Indian Hindi kids' movie **Bhoothnath** (literally 'Lord of Ghosts') adapts the story for a different culture with this morality tale of innocence and friendship between a child (Aman Siddiqui) and Nath (Amitabh Bachchan), the ghost who lives in his family's new house. A sequel, **Bhoothnath Returns**, followed in 2014.

Finally, French director Yann Samuell (**The Great Ghost Rescue**, 2011) adds to the list a goofy, effects-heavy Belgian-French co-production starring Michaël Youn. 2016's **Le fantôme de Canterville** sees a woman (Audrey Fleurot, **The Intouchables**) playing the titular role.

**The Canterville Ghost** (1986)

## THE UNINVITED

USA, 1944
Director: Lewis Allen. Screenplay: Dodie Smith, Frank Partos.
Music: Victor Young. Cinematography: Charles Lang Jr.
Cast: Ruth Hussey, Ray Milland, Donald Crisp, Barbara Everest,
Cornelia Otis Skinner, Alan Napier.

A brother and sister (Ray Milland and Ruth Hussey) move into a Welsh seaside house, despite the warnings of a local girl (Gail Russell) whose late mother used to live in the house — and might inhabit it still. They soon experience spooky 'disturbances'; could it be the girl's mother isn't the only spirit walking the halls of their new home? Quaint villages, cold drafts, séances, candlelit hallways, cries in the night, and an attractive woman haunted by the past: **The Uninvited** introduces all the staples and structure of the modern ghost film. Based on Irish author Dorothy Macardle's novel *Uneasy Freehold*, Lewis Allen's masterpiece is generally considered the first Hollywood production to take its haunting seriously. No goofball comedians poking fun at the spirits, no last act reveal that it was all a cover-up for some bootlegging operation: these ghosts are real and life-threatening. With the success of Val Lewton's RKO chillers, Paramount grew keen to produce its own supernatural scares. So keen in fact that execs reportedly added in the climax's (admittedly spooky) vaporous apparitions for shock value, proving that at no point in their history did studios trust audiences with subtlety. The story contains elements of comedy and romance, both genres until then most commonly associated with the paranormal, yet its core is a mystery with genuine chills. By today's standards it may seem somewhat tame, and some of the characters' reactions are amusingly dated (see Stella's awkward apology for not owning an ashtray: 'we're an awfully un-smoking house'); but **The Uninvited**'s influence on the classic ghost story is undeniable. Paramount hired an A-list cast and spared no expense. For their efforts, they were rewarded with commercial success, rave reviews, and an Academy Award nomination for Charles Lang's moody black and white cinematography.

## BLITHE SPIRIT

UK, 1945
Director: David Lean. Producer: Noël Coward. Screenplay: David Lean, Ronald Neame, Anthony Havelock-Allan. Music: Richard Addinsell. Cinematography: Ronald Neame. Cast: Rex Harrison, Constance Cummings, Kay Hammond, Margaret Rutherford, Hugh Wakefield, Joyce Carey.

David Lean directs Rex Harrison in one of his most memorable early film roles with this adaptation of Noël Coward's 1941 play **Blithe Spirit**. Harrison stars as novelist Charles Condomine, who, along with his wife Ruth (Constance Cummings), invites a medium (Margaret Rutherford) to perform a séance in order to research the 'tricks of the trade'. They accidentally conjure the spirit of his first wife (Kay Hammond), although she is only visible to him, and she promptly sets out to antagonize Ruth. Despite a limited cast and few locations, the movie's superb staging, clever camerawork, lavish Technicolor, and Academy Award-winning visual effects all but eclipse the story's theatrical origins. Undoubtedly inspired by the surge of spiritualism after World War I, Coward's comedy of manners pokes fun at everything from eccentric mediums, to disbelieving bourgeois, marital woes, and the BBC. Evidencing contemporary audiences' grasp of supernatural matters, mentions of exorcisms, ectoplasm and poltergeists abound — as well as an explicit reference to a character's sex life, considered so daring it was excised from the U.S. release. A box office failure, **Blithe Spirit** now stands out as a comedy classic, due to witty, biting dialogue (although Harrison's considerable charm can't entirely make up for the misogyny of some of his lines) and impeccable performances; Rutherford in particular steals the show.

EALING
Studios
The UNEXPECTED, THE TRAGIC,
THE COMIC, THE ROMANTIC,
THE DRAMATIC.....
"DEAD
OF
NIGHT"
SUITABLE
ONLY FOR
ADULTS
Michael
REDGRAVE
Googie WITHERS
MERVYN JOHNS
ROWLAND CULVER
NAUNTON WAYNE
BASIL RADFORD
SALLY ANN HOWES
FREDRICK VALK
PRODUCED BY
MICHAEL BALCON
PRINTED BY W. E. SMITH LTD. SYDNEY

## DEAD OF NIGHT

UK, 1945
Directors: Basil Dearden, Charles Crichton, Robert Hamer, Alberto Cavalcanti. Producer: Michael Balcon. Screenplay: John Baines, Angus Macphail, T.E.B. Clarke. Music: Georges Auric. Cinematography: Stan Pavey, Douglas Slocombe. Cast: Mervyn Johns, Ralph Michael, Roland Culver, Mary Merrall, Frederick Valk, Renee Gadd.

**Dead of Night**, from Ealing Studios and directors Alberto Cavalcanti, Basil Dearden, Robert Hamer and Charles Crichton, stands out not only as one of the few scary pictures produced in wartime Britain, but also as one of the most influential supernatural films ever made. An early example of horror anthology, a sub-genre it helped popularize, its linking narrative centres around an architect at a dinner party, who, although he has never met his fellow diners, remembers them from a recurring dream, and has the foreboding that something awful is about to happen to them. Various events seem to confirm the man's foresight, and the guests one by one recall supernatural events they've experienced, leading to five simple, standalone vignettes: a racing car driver avoids death in a bus crash thanks to a premonitory dream; a man is possessed by a haunted mirror; the ghost of a little boy appears at a children's Christmas party (a clear inspiration for the birthday scene of M. Night Shyamalan's **The Sixth Sense**); a golfer is pestered by his late competitor; and in what is undeniably the spookiest and most influential segment of all, a ventriloquist dummy has a mind of its own. The movie ends with a twist, and a fantastically chilling nightmare sequence. **Dead of Night** was a one-off for Ealing, which until then had mostly focused on realistic war films and on their hallmark comedies, and despite the anthology's commercial success, would never produce another horror picture.

## A PLACE OF ONE'S OWN

UK, 1945
Director: Bernard Knowles. Producer: R.J. Minney. Screenplay: Brock Williams, Osbert Sitwell. Cinematography: Stephen Dade. Cast: Margaret Lockwood, James Mason, Barbara Mullen, Dennis Price, Helen Haye, Michael Shepley.

In an age of ghostly farces, British thriller **A Place of One's Own** stands alongside America's 1944 **The Uninvited** as the only pictures of their time to earnestly depict haunted houses. Based on a 1940 novel by English author Osbert Sitwell, it marks the directorial debut of cinematographer and frequent Hitchcock collaborator Bernard Knowles, and was produced as part of a series of 1940s melodramas from Gainsborough Pictures. James Mason and Barbara Mullen star as an elderly couple whose retirement mansion appears haunted by the spirit of a past inhabitant, who eventually possesses their hired companion, played by Margaret Lockwood (who had already featured alongside Mason in previous Gainsborough production **The Man in Grey**, 1943). A box office disappointment given the clout of its stars, **A Place of One's Own** may have proven too low key and light on scares even for its contemporaries, as the New York Times review stated: 'You'll have to be awfully tolerant of old-fashioned haunted house legends to be finally satisfied with this mild film.' Mason, on the other hand, blamed himself for the disaster; he had indeed eagerly insisted on playing the elderly lead at age thirty-six, which meant he would be covered in make-up.

## THE TIME OF THEIR LIVES

USA, 1946
Director: Charles T. Barton. Producer: Val Burton. Screenplay: Val Burton, Walter DeLeon, Bradford Ropes, John Grant. Music: Milton Rosen. Cinematography: Charles Van Enger.
Cast: Bud Abbott, Lou Costello, Marjorie Reynolds, Binnie Barnes, John Shelton, Gale Sondergaard.

Bud Abbott and Lou Costello are the main attraction of this story of two eighteenth century spooks (Costello and Marjorie Reynolds) doomed to haunt the estate where they were wrongly accused and executed for treason, until proof of their innocence comes to light. Abbott features as one of the guests of the newly restored mansion in the 1940s. The script was originally written to feature a dandy and his African-American valet, but was reworked when the stars signed on. One of only two films (along with the same year's **Little Giant**) to cast Abbott and Costello as individual players rather than partners, **The Time of Their Lives** is decidedly more plot-led and less burlesque-centric than the duo's typical output. Bored with the formula, and affected by the recent strain in their professional relationship (sparked by a dispute over their earnings), the comedians embarked on this picture, which only sees them interact briefly. Convinced he'd picked the lesser part, Costello demanded to switch with Abbott and walked away for two weeks in the middle of production when his request was denied; director Charles Barton (who would team up with them again a number of times, including for **Abbott and Costello Meet Frankenstein**) worked around the character until he returned.

## THE GHOST AND MRS. MUIR

USA, 1947
Director: Joseph L. Mankiewicz. Producer: Fred Kohlmar. Screenplay: Philip Dunne. Music: Bernard Herrmann. Cinematography: Charles Lang Jr.
Cast: Gene Tierney, Rex Harrison, George Sanders, Edna Best, Vanessa Brown, Anna Lee.

1947 Twentieth Century Fox comedy **The Ghost and Mrs. Muir**, directed by Joseph L. Mankiewicz, constitutes the apex of the brief 1940s wave of romantic ghost movies. Perfectly cast — Rex Harrison, fresh off **Anna and the King of Siam**; Gene Tierney, star of **Heaven Can Wait** and of Mankiewitz's **Dragonwyck** (with a young Vincent Price); and Natalie Wood — this A-list tale of a young widow who falls for the ghost of a sea captain haunting her cottage sparkles, thanks to witty dialogue, atmospheric photography (which earned cinematographer Charles Lang an Academy Award nomination), and the remarkable chemistry of its leads. The source material, an eponymous novel published in the UK in 1945, was penned by Irish author Josephine Leslie under the pseudonym R.A. Dick, in a bid to circumvent prejudices against female writers. In both the book and the movie, Lucy Muir (whose last name means 'sea' in Gaelic) similarly finds it easier to find a publisher for Captain Gregg's memoir when using his name. Although set in England, **The Ghost and Mrs. Muir** was filmed in Palos Verdes, California, in a cottage entirely built for the production and destroyed after wrap. The set featured removable walls and ceilings, to allow in lights and cameras, and also included a greenhouse, which was never used in the movie. Leslie's novel was later adapted into a sitcom, running from 1968 to 1970 on NBC. This time the story was transposed to modern-day Maine.

## THE GHOSTS OF BERKELEY SQUARE

UK, 1947
Director: Vernon Sewell. Producer: Louis H. Jackson. Screenplay: James Seymour. Music: Hans May. Cinematography: Ernest Palmer. Cast: Robert Morley, Felix Aylmer, Yvonne Arnaud, Claude Hulbert, Abraham Sofaer, Ernest Thesiger.

The souls of a couple of eighteenth century officers (played by established character actors Robert Morley and Felix Aylmer) are doomed to haunt the walls of 50 Berkeley Square until it is visited by a British monarch in this comedy produced by the aptly named British National Films. The real-life London address had been famously haunted since the mid-nineteenth century, with various apparitions reported over the course of a century. Such was the reputation of the place that it served as inspiration for Caryl Brahms and S. J. Simon's novel *No Nightingales*, itself the basis for this movie. **The Ghosts of Berkeley Square** presents death as a bureaucracy, with rules for materializing or resting in peace, much like **Beetlejuice** would forty years later. For all its frisky comedy, patriotism, and casual racism ('A black fella! [...] Having an empire is all very well, but you don't want it in the house!'), **The Ghosts of Berkeley Square** failed to lift the spirits of post-war British audiences who, much like the spooks themselves, would have felt uncomfortably caught between nostalgia for the Kingdom's colonial glory, and the need to embrace modernity. Director Vernon Sewell would return to horror a couple of decades later with pictures such as Tigon Productions' **The Blood Beast Terror** and **Curse of the Crimson Altar** (both 1968).

## PORTRAIT OF JENNIE

USA, 1948
Director: William Dieterle. Producer: David O. Selznick. Screenplay: Paul Osborn, Peter Berneis, Leonardo Bercovici. Music: Dimitri Tiomkin. Cinematography: Joseph August. Cast: Jennifer Jones, Joseph Cotten, Ethel Barrymore, Lillian Gish, Cecil Kellaway, David Wayne.

At first optioned by MGM, Robert Nathan's 1940 novel *Portrait of Jennie*, the story of a struggling artist finding inspiration in a mysterious girl who seems to grow older with each encounter, was picked up by Academy Award-winning producer David O. Selznick (**Gone with the Wind**, **Rebecca**), who hired director William Dieterle (**The Hunchback of Notre Dame**, 1939) to tell this romantic tale. Although Vivien Leigh was originally approached to play Jennie, and the idea of filming Shirley Temple over a number of years to capture her growing up was considered, the role eventually went to Academy Award winner Jennifer Jones (**The Song of Bernadette**), whom Selznick would marry the following year. Filmed on location in New York City and Massachusetts under the title **Tidal Wave**, **Portrait of Jennie** saw its budget skyrocket during production, which was halted for five weeks while Selznick, concerned with several aspects of the picture, ordered rewrites on the script. Cinematographer Joseph H. August passed away during the shoot; the identity of his replacement for the last remaining scenes is still disputed. August was posthumously nominated for his work on the movie, which included various tints of black-and-white, and a Technicolor finale. Reviews upon release were mixed, but **Portrait of Jennie** has since grown to be seen as a nostalgic, forgotten gem.

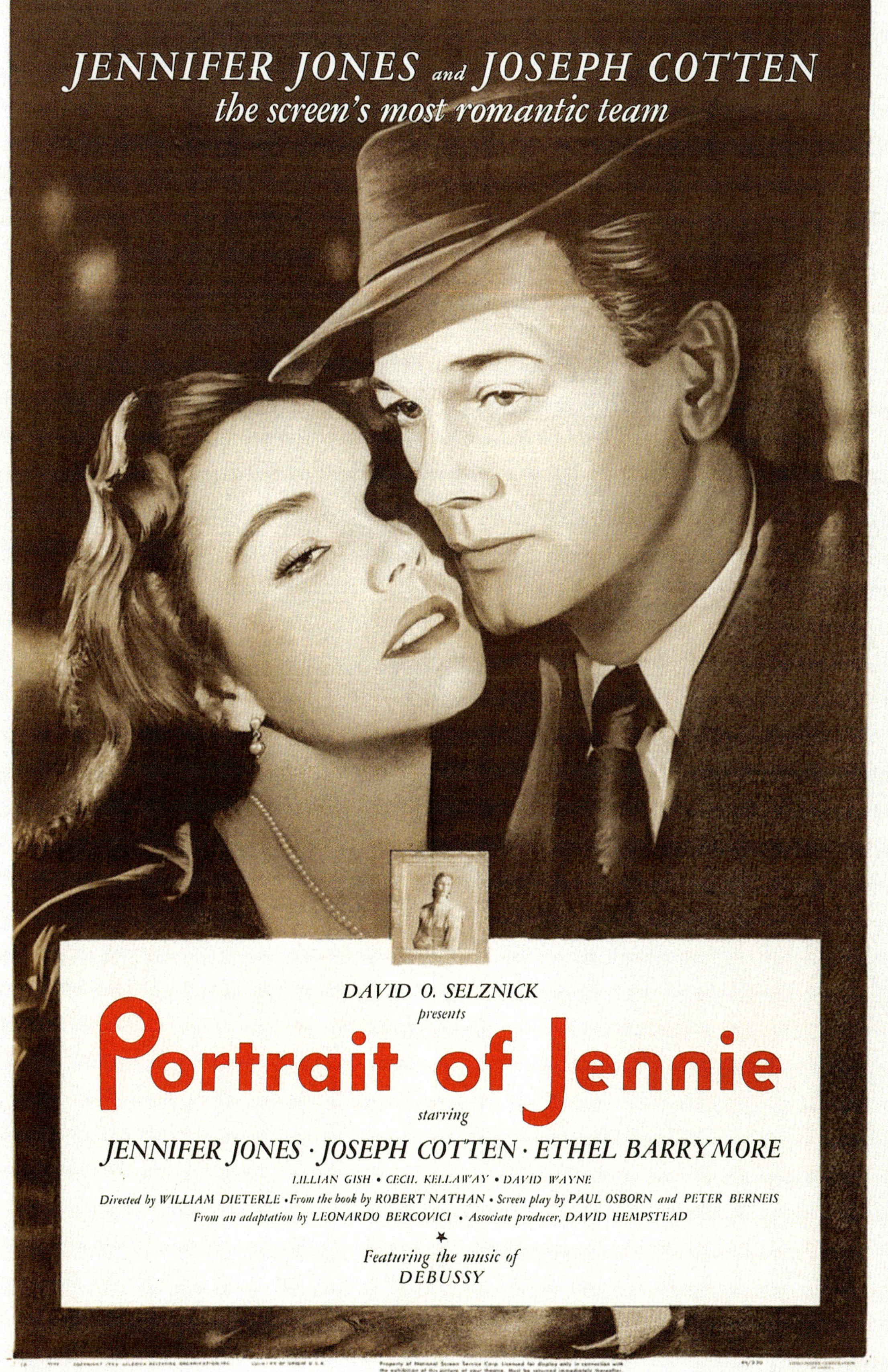
JENNIFER JONES and JOSEPH COTTEN
the screen's most romantic team
DAVID O. SELZNICK
presents
Portrait of Jennie
starring
JENNIFER JONES · JOSEPH COTTEN · ETHEL BARRYMORE
LILLIAN GISH • CECIL KELLAWAY • DAVID WAYNE
Directed by WILLIAM DIETERLE • From the book by ROBERT NATHAN • Screen play by PAUL OSBORN and PETER BERNEIS
From an adaptation by LEONARDO BERCOVICI • Associate producer, DAVID HEMPSTEAD
Featuring the music of
DEBUSSY

## GHOST OF YOTSUYA

Japan, 1949
Director: Keisuke Kinoshita. Screenplay: Eijirô Hisaita.
Music: Chûji Kinoshita. Cinematography: Hiroshi Kusuda.
Cast: Kinuyo Tanaka, Ken Uehara, Hisako Yamane, Haruko Sugimura, Chôko Iida, Osamu Takizawa.

One of the most famous ghost tales of Japanese folklore, Tsuruya Nanboku's 1825 kabuki play — the story of Iemon, an impoverished but ambitious samurai who gets rid of his wife Oiwa to climb social ranks, and is later haunted by her spirit — has been adapted a record amount of times (over thirty, many of which have been lost) since 1912. Prolific (42 movies in 23 years) and versatile director Keisuke Kinoshita's 1949 two-part version stands amongst the most memorable, as restrained and subtle as Nobuo Nakagawa's 1959 interpretation is flamboyant.

With glorious black and white cinematography from Hiroshi Kusuda, **Ghost of Yotsuya** (aka **The Yotsuya Phantom** aka **Yotsuya Kwaidan**) transposes its narrative to postwar Japan. It mainly differs from other adaptations in that Oiwa's apparitions are presented as a manifestation of her husband's bad conscience, rather than a literal spirit; Iemon is also less despicable and more human than usually depicted. The original play dealt with revenge and loyalty; Occupation policy however, while officially abolishing censorship, substituted feudal principles with democratic ideals, and Kinoshita's movie focuses on guilt, personal grudges, and the place of women in society. These themes aren't dissimilar from those underpinning Japanese horror releases of the nineties and noughties, where long-haired female ghosts exact their vengeance upon the living.

## GHOST CHASERS

USA, 1951
Director: William Beaudine.
Producer: Jan Grippo. Screenplay:
Charles R. Marion. Music: Edward J. Kay.
Cinematography: Marcel Le Picard.
Cast: Leo Gorcey, Huntz Hall, Lloyd
Corrigan, Lela Bliss, Jan Kayne,
Philip Van Zandt.

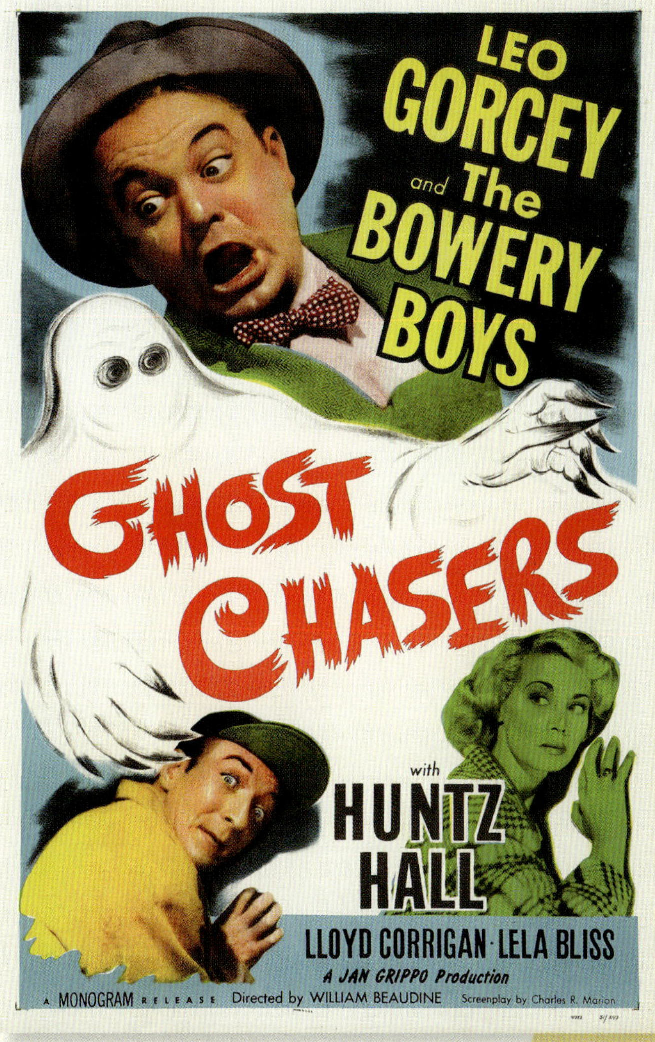


Stars of forty-eight popular comedies, the Bowery Boys, a group of New York actors led by Leo Gorcey (formerly of the East Side Kids), uncover a fake medium with the help of a 300-year-old spirit in **Ghost Chasers**, helmed by prolific B-picture director William Beaudine for Monogram Pictures. Pitting goofballs against the supernatural had proved an enduring trend since Abbott and Costello's **Hold That Ghost** (1941), with the East Side Kids facing Bela Lugosi in **Spooks Run Wild** (1941), and the ever-popular **Abbott and Costello Meet Frankenstein** (1948). The Bowery Boys themselves had already squared against ghosts the less memorable **Spook Busters** (1946), in which the Boys attempt to bust spirits out of an old mansion, only to uncover a mad scientist conducting experiments in the house. The movie is most notable for its influence on **Ghostbusters** (1984). They would trade jokes with more apparitions, vampires and gorillas in another haunted house a few years later for **Spook Chasers** (1957). **Ghost Chasers** is at its best when it mocks spiritualism, as in the scene when a ghost provides commentary on the absurdity of the séance as it unfolds, or interferes with the tricks used by the fraudulent psychic.

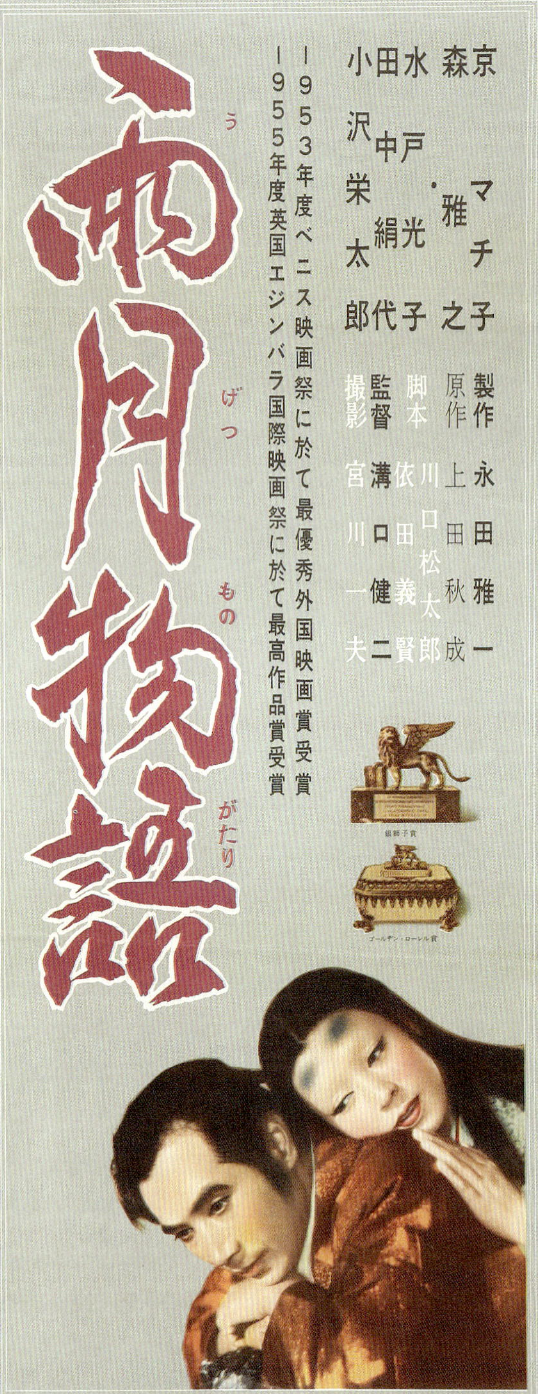

## UGETSU

Japan, 1953
Director: Kenji Mizoguchi.
Producer: Masaichi Nagata.
Screenplay: Matsutaro Kawaguchi, Yoshikata Yoda.
Music: Fumio Hayasaka.
Cinematography: Kazuo Miyagawa.
Cast: Machiko Kyo, Mitsuko Mito, Kinuyo Tanaka, Masayuki Mori, Eitaro Ozawa, Sugisaku Aoyama.

Inspired by two stories from Akinari Ueda's *Ugetsu monogatori* ('Tales of Moonlight and Rain'), as well as one by Guy de Maupassant, **Ugetsu** (literally 'moon obscured by rain clouds') is a classic jidaigeki (drama set in the Edo period) chronicling the adventures of two peasants and their wives during the civil war in late sixteenth century Japan. A morality play on the effects of war on the common people, it warns against vanity, social climbing and greed, and the impact these sins have on the loved ones of those who commit them. By that point the author of dozens of pictures and recognized as a master of Japanese cinema, director Kenji Mizoguchi chose to keep the atmosphere at once realistic and eerie, while steeping the movie in tradition. The score is derived from Kabuki theatre music. The cinematography, from DoP Kazuo Miyagawa (**Rashomon**), was inspired by Chinese painting and traditional scrolls; it is filled with long takes, typical of the filmmaker, and Miyagawa keeps the camera moving, with a reported seventy percent shot from a crane. **Ugetsu** marked the second of three awards Mizoguchi would win on three consecutive years at the Venice Film Festival (the other two being **The Life of Oharu** in 1952, and **Sansho the Bailiff** in 1954). An influential film to this day, it served as a direct reference for the misty lake scene in Martin Scorsese's **Silence** (2016).

## DIABOLIQUE

France, 1955
Director: Henri-Georges Clouzot. Producer: Henri-Georges Clouzot.
Screenplay: Henri-Georges Clouzot, Jérôme Géronimi, René Masson,
Frédéric Grendel. Music: Georges Van Parys.
Cinematography: Armand Thirard.
Cast: Simone Signoret, Véra Clouzot, Paul Meurisse, Charles Vanel,
Pierre Larquey, Michel Serrault.

Though perhaps not as widely known nowadays as some of the movies it inspired, **Diabolique** (aka **Les diaboliques**), from director Henri-Georges Clouzot (**The Wages of Fear**, 1953), is arguably one of the most influential pictures ever committed to celluloid. Based on *Celle qui n'était plus* ('She Was No More'), a 1951 novel by Pierre Boileau and Thomas Narcejac (whose work Hitchcock adapted for **Vertigo**), the film follows the wife (Véra Clouzot, real-life spouse of the filmmaker) of the sadistic headmaster (Paul Meurisse) of a country boarding school, as she murders — or does she? — her husband with the help of his mistress (Simone Signoret). Although the entire plot takes the shape of a classical ghost story, only the last few moments of the picture hint at a possible supernatural twist, open to the viewer's interpretation. Advertisements for the movie advised audiences to show up for the start of the picture, stating latecomers would be refused admission; a message at the end of the pic asked viewers not to spoil the ending for their friends. Hitchcock, who reportedly envied **Diabolique**'s international success, imitated this marketing strategy for **Psycho** (1960), itself inspired by Clouzot's film. Further offshoots include Curtis Harrington's 1967 **Games**, and Hammer Films' 1961 **Scream of Fear**, which pulls a double **Diabolique**. Tragically, Véra Clouzot, who like her character suffered from a heart condition, died of cardiac arrest just five years after the release, aged 47.

## GHOST OF KASANE

Japan, 1957
Director: Nobuo Nakagawa.
Producer: Mitsugu Ôkura. Screenplay: Kôhan Kawauchi. Music: Michiaki Watanabe. Cinematography: Yoshimi Hirano.
Cast: Kazuko Wakasugi, Takashi Wada, Tetsurô Tanba, Noriko Kitazawa, Kikuko Hanaoka.

Also known as **The Depths** or **The Ghosts of Kasane Swamp**, **Ghost of Kasane** is widely considered the best adaptation of classic tale *Shinkei Kasanegafuchi*, as told by nineteenth century horror author Encho Sanyutei. Two inferior screen versions would follow, both by Kimiyoshi Yasuda: one in black-and-white in 1960, and one in colour a decade later. The convoluted narrative shows how a murder committed by a samurai sets off a series of events that will haunt and destroy the perpetrator, his son, and his victim's daughter. This theme of curses created by guilt and extending to the next generation underpins many Japanese ghost stories, including — and especially — the J-horror wave of the late nineties and early 2000s, with movies such as the **Ring** and **Grudge** series. Best known for his *kwaidan*-inspired horror features and television films, director Nobuo Nakagawa worked with genre production company Shintoho Studios, which flourished in the late fifties before suddenly declaring bankruptcy in 1961, after the release of Nakagawa's **Jigoku**. Although ghostly apparitions are sparse and played more for its moral of karmic retribution than for scares, the violent opening scene pulls no punches, and the sense of fate closing in inexorably over the protagonists makes **Ghost of Kasane** a powerful tragedy.

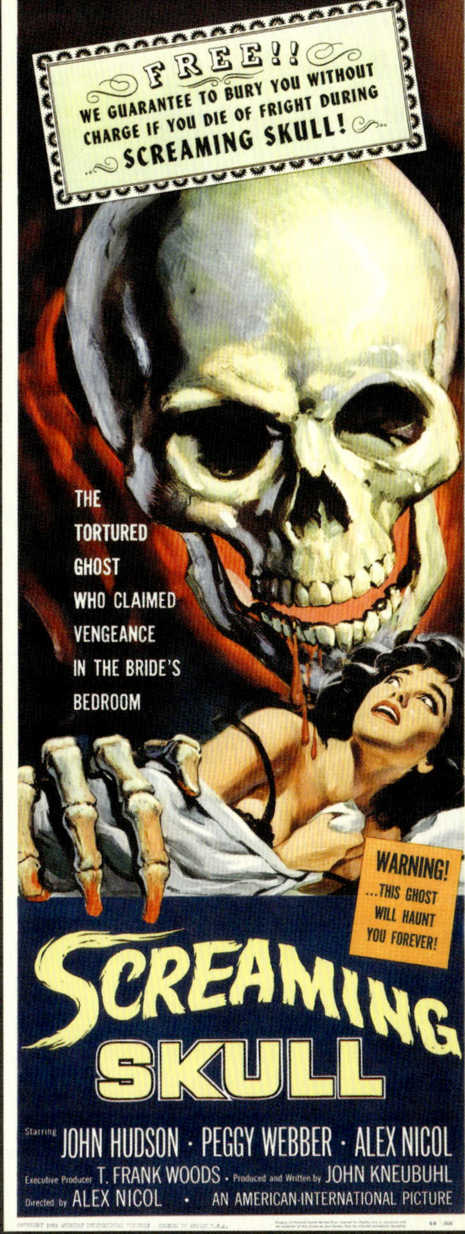


## THE SCREAMING SKULL

USA, 1958
Director: Alex Nicol. Producer: John Kneubuhl.
Screenplay: John Kneubuhl. Music: Ernest Gold.
Cinematography: Floyd Crosby.
Cast: John Hudson, Peggy Webber, Tom Johnson,
Russ Conway, Alex Nicol.

According to English folklore, floating skulls are sometimes known to appear and moan or cry at passers-by at various haunted locations. Loosely inspired by this legend, **The Screaming Skull** tells the story of widower Eric (John Hudson), who brings his wealthy new bride Jenny (Peggy Webber) to his mansion, where his first wife Marion has died. Eric claims to have moved on, but Mickey, the mentally disabled gardener (director Alex Nicol himself), reveals Marion still haunts the house... **The Screaming Skull** starts with a narration guaranteeing audience members a free burial, should they die of fright during the picture. Given the movie's very mild scares, no one was likely to claim this offer; but William Castle would use a very similar gimmick just a few months later, promising life insurance policies at screenings of **Macabre** and parking hearses outside theatres. For his first directing effort, Nicol, a Broadway and screen actor unsatisfied with the parts he was offered, demonstrated a great ability to spot talent, hiring the likes of future Oscar-winning cinematographer Floyd Crosby; and composer Ernest Gold, soon to be known for his work on Otto Preminger's **Exodus**. For the movie's main theme, Gold borrowed from Berlioz's Symphonie Fantastique, which Stanley Kubrick's **The Shining** would also copy twenty-two years later. The result is an atmospheric yet unevenly paced, barely feature-length piece, replete with eerie pictures of superimposed skulls.

## HOUSE ON HAUNTED HILL

USA, 1959
Director: William Castle.
Producer: William Castle.
Screenplay: Robb White. Music: Von Dexter.
Cinematography: Carl Guthrie.
Cast: Vincent Price, Carol Ohmart, Richard Long, Alan Marshal, Carolyn Craig, Elisha Cook Jr.

Arguably master of gimmicks William Castle's best known directing effort, **House on Haunted Hill** is the movie equivalent of a funhouse, using its threadbare plot to lead viewers from spooky sound effects to schlocky frights. A gleefully evil Vincent Price plays Frederick Loren, a millionaire who, along with his wife Annabelle (Carol Ohmart), invites five strangers to a haunted house, promising a reward of $10,000 to anyone who remains the entire night. Naturally, they soon find themselves locked inside, to the mercy of their hosts... and of the house's ghosts. In true Castle fashion, screenings culminated in a trick gone down in history as Emergo: an inflatable skeleton flying over the audience during the climax, in which a corpse floats out of an acid vat to attack the treacherous Annabelle. However, the scene today pales in comparison with the wonderfully creepy apparitions, earlier in the story, of the blind caretaker of the house. On a budget of $150,000, Castle used Frank Lloyd Wright's famous Ennis house in Los Feliz for the haunted abode's exteriors, and filmed the bulk of the picture on a soundstage. Despite poor reviews and an often-uncooperative Emergo, **House on Haunted Hill** had punters line around the block, paving the way for further Castle antics.

## GHOST OF DRAGSTRIP HOLLOW

USA, 1959
Director: William Hole Jr. Producer: Lou Rusoff. Screenplay: Lou Rusoff. Music: Ronald Stein. Cinematography: Gilbert Warrenton.
Cast: Jody Fair, Martin Braddock, Russ Bender, Leon Tyler, Elaine Dupont, Henry McCann.

Part of a wave of hot rod movies popular in the fifties (including 1958's **Hot Rod Gang**, to which this is a sequel of sorts, sharing some of its characters) and a forerunner to the beach party movies of the sixties, **Ghost of Dragstrip Hollow** is a pure product of its time exploiting the nascent teen culture, while not necessarily being its finest representative. A Los Angeles drag-racing gang organizes a party in a reputedly haunted house, and plenty of goofy comedy, suspicious slang, and rock and roll scenes ensue. Director William Hole keeps his micro-budget in check by skimping on fast cars, races, and ghostly effects, which are for the most part reduced to shadows, cries in the night, moving objects, and a pair of glowing eyes. The spirit is eventually revealed, in grand Scooby-Doo fashion, to be an unemployed monster actor... until a real spook makes its presence known. Writer and producer Lou Rusoff, brother-in-law of Sam Arkoff of American International Pictures (who released the movie on a double bill with **Diary of a High School Bride**) spent most of his career penning scripts for Arkoff and Roger Corman (most notably on **It Conquered the World**, 1956; and a number of hot rod and beach pictures, such as 1956's **The She-Creature** and 1963's **Beach Party**).

## GHOST OF YOTSUYA

Japan, 1959
Director: Nobuo Nakagawa. Producer: Mitsugu Ôkura. Screenplay: Masayoshi Ônuki, Yoshihiro Ishikawa. Music: Michiaki Watanabe. Cinematography: Tadashi Nishimoto.
Cast: Shigeru Amachi, Katsuko Wakasugi, Shuntarô Emi, Ryûzaburô Nakamura, Noriko Kitazawa, Junko Ikeuchi.

Two years after **Ghost of Kasane**, Nobuo Nakagawa returns to ghost stories with another oft-adapted *kwaidan*, **Ghost of Yotsuya**. This tale of revenge follows the tragic fates of cruel and ambitious samurai Iemon (Shigeru Amachi) and his long-suffering wife Oiwa (Katsuko Wakasugi) in Yotsuya, an area of Tokyo. The original story was reportedly based on two real life double murder cases: in one, two servants killed their masters; in the other, a samurai murdered his concubine and her lover. The play was an immediate success, yet much like Macbeth in the West, its production was said to bring ill luck. To appease Oiwa's spirit, thought to be the cause of theatre troops' misfortunes, pilgrimage to her grave to ask for her blessing became customary. Produced, like **Kasane**, by Shintoho Studios, **Ghost of Yotsuya** was filmed in vivid Eastmancolor, the same process used by Hammer films, whose first genre hits **The Curse of Frankenstein** (1957) and **Dracula** (1958) clearly inspired this rather graphic picture. The drama unfolds slowly in its first half, but the last half hour truly delivers: blood runs bright red, poison melts faces, and the vengeful ghosts' appearances provide genuine chills. One of the best and spookiest *kwaidan* adaptations ever made, it is a must-see for those interested in the origins of J-horror scare tactics, as the continuation between **Yotsuya** and movies such as **Ring** is rather clear.

## THE HEADLESS GHOST

UK, 1959
Director: Peter Graham Scott.
Producer: Jack Greenwood.
Screenplay: Kenneth Langtry [Aben Kandel], Herman Cohen. Music: Gérard Schurmann.
Cinematography: John Wiles.
Cast: Richard Lyon, Liliane Sottane, David Rose, Clive Revill, Jack Allen, Alexander Archdale.

Having known some success with cheap B-pictures such as **I Was a Teenage Werewolf**, **I Was a Teenage Frankenstein** (both 1957), and **How to Make a Monster** (1958) for American International Pictures, producer Herman Cohen was in the midst of delivering **Horrors of the Black Museum** (1959) to the distributor when AIP's James H. Nicholson commissioned him to come up with a black-and-white supporting feature, to turn the release into a double bill. Written in two weeks by Cohen himself (with frequent collaborator Aben Kandle, under a pseudonym), and filmed in three, on location and using some of **Black Museum**'s sets at Merton Park Film Studios, **The Headless Ghost** filled the bill with its light-hearted story of three foreign exchange students (Richard Lyon, David Rose and Liliane Sottane) who spend the night in a reputedly haunted castle in England ('there's nothing like this in Michigan!'), and essentially learn a history lesson as they endeavour to reunite the body of a decapitated, 600-year-old ghost with his head. Despite its rushed production and run-of-the-mill plot, **The Headless Ghost** does boast commendable cinematography and a great-looking fortress. Director Peter Graham Scott would go on to sign smugglers' tale **Captain Clegg** for Hammer Films in 1962.

## 13 GHOSTS

USA, 1959
Director: William Castle.
Producer: William Castle. Screenplay: Robb White.
Music: Von Dexter. Cinematography: Joseph Biroc.
Cast: Charles Herbert, Jo Morrow, Martin Milner, Rosemary DeCamp, Donald Woods, Margaret Hamilton.

Here is another haunted house spookshow from director/showman William Castle, complete with ghostly wails, expository dialogue, cheesy acting, and of course, a new gimmick. An impoverished family — the very likable Zorbas, played by Charles Herbert, Jo Morrow, Donald Woods and Rosemary DeCamp — inherit a fully furnished mansion from a forgotten uncle, who happened to be an occultist. Once moved in, they are told their new home is inhabited by twelve ghosts, and indeed start seeing them after discovering a pair of goggles enabling them to view the supernatural. But also hidden within the abode's walls is a treasure, and a very real killer on the lookout for it. The goggles, of course, are key to the movie's trick, the Illusion-O: audiences were invited through on-screen prompts to watch parts of the black-and-white presentation through coloured glasses, to either enhance (the 'ghost viewer') the appearance of the spirits (colourized in blue), or minimize them (the 'ghost remover') if the experience seemed too intense. Schlocky but charming, **13 Ghosts** holds up today thanks to a plot which rattles along, and well-designed, memorable spectres, including clutching hands, flaming skeletons, a chef chopping his wife and her lover with a meat cleaver, an executioner, and a headless tamer with his lion.

2001 saw the release of **Thir13en Ghosts**, a remake produced by Joel Silver and Robert Zemeckis' Dark Castle, the company behind the 1999 re-imagining of William Castle's **House on Haunted Hill**. It is mostly notable for its production design, and for the ghosts themselves, each visually different from the others and given its own backstory.

## THE LIVING COFFIN

Mexico, 1959
Director: Fernando Méndez.
Producers: Alfredo Ripstein Jr., César Santos Galindo.
Screenplay: Ramón Obón. Music: Gustavo César Carrión.
Cinematography: Víctor Herrera.
Cast: Gastón Santos, María Duval, Pedro de Aguillón, Hortensia Santoveña, Carolina Barret, Antonio Raxell.

Bullfighter-turned-actor Gastón Santos shares top billing with his horse Rayo De Plata ('Ray of Silver') in **The Living Coffin** (aka **El grito de la muerte** — literally, 'The Scream of Death'), the tale of a lawman investigating a mysterious dilapidated hacienda said to be haunted by the spirit of the Weeping Woman, La Llorona. Director Fernando Méndez had previously helmed Abel Salazar's hit **El vampiro** (1957), as well as mad scientist horror **The Black Pit of Dr. M** (**Misterios de ultratumba**, 1959), also starring Santos. The leading man may be unconvincing, and the Scooby-Doo plot lead to the predictable revelation that the supposed phantom is a cover-up for criminal activities, but **The Living Coffin** is an amusing effort, at no point taking itself too seriously, remarkable for its colour cinematography, striking and unusual for its time, and as an early example of horror Western. Around the same time, Mexico, then in the midst of a golden age for horror, would also produce Old West mysteries **El jinete sin cabeza** and **La cabeza de Pancho Villa** (both 1957), as well as cowboys-versus-dinosaur romp **The Beast of Hollow Mountain** (**La bestia de la montana**, 1956); while in the U.S., Universal Pictures pitted a doctor against a vampire in **Curse of the Undead** (1959).

## THE ENCHANTING SHADOW

Hong Kong, 1960
Director: Li Han-hsiang. Producer: Run Run Shaw.
Screenplay: Wang Yueh-ting. Music: Yao Min.
Cinematography: Ho Luk-ying.
Cast: Betty Loh Tih, Chao Lei, Yang Chih-ching,
Li Kuo-hua, Su Hsiang, Tong Yeuk-ching.

Since dipping their toes into horror in 1954 with **Beyond the Grave**, the Shaw Brothers produced a number of supernatural adventures. Amongst their most successful efforts is **The Enchanting Shadow**, based on a story from Pu Songling's collection of legends *Strange Tales from a Chinese Studio* (1740). Unable to find overnight accommodation, a traveling scholar spends the night in a haunted temple, where he meets a beautiful, mysterious woman. The theme of the ghostly seductress, common in Chinese legends, can also be found in movies such as **The Painted Skin** (1966), and **A Chinese Ghost Story** (1987), which is largely considered an unofficial remake of this classic, sharing not only its storyline but also several key moments. Drawing inspiration from the East (Nobuo Nakagawa's **Ghost of Yotsuya**, 1959), as well as the West (Hammer Horror), and filmed in gorgeous Eastmancolor, **The Enchanting Shadow** is signed by award-winning director Li Han-hsiang, best known for his musical adaptations of Huangmei opera (**The Love Eterne**, 1963). So impressive are its technical accomplishments — lush cinematography, top-notch cast and production design — that it was sent to the Cannes Film Festival as 'the first Chinese colour film entered in international competition, representing Nationalist China', and was also Hong Kong's selection to the Academy Awards the following year.

## LA LLORONA

Mexico, 1960
Director:
René Cardona.
Producer:
José Luis Bueno.
Screenplay:
Adolfo Torres Portillo.
Music:
Luis Mendoza López.
Cinematography:
Jack Draper.
Cast:
María Elena Marqués,
Eduardo Fajardo,
Luz María Aguilar,
Carlos López Moctezuma,
Mauricio Garcés,
Emma Roldán.

Mexicans have long been avid consumers of horror entertainment, and with some help from rising stars such as actor-producer Abel Salazar, the late 1950s and early 1960s saw a boom in the production of genre pictures, with titles such as **La bruja** (1954), **El vampiro** (1957), **The Vampire's Coffin** (1958), **The Aztec Mummy** (1957) and its sequels, and **The Brainiac** (**El baron del terror**, 1961). They were generally outlandish, filled with monsters, and shot black and white. It was only a matter of time until the legend of the Weeping Woman would be once more brought to the screen. Based on a stage play by popular writer Carmen Toscano, **La Llorona**, from prolific Cuban director René Cardona (who would go one to direct several more horror pictures, as well as a handful of Santo and Blue Demon movies), offers an early iteration of the now well-established murderous babysitter sub-genre. The infamous ghost (played by striking actress-singer María Elena Marqués) indeed appears in 1960s Mexico to be hired as nanny to a little boy (actually played by a girl), only to repeatedly attempt to kill the baby. Slow-paced and more dramatic than scary, **La Llorona** is mostly known for its middle section, which shows a faithful retelling of the original 16th century story.

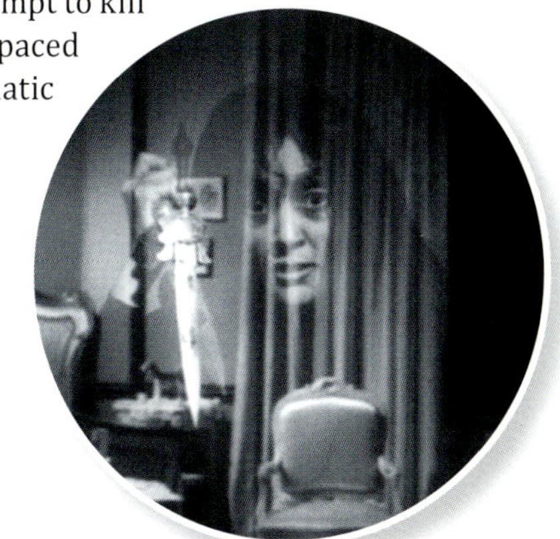

## TORMENTED

USA, 1960
Director: Bert I. Gordon. Producers: Bert I. Gordon, Joe Steinberg. Screenplay: George Worthing Yates.
Music: Albert Glasser. Cinematography: Ernest Laszlo.
Cast: Richard Carlson, Juli Reding, Susan Gordon, Lugene Sanders, Joseph Turkel, Lillian Adams.



'Tormented By The She-Ghost of Haunted Island!' A jazz pianist (Richarld Carlson, of **Creature from the Black Lagoon** fame) blackmailed by his ex girlfriend Vi (Juli Reding) refuses to save her life when the railing she leans against at the top of a lighthouse collapses. She falls to her death, and her vengeful spirit soon starts following him around, manifesting in amusing and rather harmless ways: footsteps in the sand, seaweed on a wedding dress, a disembodied hand, a floating head, a face on a picture, none of them particularly well executed. Affectionately known as Mister B.I.G. for movies such as **The Amazing Colossal Man**, 1957, **Village of the Giants**, 1965, and **Empire of the Ants**, 1977, Bert I. Gordon took a quick break from oversized monster to produce and direct this light, melodramatic yarn (the screenplay, based on his idea, was penned by **Them!** writer George Worthing Yates). His own eleven-year-old daughter Susan, who also appeared in **Attack of the Puppet People** (1958) shines as the pianist's future sister-in-law. Now largely forgotten and in the public domain, **Tormented** knew a brief regain of popularity in the early nineties, when American television series *Mystery Science Theater 3000* selected it for an episode.

## THE CURSE OF THE CRYING WOMAN

Mexico, 1961
Director: Rafael Baledón. Producer: Abel Salazar. Screenplay: Rafael Baledón, Fernando Galiana. Music: Gustavo César Carrión. Cinematography: José Ortiz Ramos.
Cast: Rosita Arenas, Abel Salazar, Rita Macedo, Carlos López Moctezuma, Mario Sevilla, Enrique Lucero.

Mexico offers yet another treatment of the myth of La Llorona, the Crying Woman; this time mixing it with elements of witchcraft in the story of a widow (Rita Macedo) attempting to use her niece in a ritual to bring back to life the mummy of a legendary sorceress — the infamous weeping woman — from whom she hopes to gain power. Filmed in 1961 but not released until two years later, **The Curse of the Crying Woman** (aka **La maldición de la llorona**) is the work of actor-turned-director Rafael Baledón, who would in those years churn out a healthy average of five movies a year. An old house, a dysfunctional aristocratic family, a haunted mirror, bats in the belfry: the film sits comfortably in the wave of Gothic horror which engulfed the world in the first half of the decade. The opening scene, with its black-clad woman standing in the fog, holding hounds on leashes, will feel familiar to Bava fans: it is practically lifted from his 1960 **Black Sunday**. Yet the production adds a flavour of Mexican folklore, and features some striking images: most memorable are the close-ups on the witch's entirely black eyes. The legendary wraith would return to the screen a number of times over the years, including 1974's **La venganza de la llorona**, where she squares off against famed masked wrestler Santo, and 2011 popular cartoon **La leyenda de la llorona**.

## HOUSE OF MYSTERY

UK, 1961
Director: Vernon Sewell. Producers: Julian Wintle, Leslie Parkyn. Screenplay: Vernon Sewell.
Music: Stanley Black. Cinematography: Ernest Steward.
Cast: Jane Hylton, Peter Dyneley, Nanette Newman, Maurice Kaufmann, Colin Gordon, Molly Urquhart.

Adapted from French play 'L'Angoisse' by Pierre Mills and Celia de Vilyars, **House of Mystery** revolves around a house-hunting couple (Ronald Hines and Colette Wilde) visiting a countryside cottage, and learning about its haunted history. The story is told through a series of flashbacks. UK director Vernon Sewell (**The Ghosts of Berkeley Square**, 1947; **Curse of the Crimson Altar**, 1968) had already filmed three versions of this story (**The Medium**, 1934; **Latin Quarter**, 1945; **Ghost Ship**, 1952) before getting to this production, one of the last quota quickies, made to guarantee a percentage of British feature-length productions in theatres. Independent Artists, created by producers Leslie Parkyn and Julian Wintle, is the company behind such horror and B-movies as **Circus of Horrors** (1960) and **Night of the Eagle** (aka **Burn, Witch, Burn**, 1962). Also of note is the psychic investigator (Colin Gordon) enlisted to study the house through scientific means: one of the first characters to do so in a ghost story, soon after Nigel Kneale's **Quatermass** series and years before **The Stone Tape** (1972) or **The Legend of Hell House** (1973). With a running time just under 55 minutes, **House of Mystery** aired in the U.S. as part of NBC anthology series *Kraft Mystery Theater.*

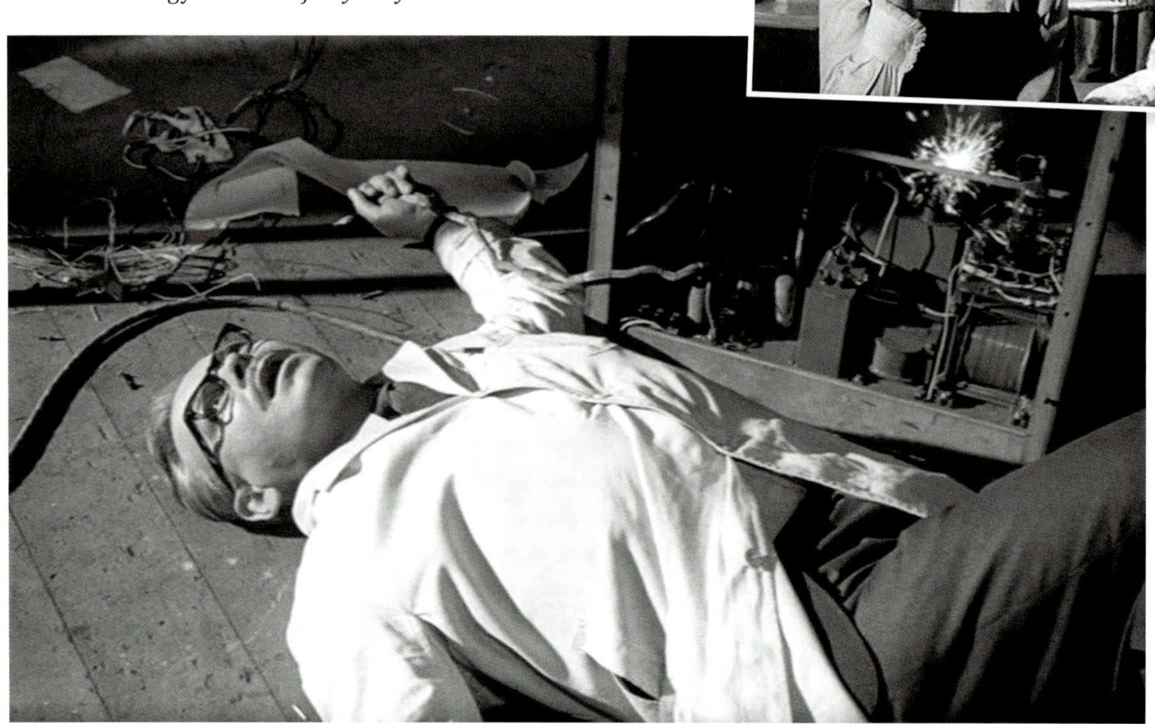

## THE INNOCENTS

UK, 1961
Director: Jack Clayton. Producer: Jack Clayton.
Screenplay: William Archibald, Truman Capote, John Mortimer.
Music: Georges Auric. Cinematography: Freddie Francis.
Cast: Deborah Kerr, Michael Redgrave, Peter Wyngarde, Megs Jenkins, Pamela Franklin, Martin Stephens.

'All I want to do is save the children, not destroy them.' This line, spoken by the neurotic Miss Giddens (Deborah Kerr), encapsulates the dilemma at the heart of **The Innocents**, director/producer Jack Clayton's subtle, elegant psychological study. Is she saving the children under her care, or is she condemning them? Are the ghosts threatening them real, or the product of her imagination? Upon taking up a position as a governess in a large countryside house, Miss Giddens finds her first charge, Flora (Pamela Franklin), is a charming, quiet little girl. But the mood changes when her brother Miles (Martin Stephens) returns after being expelled from school. The children grow secretive, mysterious presences are felt, and Miss Giddens herself seems to hide a haunting past. She soon suspects the siblings are possessed by the ghosts of the previous governess, and of the valet she had a liaison with. Co-written by Truman Capote, this adaptation of Henry James's *The Turn of the Screw* adds ambiguity to the classic ghost story. Has Miss Giddens simply lost her grip on reality? As her character slowly descends into madness, Kerr superbly conveys a sense of repressed sexuality and contained hysteria. Yet imagined or real, the late governess's appearances on the lake are quietly chilling, and the valet's floating face in the window jangles the nerves. Freddie Francis' cinematography, making full use of CinemaScope (imposed upon Clayton because Twentieth Century-Fox owned the format), is a masterclass in composition and black-and-white lighting. Highly regarded and influential, **The Innocents** paved the way for more obvious Gothic scares in its successors, from **The Haunting** and **The Legend of Hell House** to **The Orphanage** and **Crimson Peak**.

## CARNIVAL OF SOULS

USA, 1962
Director: Herk Harvey.
Producer: Herk Harvey.
Screenplay: John Clifford.
Music: Gene Moore.
Cinematography: Maurice Prather.
Cast: Candace Hilligoss, Herk Harvey, Frances Feist, Sidney Berger, Stan Levitt, Art Ellison.

The only survivor of a drag race car crash, Mary Henry (Candace Hilligoss) drives to Salt Lake City, where she is hired as a church organist. On her way, she is startled by the apparition of a ghoulish man with pasty white skin and black-rimmed eyes. The man keeps haunting her over the next days, and lures her towards an abandoned carnival on the outskirts of town. **Carnival of Souls**, industrial film director Herk Harvey's only feature, is the very definition of eerie.

With just $30,000 and six crew members at his disposal, Harvey eschewed lavish production design and special effects in favour of simple, effective make-ups (the writer-producer himself playing the lead ghoul) and a haunting organ soundtrack, to craft a nightmarish atmosphere and striking, dream-like imagery, where the supernatural occurs in the most banal, everyday settings. Released in a clipped version as a drive-in double bill with Lon Chaney Jr. vehicle **The Devil's Messenger**, the movie failed to connect with its audience at the time, but soon became a cult classic, its influence evident on movies as diverse as **Night of the Living Dead** (1968), **Lost Highway** (1997) or **The Sixth Sense** (1999). As the original U.S. release failed to include a copyright on the prints, the film automatically fell into public domain, which explains why it appears on characters' television screens in countless movies, this author's own **Tales of Halloween** segment included.

## TOWER OF LONDON

USA, 1962
Director: Roger Corman.
Producer: Gene Corman.
Screenplay: Leo Gordon, Amos Powell, James B. Gordon. Cinematography: Arch R. Dalzell.
Cast: Vincent Price, Michael Pate, Joan Freeman, Robert Brown, Justice Watson, Sarah Selby.

In the early 1960s, veteran producer Edward Small, tempted to cash in on the success of AIP's Poe adaptations with a picture inspired by another literary classic, approached Roger Corman with a loose adaptation of Shakespeare's Richard III. Small would produce along with Corman's brother Gene; Vincent Price, who had already appeared in a small part in a 1939 Boris Karloff vehicle of the same title, would star as murderous King Richard III, driven mad by guilt and haunted by the ghosts of his victims. Armed with a distribution deal with United Artists, Small, a prolific man if there ever was one, envisioned this **Tower of London** as part of a short series of horror pictures he produced around the same time, alongside **Doctor Blood's Coffin** (with Hazel Court), **Diary of a Madman**, and **Twice-Told Tales**, the latter two also starring Price. The budget, however, was low even by Corman's standards. Right before the start of his fifteen-day shoot, the director was informed he would be filming in black and white, which was all finances allowed. Corman resented the decision — rightfully so, as it turned out to be a commercial mistake. One can only dream of what the movie's elaborate sets (which took up most of the budget), its superimposed ghosts, and Price's haunted performance would have looked like in the filmmaker's trademark Technicolor.

## BLACK SABBATH

Italy/France/USA, 1963
Director: Mario Bava. Screenplay: Marcello Fondato, Alberto Bevilacqua, Mario Bava, Ugo Guerra.
Music: Roberto Nicolosi, Les Baxter [U.S. version].
Cinematography: Ubaldo Terzano.
Cast: Boris Karloff, Mark Damon, Michele Mercier, Jacqueline Soussard, Milly, Lidia Alfonsi.

One of the highlights of iconic Italian filmmaker Mario Bava's illustrious career, AIP production **Black Sabbath** is an anthology movie of three half hour stories, framed by deliberately schlocky introductions from a delightfully hammy Boris Karloff. Exquisitely shot in sumptuous Technicolor, the feature is strong throughout, each segment offering a unique take on a different horror sub-genre, as suggested by its original title, **I tre volti della paula** ('The Three Faces of Fear'). Yet undeniably the most memorable part of the film is **The Drop of Water**, an exercise in fright in which a nurse steals a ring from an old medium whose body she was called in to prepare for her burial.

While the rather straightforward script offers few surprises, the payoff being very much what the audience is led to anticipate, there is nothing ordinary about its execution. Bava chose to set this very modern story in a surreal version of 1910s London; a world of antique toys, phonographs and faded wallpapers, where everything is so heightened that the corpse itself isn't played by an actor but by a doll. This, along with the lavish production design and remarkably unnerving use of sound, combines to create an atmosphere of genuine terror and some unforgettable imagery.

## THE HAUNTING

USA/UK, 1963
Director: Robert Wise. Producer: Robert Wise. Screenplay: Nelson Gidding. Music: Humphrey Searle. Cinematography: Davis Boulton. Cast: Julie Harris, Claire Bloom, Richard Johnson, Russ Tamblyn, Lois Maxwell, Fay Compton.

Robert Wise's masterpiece **The Haunting** may have received mixed praise upon initial release, but it has since taken pride of place amongst the highest rated pictures in the genre. The simple storyline follows a scientist (Richard Johnson) and his guests investigating the reputedly haunted Hill House, focusing more specifically on Eleanor (Julie Harris), a meek, psychologically fragile middle-aged woman who feels drawn to the house. Author Shirley Jackson, whose fantastic 1959 novel *The Haunting of Hill House* served as basis for this classic, envisioned the tale as a pure ghost story; screenwriter Nelson Gidding however chose to emphasize Eleanor's mental breakdown and leave some ambiguity as to the reality of the haunting. At the time he discovered the book, Wise was under contract with MGM. The budget the studio offered, however, seemed too low for the material; yet MGM's UK branch ended up making a slightly higher offer, which is how the filmmaker ended up shooting in England. Ettington Park was chosen as main location. Best known for his larger budget dramas, musicals and sci-fi epics, Wise had directed two scary movies, both for RKO producer Val Lewton: **The Curse of the Cat People** (1944) and **The Body Snatcher** (1945). Lewton's understated approach to the genre clearly influenced the filmmaker; **The Haunting** is all about eeriness, subtlety and unseen menace, rather than explicit horror. Wise builds atmosphere through low angles and elaborate moves, using custom made dolly tracks, infrared film, handheld cameras, and an experimental 28mm anamorphic wide angle lens which distorted some shots, adding to the picture's eeriness and sense of creeping insanity. To guide the actors' performances, a recorded track of sound effects was played, so they would know what noises to react to.

**The Haunting** was remade by Jan de Bont in 1999; but the new version's all-out use of computer-generated imagery and loud scares only served to highlight the effectiveness of Wise's light touch. Stephen King miniseries **Rose Red** (2002) was originally conceived as a reimagining of the story, but creative differences between King and producer Steven Spielberg led to the project being shelved, and later rewritten with just a passing resemblance to the source material.

## THE TERROR

USA, 1963
Director: Roger Corman. Producer: Roger Corman. Screenplay: Leo Gordon, Jack Hill, Roger Corman [uncredited]. Music: Ronald Stein. Cinematography: John Nickolaus Jr., Floyd Crosby [uncredited].
Cast: Jack Nicholson, Boris Karloff, Sandra Knight, Richard Miller [Dick Miller], Dorothy Neumann, Jonathan Haze.

After wrapping **The Raven** ahead of schedule, Roger Corman, true to his thrifty persona, decided to film another movie to make full use of Boris Karloff's remaining time under contract. Cobbled together in a few weeks, **The Terror** started filming without a finished script, which likely explains why photography took nearly nine months to complete. A young Jack Nicholson plays Andre Duvalier, a soldier in Napoleon's army, who somehow finds himself separated from his regiment and lost on an isolated beach. The first soul he encounters is Helene (Sandra Knight, then married to Nicholson and pregnant in certain scenes), who runs away from him, into the sea. Desperate to find her, Duvalier asks the locals, who deny her existence. Yet she is the living portrait of Ilsa, the baron (Karloff)'s wife, who has been dead for twenty years. Taking advantage of sets leftover from **The Raven** and **The Haunted Palace**, Corman also enlisted UCLA graduates Francis Ford Coppola and Jack Hill to film cliffside scenes and quicksand shots, respectively (Coppola filmed in Big Sur, Hill used in his own backyard). Monte Hellman and Nicholson himself are also rumoured to have directed sequences. The result is more coherent and entertaining than one would expect from such a chaotic production, though the ghostly elements of the story are, characteristically for the time, underplayed. Released under a host of alternative titles including **The Night of Terror** and **The Haunting**, **The Terror** is in the public domain; some of Karloff's scenes later appeared in Peter Bogdanovich's **Targets** (1968).

## THE WHIP AND THE BODY

Italy/France, 1963
Director: Mario Bava.
Producer: Tom Rhodes.
Screenplay: Ernesto Gastaldi, Ugo Guerra, Luciano Martino.
Music: Carlo Rustichelli.
Cinematography: Ubaldo Terzano.
Cast: Daliah Lavi, Christopher Lee, Luciano Stella, Evelyn Stewart, Harriet White, Gustavo De Nardo.

Tasked by producers to come up with a script in the vein of Roger Corman's **Pit and the Pendulum**, screenwriter Ernesto Gastaldi penned the tale of a debauched aristocrat returning to his family castle to reclaim an inheritance, and gave it both a spectral twist and a sadomasochistic flavour. The resulting movie, Mario Bava's **The Whip and the Body** (**La frusta e il corpo** in Italy, and also known as **What!** in the U.S. and **Night Is the Phantom** in the UK — while the first couple of drafts were titled **The Knife in the Body** and **Spectral**, respectively), has long been surrounded by an aura of scandal. Pulled from theatres and confiscated in Italy for its BDSM undertones, this French-Italian production also saw several sequences of sexual violence excised from international prints, mangling it beyond story logic. Indeed at the core of the movie is the doomed, sadomasochistic relationship between Kurt (Christopher Lee) and former lover Nevenka (Daliah Lavi); and sequences of whipping, underlined by romantic music and clearly showing pleasure from the woman receiving the lashing, are the highlights of the picture. **The Whip and the Body** features the vivid colours and lush production design typical of Bava, who shot the movie himself — though it is his cameraman, Ubaldo Terzano, who received cinematographer credit.

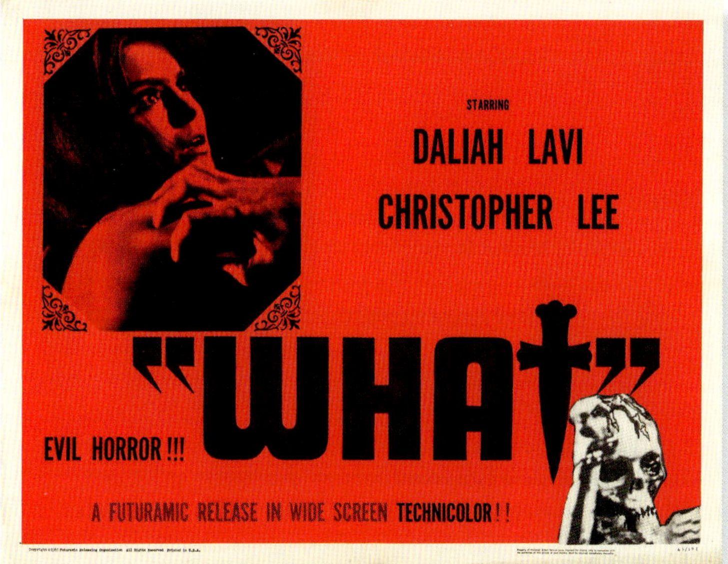

THE LIVING AND DEAD CHANGE PLACES IN AN ORGY OF TERROR IN

EDGAR ALLAN POE'S

CASTLE OF BLOOD

They love only for blood!

Starring
BARBARA STEELE · GEORGE RIVIERE with MARGRETE ROBSAHM · HENRY KRUGER · MONTGOMERY GLEEN
SYLVIA SORENT · RAUL H. NEWMAN Music Composed and Directed by RITZ ORTOLANI · Produced by FRANK BELTY
and WALTER SARCH · Directed by ANTHONY DAWSON · A WOOLNER BROS. RELEASE



64/152

## CASTLE OF BLOOD

Italy/France, 1964
Director: Anthony Dawson [Antonio Margheriti].
Producers: Frank Belty [Franco Belotti],
Walter Sarch [Walter Zarghetta].
Screenplay: Jean Grimaud [Giovanni Grimaldi],
Gordon Wilson Jr. [Sergio Corbucci].
Music: Ritz [Riz] Ortolani. Cinematography:
Richard Kramer [Riccardo Pallottini].
Cast: Barbara Steele, George Riviere [Georges Rivière], Margrete Robsahm, Raul H. Newman [Umberto Raho], Sylvia Sorent [Sylvia Sorrente], Montgomery Gleen [Silvano Tranquilli].

One of 1960s gothic horror's unsung heroes, Italian filmmaker Antonio Margheriti never quite reached the popularity of Bava and Corman, despite significant contributions to the ghost movie sub-genre. **Castle of Blood** (aka **Danza macabra** or **Edgar Allan Poe's Castle of Blood**, as the English title card reads), the director's first foray into horror, was original penned for Sergio Corbucci (**Django**, 1966). But when another company hired him for a peplum just before cameras were set to roll, he passed the baton to his friend Margheriti. Corbucci ended up directing one scene of the picture, which was shot in a mere fifteen days using four cameras rolling at once for each scene, much like a television show. Derivative of Corman and earlier haunted house staples, **Castle of Blood**, which follows a journalist (Georges Rivière) challenged by a friend of Edgar Allan Poe to spend the night at a haunted castle, is notable for including several then-controversial scenes of seduction, nudity and lesbianism. Its most explicit scene was cut from the Italian print, but made it into international releases. Margheriti remade **Castle of Blood** in colour as **Web of the Spider** (1971), starring Klaus Kinski and Michele Mercier; a movie the director would regret making.

## KWAIDAN

Japan, 1964
Director: Masaki Kobayashi. Producer: Shigeru Wakatsuki.
Screenplay: Yôko Mizuki. Music: Tôru Takemitsu.
Cinematography: Yoshio Miyajima.
Cast: Michiyo Aratama, Misako Watanabe, Rentarô Mikuni, Keiko Kishi, Tatsuya Nakadai, Katsuo Nakamura.

A four-part anthology based on folk tales collected by author Lafcadio Hearn, **Kwaidan** is one of the best-known and acclaimed movies in the Japanese sub-genre. Produced by Toho, the company behind the **Godzilla** series, it not only received the Special Jury Prize in Cannes, but was also nominated to an Academy Award for Best Foreign Language Film. Yet production had been a struggle for director Masaki Kobayashi who, after many social and political dramas (among which classic samurai film **Harakiri** (aka **Seppuku**, 1962), winner of the Cannes Jury Prize), took several years to complete what he considered his magnum opus. The most expensive film made in Japan up to that point, **Kwaidan** was filmed in a former airplane hangar, the only space large enough to accommodate its large hand-painted sets, which gave the movie its distinctive, heightened look. Much has been said about its vivid use of colour and artificial aesthetics, which find roots in Japanese theatre. Anchored in familiar themes — the consequences of greed and ambition, vengeful ghosts, spooky long-haired women — **Kwaidan** builds on its simple tales an expressionist succession of slow-moving, surreal, striking tableaux. Interestingly, the plot of the 'Lover's Vow' chapter from **Tales from the Darkside: The Movie** (1990) was practically identical to 'The Woman of the Snow', a segment omitted from the original U.S. release, to cut down on the three-hour running time.

## THE LONG HAIR OF DEATH

Italy, 1964
Director: Anthony Dawson [Antonio Margheriti].
Producer: Felice Testa Gay. Screenplay: Robert Bohr [Tonino Valerii].
Music: Evirust [Carlo Rustichelli].
Cinematography: Richard Thierry [Riccardo Pallottini].
Cast: Barbara Steele, George [Giorgio] Ardisson, Halina Zalewska,
Robert Rains [Umberto Raho], Laureen Nuyen [Laura Nucci],
Jean Rafferty [Giuliano Raffaelli].

Wrongfully convicted of murder and burned at the stake, Adele Karnstein (Halina Zalewska), in her last moments, curses her accusers Count Humboldt (Giuliano Raffaelli) and his son Kurt (George Ardisson). At the same time, her daughter Helen (Barbara Steele) is killed trying to save her. Years later, Adele's youngest child Lisabeth (Zalewska in a dual role) is forced into marriage with Kurt as a plague spreads upon the area, and a mysterious woman, who looks strangely like Helen, appears at the gates of the Humboldt castle. For his second contribution to the sub-genre, after **Castle of Blood**, Antonio Margheriti again cast Steele as a woman returning from the dead. The convoluted plot somewhat sags in the middle, yet **The Long Hair of Death** (aka **I lunghi capelli della morte**) bears all the hallmarks of gothic horror — ancient curses, chiaroscuro lighting, maidens tiptoeing down candlelit hallways in medieval castles — and adds an air of sexuality and scandal, with themes of rape, adultery and domestic abuse, and enough impressive set pieces, including a shocking, satisfying ending, to reward viewers' patience. The castle sets are remarkable, as is the dramatic score by Carlo Rustichelli, an incredibly prolific composer whose most notable contributions include Bava's **The Whip and the Body**, **Kill, Baby... Kill!**, and **Blood and Black Lace**.

## THE TOMB OF LIGEIA

UK, 1964
Director: Roger Corman. Producer: Pat Green. Screenplay: Robert Towne. Music: Kenneth V. Jones. Cinematography: Arthur Grant.
Cast: Vincent Price, Elizabeth Shepherd, John Westbrook, Derek Francis, Oliver Johnston, Richard Vernon.

Following the death of his wife Ligeia (Elizabeth Shepherd), Verden Fell (Vincent Price) has become a recluse, overly sensitive to light, wrapped in his grief, and obsessed with her promise to return from the dead. He remarries, but no sooner have he and his young bride come back from their honeymoon that Fell returns to his morbid thoughts and seems haunted by the spirit of his late spouse. Wigged and made up to appear younger than his 52 years, Price delivers a powerful, tortured performance on which the entire movie hinges; in fact, the supernatural is so subtle that the story could be interpreted as a tale of grief and obsession, if not for a subplot involving the soul of Ligeia ostensibly possessing a black cat. The last of Roger Corman's eight Edgar Allan Poe adaptations for American International Pictures, **The Tomb of Ligeia** breaks with tradition in its relative restraint — compared to the lurid Gothic excesses of his previous pictures — and its use of outdoors locations. Largely filmed in and around Norfolk's Castle Acre Priory (as well as Shepperton Studios, for the interiors), it also features daytime scenes in the English countryside and at Stonehenge. Still, the movie is characteristically lush, with Corman's careful framing and deliberate use of vibrant colours, and atmospheric opening titles.

AMERICAN INTERNATIONAL
presents
VINCENT PRICE
ELIZABETH SHEPHERD
STARRING IN
EDGAR ALLAN POE'S
TOMB of LIGEIA
IN
COLORSCOPE
Screenplay by ROBERT TOWNE · From the Story by EDGAR ALLAN POE · Produced and Directed by ROGER CORMAN

angielski film grozy
GROBOWIEC LIGEI
wg. Edgara Allana Poe
Reżyseria: Roger Corman
w rolach głównych:
Vincent Price
Elisabeth Shepherd
Derek Francis
Produkcja
Alta Vista
Roger Corman

## DR. TERROR'S HOUSE OF HORRORS

UK, 1965
Director: Freddie Francis. Producers: Milton Subotsky, Max J. Rosenberg.
Screenplay: Milton Subotsky. Music: Elisabeth Lutyens.
Cinematography: Alan Hume.
Cast: Peter Cushing, Christopher Lee, Roy Castle,
Max Adrian, Michael Gough, Neil McCallum.

In the mid sixties, leading horror company Hammer Films was staring down the barrel of a decade-long identity crisis; its Gothic, period chills now considered somewhat quaint by contrast with the increasingly daring releases of the time, in the wake of **Psycho** and its British counterpart, **Peeping Tom** (both 1960). Milton Subotsky and Max J. Rosenberg, founders of Amicus Productions, worsened the issue when they turned their attentions from low-brow comedies to horror,

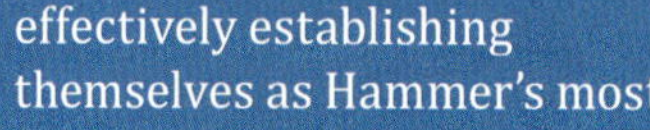

effectively establishing themselves as Hammer's most

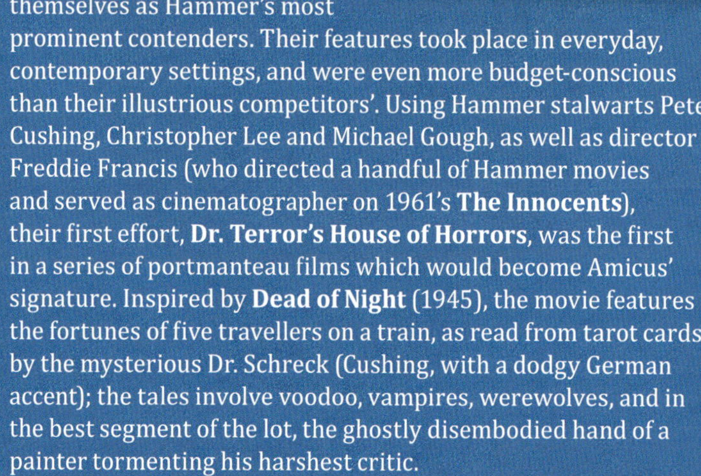

prominent contenders. Their features took place in everyday, contemporary settings, and were even more budget-conscious than their illustrious competitors'. Using Hammer stalwarts Peter Cushing, Christopher Lee and Michael Gough, as well as director Freddie Francis (who directed a handful of Hammer movies and served as cinematographer on 1961's **The Innocents**), their first effort, **Dr. Terror's House of Horrors**, was the first in a series of portmanteau films which would become Amicus' signature. Inspired by **Dead of Night** (1945), the movie features the fortunes of five travellers on a train, as read from tarot cards by the mysterious Dr. Schreck (Cushing, with a dodgy German accent); the tales involve voodoo, vampires, werewolves, and in the best segment of the lot, the ghostly disembodied hand of a painter tormenting his harshest critic.

## HOUSE OF TERRORS

Japan, 1965
Director: Hajime Satô. Producer: Hiroshi Ohkawa. Screenplay: Hajime Takaiwa. Music: Shunsuke Kikuchi. Cinematography: Shôei Nishikawa.
Cast: Kô Nishimura, Yûko Kusunoki, Yoko Hayama, Masumi Harukawa, Shinjirô Ebara, Kazuo Kitamura.

**House of Terrors**, also known as **The Ghost of the Hunchback** or **Satan's Pit** (after the house the story takes place in), breaks away from the Edo period *kwaidan* with this modern day story of three visitors to an old isolated house, who won't heed the warnings of a hunchback caretaker telling them about the homicidal ghosts of the mansion's former occupants. Rather than drawing inspiration from traditional tales, director Hajime Satô turned to recent successes of the West.

If **Kwaidan**'s Masaki Kobayashi took a leaf out of Hammer Films' book, Satô turned to the roller coaster fun of **House on Haunted Hill** (1959) and the Gothic horrors of Mario Bava or Antonio Margheriti. Cue flickering lights, quick zoom-ins, readings of wills, silhouettes projected on the walls, cartoonish corpses, ghostly apparitions, and bulging doors directly lifted from **The Haunting** (1963). Censorship laws for depictions of sexual violence were evidently more lax in Japan than they were in the West, and a scene of a woman assaulted and strangled with her own pearls comes across as rather jarring in this otherwise inoffensive, schlocky context. Satô would go on to direct **Terror Beneath the Sea** and **The Golden Bat**, both starring Sonny Chiba, the following year.

## NIGHTMARE CASTLE

Italy, 1965
Director: Mario Caiano. Producer: Carlo Caiano.
Screenplay: Mario Caiano, Fabio De Agostini.
Music: Ennio Morricone. Cinematography: Enzo Barboni.
Cast: Barbara Steele, Paul Muller, Helga Liné,
Lawrence Clift [Marino Masé], Rik Battaglia, Giuseppe Addobbati.

Exploitation director Mario Caiano's **Nightmare Castle** (**Amanti d'oltretomba**, also known in the UK as **Night of the Doomed**), boasts one of those convoluted, improbable plots only 1960s Italian cinema could bless us with. A mad scientist (Paul Muller) tortures and kills his wife (Barbara Steele) and her lover, uses their hearts in his experiments, and marries his late wife's sister (Steele in a blond wig), who inherited the castle, only to find himself tormented by the ghosts of his victims. Caiano, who also co-wrote the script, acknowledged drawing inspiration from the works of Edgar Allan Poe. The author's influence however is less obvious than Mario Bava's, whose films he claimed to be unfamiliar with. Caiano's father Carlo produced the picture for a relatively low budget, allowing the filmmaker, whose credits include such exotic titles as **Bullets Don't Argue** (1964) and **Nazi Love Camp 27** (1977), an eighteen-day shoot in a studio in Rome, and on location in the suburbs. The plot meanders, but is supported by Steele's always reliable performance as well as moody black-and-white photography by Enzo Barboni, who would go on to direct a series of Terence Hill and Bud Spencer vehicles. Also of note is the soundtrack, which marks one of Ennio Morricone's earliest full film scores.

## BUT YOU WERE DEAD

Italy, 1966
Director: Gianni Vernuccio.
Producer: Gianni Vernuccio. Screenplay: Enzo Ferrari, Gianni Vernuccio. Music: Giorgio Gaslini.
Cinematography: Gianni Vernuccio.
Cast: Alba Rigazzi, Alex Morrison [Sandro Luporini], Walter Pozzi, Jeanine, Tony Bellani, Cristina Gaioni.

**But You Were Dead** (the less-spoilerific original title translates as **The Long Night of Veronique**) is one of the last credits in Cairo-born filmmaker Gianni Vernuccio's long filmography, which mainly includes adventure films (**The Treasure of Bengal**, 1953), dramas (**Los amantes del desierto**, 1957), and love stories (**Un amore**, 1965). In true micro-budget fashion, he not only directed and produced, but also shot and edited the picture, which was filmed in Lombardy with a cast of unknowns. Visiting his grandfather, Count Anselmi (Walter Pozzi), to fulfil his mother's will after his parents' death, Giovanni (Alex Morrison) witnesses the apparition of the spirit of Veronique (Alba Rigazzi), who died during the First World War and now haunts the old villa, looking for her lost love. Clearly inspired by the Gothic horrors of Mario Bava or Antonio Margheriti released around the same time, **But You Were Dead**, however, has a contemporary setting (regardless of what its poster suggested) and is more akin to a slow romance than a scary movie, despite a handful of eerie moments. Largely forgotten today and nearly impossible to find, Vernuccio's movie perhaps evidences the extent to which Bava's influence and success permeated Italian cinema at the time, with non-genre filmmakers peppering their love stories with castles and ghostly inamoratas.

## THE GHOST AND MR. CHICKEN

USA, 1966
Director: Alan Rafkin. Producer: Edward J. Montagne.
Screenplay: James Fritzell, Everett Greenbaum, Andy Griffith [uncredited].
Music: Vic Mizzy. Cinematography: William Margulies.
Cast: Don Knotts, Joan Staley, Liam Redmond, Skip Homeier, Dick Sargent, Reta Shaw.

For his first feature-length production for Universal Studios, television comedian Don Knotts (*The Andy Griffith Show*) stars as a cowardly small-town newspaper reporter assigned to spend the night in a reputedly haunted murder house. A brief return to the goofy, fake (or-is-it?) ghost sub-genre which flourished in the forties, **The Ghost and Mr. Chicken**, also known under its working title **Running Scared**, was shot in seventeen days by *Andy Griffith Show* director Alan Rafkin, who brought along much of the team; Griffith himself writing a draft of the script. For his haunted mansion, Rafkin selected a house on the famed Colonial Street on the Universal backlot, next door to the *Munsters* house, where Joe Dante's **The 'Burbs** (1989) and **Desperate Housewives** would later be filmed. Vic Mizzy, whose name will go down in history for the *Addams Family* theme, not only composed an upbeat, comical soundtrack, but also contributed unexpected chills with an organ piece which traumatized a generation and became a Halloween party staple. Released double-billed with similarly spooky family movie **Munster, Go Home!** in the summer of 1966, **The Ghost and Mr. Chicken** was a big hit, which led Knotts to star in four more pictures for Universal.

## KILL, BABY... KILL!

Italy, 1966
Director: Mario Bava.
Producers: Nando Pisani, Luciano Catenacci.
Screenplay: Romano Migliorini, Roberto Natale, Mario Bava.
Music: Carlo Rustichelli. Cinematography: Antonio Rinaldi.
Cast: Erika Blanc, Giacomo Rossi Stuart, Fabienne Dali,
Giana Vivaldi [Giovanna Galletti], Piero Lulli,
Max Lawrence [Luciano Catenacci].

A coroner (Giacomo Rossi Stuart) is sent to a remote village in the Carpathian mountains to help investigate the death of a woman, rumoured by the locals to have fallen prey to the murderous ghost of a child. This very simple plot line allows Mario Bava to craft a masterpiece of eeriness and atmosphere, a tale of superstition and village hysteria which turns on its head clichés of the malevolent old witch and the angelic fair-haired child. Shot in a mere twelve days on a shoestring budget (production ran out of money in the middle of filming, the cast and crew agreeing to complete the picture out of loyalty to Bava), **Kill, Baby... Kill!** (aka **Curse of the Living Dead** and **Operazione paura**) marks the filmmaker's third collaboration with cinematographer Antonio Rinaldi, whose camera swoops down spiral staircases, moves along brick houses and down cobblestone streets, and brutally zooms onto distraught faces. Rinaldi exclusively worked for Bava throughout his entire career, from 1965's **Planet of the Vampires** to 1972's **Baron Blood**. One of Bava's most revered films, **Kill, Baby... Kill!**'s influence can be felt on stories such as **The Wicker Man** (1973) and **Sleepy Hollow** (1999). Tobe Hooper's 1979 **Salem's Lot** and Guillermo del Toro's 2001 **The Devil's Backbone** each riff on the famous image of the killer child in the window; while Scorsese and Fellini both admitted drawing inspiration from Bava's movie.

## THE PAINTED SKIN

Hong Kong, 1966
Director: Bao Fang. Screenplay: Wong Biu-Yi.
Music: Yue Lun. Cinematography: Cho Chi.
Cast: Zhu Hong, Kao Yuen, Chen Juan-Juan, Weng Wu, Jiang Ming, Tung Ngai.

Established in 1953, leftist Hong Kong studio Feng Huang generally focused on serious literary adaptations, but also put out bigger budget entertainment, of which **The Painted Skin** (aka **Hua Pi**) is a prominent example. Like **The Enchanting Shadow** (1960), the movie is based on a story from *Strange Tales from a Chinese Studio* (1740) by Chinese author Pu Songling, who reputedly collected the legends from passers-by; a process we witness in the movie's opening scene, where Pu himself is told the tale of Wang (Kao Yuen), a scholar seduced by a demon (or vampire, or ghost — its exact nature is debatable) assuming the shape of a beautiful woman. So popular is the original story of The Painted Skin, that its title has entered the Chinese vocabulary to depict the duplicity of a devil in disguise. And indeed, in an effective scene in the third act of the film, the despicable creature is seen putting on its human costume. Light on scares, at least until its climax, yet colourful and full of old-fashioned charm, **The Painted Skin** is the work of actor-director Bao Fang, who later appeared in **The Bride with White Hair**, 1993, and Jackie Chan classic **The Legend of the Drunken Master**, 1994. Another feature incarnation of the tale, directed by King Hu, came out in 1993; also notable are a television series in 2011, and a big-budget epic starring Donnie Yen in 2008, which received a sequel, **Painted Skin: The Resurrection**, in 2012.

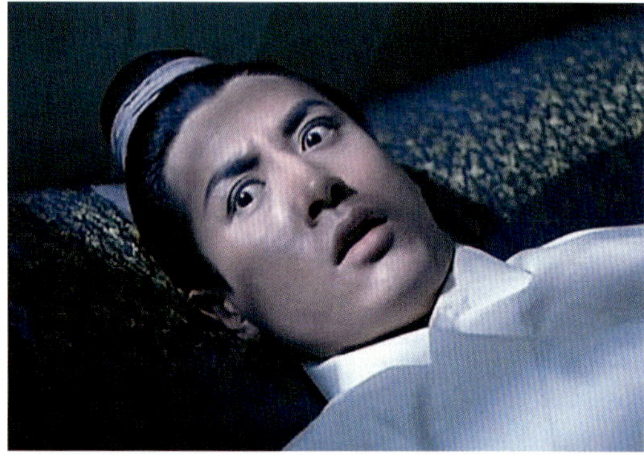

## SPIRITS OF THE DEAD

France/Italy, 1967
Directors: Roger Vadim, Federico Fellini, Louis Malle.
Producer: Raymond Eger. Screenplay: Roger Vadim, Pascal Cousin, Louis Malle, Daniel Boulanger, Federico Fellini, Bernardino Zapponi. Music: Jean Prodromidés, Diego Masson, Nino Rota. Cinematography: Claude Renoir, Tonino Delli Colli, Giuseppe Rotunno. Cast: Jane Fonda, Terence Stamp, Peter Fonda, Carla Marlier, Françoise Prévost, James Robertson Justice.

For a brief time in the late sixties and early seventies, omnibus films, which offered the commercial prospect of grouping star directors and cast into one picture, were all the rage. **Spirits of the Dead** (aka **Histoires extraordinaires**) capitalizes on the trend by bringing together some of the greatest names in cinema history on both sides of the camera, for a series of tales loosely based on Edgar Allan Poe: *Metzengerstein* reunites **Barbarella** team Roger Vadim and Jane Fonda; *William Wilson*, by Louis Malle, features Alain Delon and Brigitte Bardot; and *Toby Dammit, or Never Bet the Devil Your Head*, by Federico Fellini, stars Terence Stamp. Orson Welles was originally attached, as well as a few others (Chabrol, Visconti), who dropped out and were replaced in development. The filmmakers worked separately from each other, unaware of the others' choices. Fellini's segment, arguably the most overtly ghostly of the three, was inspired by the ball-bouncing spirit in Mario Bava's **Kill, Baby... Kill!** This Italy-France co-production was released in the U.S. in 1969 by AIP, who, amongst other changes, added a voice-over by an uncredited Vincent Price reading quotes from Poe's poem over the main and end titles. Acquired shortly after the creation of the Motion Picture Association of America (MPAA), **Spirits of the Dead** was the first horror movie to receive an R (Restricted) rating.

## HASTA EL VIENTO TIENE MIEDO

Mexico, 1968
Director: Carlos Enrique Taboada.
Producer: Jesús Grovas.
Screenplay: Carlos Enrique Taboada.
Music: Raúl Lavista.
Cinematography: Agustín Jiménez.
Cast: Marga López, Alicia Bonet, Maricruz Olivier, Norma Lazareno, Renata Seydel, Irma Castillón.

Mexico's love affair with female ghosts continues with this story of a schoolgirl (Alicia Bonet) who believes herself to be haunted, and eventually possessed, by the spirit of a former student who hung herself years before in a tower of the boarding school. Written and directed by Carlos Enrique Taboada (**El libro de piedra / The Book of Stone**, 1969; **Más negro que la noche / Blacker Than Night**, 1975), **Hasta el viento tiene miedo** (which translates as 'Even the Wind Is Afraid') is one of the country's more subtle, atmospheric efforts, at a age when Mexican horror was by and large defined by monsters, wrestlers, and schlock. A slow burn with an almost exclusively female cast, it is in tone, pacing and themes very much aligned with the Gothic stories produced in Italy and Great Britain around the same time.

Taboada, disillusioned by the initial reception of his directing work, turned to television writing in the last stage of his career. He is today recognized as a major genre talent in his country, his influence acknowledged by the likes of Guillermo del Toro, and the movie has become a Day of the Dead perennial. In 2007, **Hasta el viento tiene miedo** received a low-budget, R-rated remake, in which Bonet cameos.

## KURONEKO

Japan, 1968
Director: Kaneto Shindô. Producers: Nobuyo Horiba, Kazuo Kuwahara, Setsuo Noto. Screenplay: Kaneto Shindô. Music: Hikaru Hayashi. Cinematography: Kiyomi Kuroda. Cast: Kichiemon Nakamura, Nobuko Otowa, Kiwako Taichi, Kei Satô, Hideo Kanze, Taiji Tonoyama.

**Yabu no naka no kuroneko** ('A Black Cat in a Bamboo Grove'), distributed internationally as **Kuroneko** ('Black Cat'), starts with the brutal rape and murder of a villager and her daughter by a group of samurai. As the house burns, their bodies remain inexplicably intact and a black cat appears to lick the blood and ashes off the victims. They return as *onryō*, vengeful ghosts who lure men to their home in a bamboo grove, seduce them, and kill them. War hero Gintoki (Kichiemon Nakamura) is dispatched to investigate the men's disappearances. Shot in Toho Scope, this oneiric masterpiece of Japanese cinema is the work of acclaimed and prolific writer-director Kaneto Shindô (**Onibaba**, 1964); minimalist in its production design — all stark straight lines like a Noh theatre set — and its music, it is on the other hand explicit in its use of blood, flashes of violence, and eroticism. Although not a direct adaptation of a traditional *kwaidan*, **Kuroneko** takes its place in a long line of *yurei*, *onryō*, and *kaibyô* (ghost cat) films. It was entered in the 1968 Cannes Festival competition, but the event was cancelled halfway through that year due to the country's social unrest, and the movie was later released outside Japan without the clout of a prestigious festival screening.

## THE SNOW WOMAN

Japan, 1968
Director: Tokuzô Tanaka. Producers: Ikuo Kubodera, Masaichi Nagata. Screenplay: Fuji Yahiro.
Music: Akira Ifukube. Cinematography: Chikashi Makiura.
Cast: Shiho Fujimura, Akira Ishihama, Machiko Hasegawa, Taketoshi Naitô, Mizuho Suzuki, Fujio Suga.

Also known as **Ghost Story of the Snow Witch**, **The Snow Woman** is another classic *kwaidan* based on the folklore figure of Yuki-onna. As described by Lafcadio Hearn in his collection of tales, the snow woman, here played by Shiho Fujimura, is a beautiful long-haired, white-clad woman who appears in snow storms and freezes her victims to death with her white breath. In early versions of the story, the eerie creature was presented as a purely evil force, but screen incarnations have given her more compassionate, tragic qualities. Essentially an expanded retelling of the Woman of the Snow chapter from **Kwaidan** (1964), **The Snow Woman** places emphasis on drama and social commentary, contrasting Yuki-onna's supernatural nature with human cruelty as a brutal samurai hell-bent on ruining her marriage will stop at nothing to claim her for his own. **The Snow Woman** was produced by Daiei Film (**Rashomon**, 1950; **Ugetsu**, 1953), one of the major studios during Japan's Golden Age; though by then it already teetered on the brink of bankruptcy. Prolific sixties director Tokuzô Tanaka, who started his career as an assistant director to Akira Kurosawa, would go on to helm **The Haunted Castle** (1969), inspired by the tale of the vampire cat of Nabeshima and also for Daiei, as well as entries in the **Zatoichi** series.

## WHISTLE AND I'LL COME TO YOU

UK, 1968
Director: Jonathan Miller. Producer: Jonathan Miller.
Screenplay: Jonathan Miller. Cinematography: Dick Bush.
Cast: Michael Hordern, Ambrose Coghill, George Woodbridge, Nora Gordon, Freda Dowie.

On an off-season stay at a remote coastal resort, bumbling academic Professor Parkin (Shakespearian actor Michael Hordern, in a pitch-perfect performance) finds an ancient bone whistle in the sand. An inscription on its side reads, 'Who is it who is coming?' and when the staunch rationalist blows the whistle, he is surprised to experience nightly disturbances… Filmmaker Jonathan Miller, a trained neurologist-turned-theatre and television director, is economical in his use of (largely improvised) dialogue and indulges in few stylistic flourishes. Yet he creates a mounting sense of dread with minimal resources: few movies can elicit such absolute horror with a pulsing sound, sharp editing, and a rag cloth on a stick. Sadly, Miller never returned to the genre, instead turning his attention to operas and documentaries. Often jumbled in with the BBC's subsequent yearly series **A Ghost Story for Christmas**, this adaptation of M.R. James's 1904 *Oh, Whistle, and I'll Come yo You, My Lad* was in fact part of arts documentary program **Omnibus**, which explains the opening voice-over educating viewers on James's works, and highlighting the story's moral value, stating that it 'hints at the dangers of intellectual pride'. In 2010 the BBC attempted a new adaptation of the material, starring John Hurt and Gemma Jones, but failed to match the elegant, subtle terror of the original.

## LET'S SCARE JESSICA TO DEATH

USA, 1971
Director: John Hancock. Producer: Charles B. Moss Jr. Screenplay: Norman Jonas [Lee Kalcheim], Ralph Rose [John Hancock]. Music: Orville Stoeber, Walter Sear. Cinematography: Robert M. Baldwin. Cast: Zohra Lampert, Barton Heyman, Kevin O'Connor, Gretchen Corbett, Alan Manson, Mariclare Costello.

First of the low-key slow burns which would become a hallmark of 1970s ghost stories, in stark contrast with the decade's opposing trend of bloody, sensationalist shockers *à la* **The Last House on the Left**, **Let's Scare Jessica to Death** is an early entry into the is-this-real-or-is-she-mad sub-genre. Following a nervous breakdown, Jessica (Zohra Lampert, in a polarizing performance) is released from a mental institution into the care of her husband. Together with an old friend, they move into a farmhouse on a remote island, but as soon as they settle, she starts hearing voices and experiencing visions, particularly of a drowned woman in the nearby lake. The title makes one suspect a **Diabolique**-type ploy, but the true nature of the threat — vampire? spirit? succubus? — is unclear, though the movie makes ample use of classical ghost story trappings. Despite its Gothic eeriness reminiscent of the **Carnival of Souls** and **The Innocents** of the past decade, director John Hancock's first feature feels very modern, with hippie characters, Jessica's inner monologue as voice-over, and underlying themes of depression and marital infidelity. Although unfairly overlooked at the time, Stephen King singled it out ten years later as one of the best horror movies ever made in his book *Danse Macabre*, and it is now regarded as a hidden gem.

## THE STONE TAPE

UK, 1972
Director: Peter Sasdy.
Producer: Innes Lloyd.
Screenplay: Nigel Kneale.
Cast: Michael Bryant, Jane Asher, Iain Cuthbertson, Michael Bates, Reginald Marsh, Tom Chadbon.

Playwright Nigel Kneale (**Quatermass and the Pit**) always excelled at showcasing the clash of science and the supernatural, a theme at the very core of this minimalist *huis clos*, aired on the BBC on Christmas Day 1972. Peter Brock (Michael Bryant) is the brash leader of a team of scientists developing a recording technology. As soon as she enters their new research facility, an old Victorian mansion, the only woman amongst them, Jill (played by Jane Asher), in tears and hysterics from start to finish, witnesses the ghost of a maid running away and falling off some steps. Brock believes the apparition to be little more than the playback of a tragic event preserved by the stone wall, and they set off to figure out how to reproduce the phenomenon. Despite its barebones direction and some theatrical acting, **The Stone Tape** made a deep impression. John Carpenter's **Prince of Darkness** (which even references a fictional Kneale University), Tobe Hooper's **Poltergeist**, and Hammer Films' 2014 **The Quiet Ones**, as well as Stephen Volk's 1992 TV phenomenon **Ghostwatch**, all have roots in this little TV special. But its influence went beyond the movie world: residual haunting, Cambridge archaeologist T.C. Lethbridge's theory that ghosts are mere recordings of past traumatic events, stored by the environment and replayed under the right circumstances, has since been widely known as the stone tape theory.

## THE TURN OF THE SCREW

*Various adaptations*

Originally published in 1898, Henry James's novella *The Turn of the Screw* is the first-person account of a young governess driven to madness by the ghostly happenings at the country estate she shares with her two charges, Flora and Miles. Subtle, ambiguous and psychological, it may not have immediately seemed to easily transpose to the screen, and with the exception of a 1950 Broadway play and a chamber opera from English composer Benjamin Britten in 1954, it isn't until 1959 that the first adaptation of note would appear, with John Frankenheimer's live NBC play starring Ingrid Bergman. Broadcast in colour, this version only survives in a black-and-white recording of the presentation. More than a dozen would follow.

In 1961, Jack Clayton directed what remains to this day the finest adaptation of Henry James's piece: **The Innocents**, which best preserves doubt as to the presence of the spirits, and the sanity of its sexually repressed lead. Far from discouraging filmmakers from trying to top its success, **The Innocents** appears to have shown them the way, launching an on-going slew of film and television versions from France (**Le tour d'écrou**, 1974) to Spain (**Otra vuelta de tuerca**, 1985; **Presence of Mind**, 1999, starring Lauren Bacall, Jude Law and Sadie Frost) and Mexico (miniseries, 1981); not to mention Michael Winner's **The Nightcomers** (1971), a controversial prequel focusing on the relationship between Quint (Marlon Brando) and Miss Jessel (Stephanie Beacham).

Amongst the most significant is Dan Curtis's (**Dark Shadows**) two-part television movie starring Lynn Redgrave and Megs Jenkins. Aired in April 1974 as part of ABC's Wide World Mystery anthology, Curtis's **The Turn of the Screw** was filmed on location in an old country house in Hinwick, a small town outside London, which would hamper the traditional television way of shooting, with three cameras working simultaneously on each scene. Limited by time and money, the filmmaker made a number of small adjustments to the story, relinquishing the ambiguity Clayton had sought to preserve. Amusingly, the novella would also inspire a December 1968 episode of **Dark Shadows**.

In 1999, Jodhi May and Colin Firth appeared in an ITV adaptation from television director Ben Bolt, who generally sticks close to the text of the novella; so much so in fact that for its U.S. broadcast, as part of PBS's Masterpiece Theater program, the piece was introduced as a 'filmed text'.

The BBC's 2009 adaptation is framed by discussions between a psychiatrist and his patient (future **Downton Abbey** favourites Michelle Dockery and Dan Stevens), as the latter recalls her misfortunes in flashbacks. Set after the first World War, this version, from television director Tim Fywell and aired in December as one of the network's traditional Christmas ghost stories, remains nonetheless fairly faithful to the original.

Finally, although by no means literal transpositions, it is worth noting that Alejandro Amenábar's **The Others** and Nick Murphy's **The Awakening** certainly owe a debt of gratitude to Henry James's story.

## FROM BEYOND THE GRAVE

UK, 1973
Director: Kevin Connor.
Producers: Max J. Rosenberg, Milton Subotsky.
Screenplay: Robin Clarke, Raymond Christodoulou.
Music: Douglas Gamley. Cinematography: Alan Hume.
Cast: Peter Cushing, David Warner, Wendy Allnutt, Donald Pleasence, Ian Bannen, Diana Dors.

Last and best in British production company Amicus's long-running series of anthologies, **From Beyond the Grave** stars Peter Cushing as the owner of antique shop Temptations Limited ('Offers you can't resist!'), who curses patrons who dare attempt to trick him. This linking device leads to four stories relating the fates of cheating customers, two of whom run afoul of ghosts: In 'The Gatecrasher', a man (David Warner) finds himself compelled to kill women after an impromptu séance, under the influence of a spirit inhabiting an old mirror he bought for a steal. Likely inspired by **Dead of Night**, this is easily the spookiest tale of the lot, in no small part thanks to Marcel Steiner's remarkably frightful mirror ghost. In 'The Door', a writer (Ian Ogilvy) buys an ornate door from the shop, intending to convert it into a stationery closet. But his plan is thwarted when his purchase mysteriously opens onto a secret room harbouring the ghost of a 17th century occultist (Jack Watson), who soon escapes. **From Beyond the Grave** is a fun, polished piece, complemented by an all-star cast, and **The Legend of Hell House** cinematographer Alan Hume's rich, colourful pictures. First-time director Kevin Connor went on to helm Amicus's last releases as well as cult classic **Motel Hell**, while pursuing a successful TV career.

## HIGH PLAINS DRIFTER

USA, 1973
Director: Clint Eastwood.
Producer: Robert Daley.
Screenplay: Ernest Tidyman.
Music: Dee Barton.
Cinematography:
Bruce Surtees.
Cast: Clint Eastwood,
Verna Bloom, Marianna Hill,
Mitchell Ryan, Jack Ging,
Stefan Gierasch.

For his second feature (and first Western) in the director's seat, Clint Eastwood stars as a mysterious, nameless gunslinger on a quest for tit for tat justice against a band of outlaws in a small mining town. Earlier drafts of the script, penned by Academy Award winner Ernest Tidyman (**The French Connection**, 1971), identified the Stranger as the brother of the sheriff whose murder he seeks to avenge; Eastwood removed such mentions to keep the character's very nature — largely interpreted as the spirit of the victim himself — open to interpretation. For that reason, it is regularly referred to as a Gothic horror, or a ghost story, under the unusual guise of a bleak, gritty Western which blurs the lines between good and evil, hero and villain, sympathetic and despicable; the polar opposite of John Wayne's Old West. **High Plains Drifter** was filmed on location around Mono Lake, California, against Universal's wishes to have it lensed on the backlot; an entire town had to be built from scratch in under three weeks. Production lasted six weeks and the movie was shot in sequence. Eastwood would create another subtly ghostly character with **Pale Rider**'s scarred Preacher (1985), whose backstory is unclear, but whom the director himself depicts as a spirit.

## THE LEGEND OF HELL HOUSE

UK, 1973
Director: John Hough. Producers: Albert Fennell, Norman T. Herman. Screenplay: Richard Matheson. Music: Brian Hodgson, Delia Derbyshire. Cinematography: Alan Hume. Cast: Clive Revill, Pamela Franklin, Roddy McDowall, Gayle Hunnicutt, Roland Culver, Peter Bowles.

More visceral than **The Haunting**, its most direct influence, and every bit as tense, **The Legend of Hell House**, a faithful adaptation by Richard Matheson of his own 1971 novel *Hell House*, is often unjustly overlooked. Giving traditional ghost story staples — cobwebs, black cats, Gothic mansions — a modern twist, this scary masterpiece hints at the failure of science to explain or defeat the supernatural, and adds to the proceedings a touch of debauchery (though this aspect is admittedly toned down compared to the novel.) Hired by a dying millionaire to investigate the possibility survival after death, Lionel Barrett (Clive Revill), an insufferably smug physicist, spends Christmas week at Hell House, the 'Mount Everest of haunted houses' and former home of depraved giant Emeric Belasco, whose malevolent spirit remains within its walls. Barrett brings along his oddly coiffed wife Ann (Gayle Hunnicut), mental medium Florence Tanner (Pamela Franklin), and Ben Fischer (Roddy McDowall), the only survivor of a previous research team. It isn't long before a ghostly presence reveals itself to the team. Is Belasco really the only soul trapped in Hell House? John Hough's (**Twins of Evil**, **The Watcher in the Woods**) movie is technically impeccable, with mind-boggling practical effects, sumptuous sets, and Alan Hume's brightly coloured cinematography, all in low angles, menacing foreground elements, and uncomfortable close-ups. But it is Roddy McDowall's terrific performance which truly gives the film its heart, as the timid, closed-off psychic who overcomes his fear and rises to the occasion.

## VOICES

UK, 1973
Director: Kevin Billington. Producer: Robert Enders.
Screenplay: George Kirgo, Robert Enders.
Music: Richard Rodney Bennett.
Cinematography: Geoffrey Unsworth.
Cast: David Hemmings, Gayle Hunnicutt, Lynn Farleigh, Russell Lewis, Eva Griffith, Adam Bridge.

Another entry into the 'woman goes mad and hears voices after the death of her child' sub-genre, **Voices**, also known in the U.S. as **Nightmare**, stars real-life husband and wife David Hemmings (**Blow-Up**, **Deep Red**) and Gayle Hunnicutt (**The Legend of Hell House**) as a couple trying to reconnect in their fog-shrouded country house after her release from a mental institution. Though its premise is similar to nearly every ghost story made in the seventies (one is particularly reminded of **Let's Scare Jessica to Death**), its focus on the couple's disintegration, and its twist ending, set it apart. Based on *The Others*, a 1967 30-minute play by Richard Lortz, this British production by television and theatre director Kevin Billington wears its stage origins on its sleeve, devoting most of its time to the couple's bickering inside one room of the house. Before **Voices**, *The Others* was adapted into an episode of British series **Armchair Theatre** (1970) directed by Piers Haggard (**The Blood on Satan's Claw**, 1971).

Possibly influenced by **Carnival of Souls** (1962) and Bava's **Kill, Baby... Kill!** (1966), the story — whether as *The Others* or **Voices** — is widely thought to have served as inspiration for Amenábar's masterpiece **The Others** (2001).

## BLOOD REINCARNATION

Hong Kong, 1974
Director: Ting Shan-hsi.
Producer: Yu Feng-chih. Screenplay: Ting Shan-hsi.
Music: Chou Fu-liang. Cinematography: Chen Ching-chu.
Cast: Shih Tien, Shirley Huang, Chi Shih-ying, Wang Lai,
Chiang Nan, Meng Li.

'Charm can do nothing on ghost. You better believe it. This film is based on Cantonese legend and asks people to do good deeds'. So starts **Yinyang jie** (also known as **Blood Reincarnation**), a three-part horror anthology from Hong Kong writer-director Ting Shan-hsi. Each of its simple vignettes unfolds like a Buddhist-inspired morality play (a wise woman even explains that people should worship Buddha in order to avoid ghosts), with the sinners punished by the souls of those they offended. In the first story, 'The Treasure', the baby of a couple who killed an old woman to steal her buried treasure is possessed by the spirit of their victim. Rather bloody (including the decapitation of a chicken), it is told in a non-linear fashion. The second and more comedic tale, 'Wanton', sees a woman and her lover haunted by the ghost of her husband, whom they murdered when he found them out. She ends up bitten to death by her inamorato, somehow possessed by a dog. Finally in 'Lau Tin Sok', by far the longest and most sentimental story, a doctor executed for a crime he didn't commit is granted seven days on earth through the process of blood reincarnation to exact revenge upon his accusers.

## BURNT OFFERINGS

USA, 1976
Director: Dan Curtis.
Producer: Dan Curtis.
Screenplay: William F. Nolan,
Dan Curtis. Music: Robert Cobert.
Cinematography:
Jacques R. Marquette.
Cast: Karen Black, Oliver Reed,
Burgess Meredith, Eileen Heckart,
Lee Montgomery, Dub Taylor.

Arguably more a possessed house than an actual haunting story, **Burnt Offerings**, based on the homonymous book by Robert Marasco (reportedly an influence on Stephen King's *The Shining*), follows Ben and Marian Rolf (Oliver Reed and Karen Black) and their family (Lee H. Montgomery and Bette Davis) as they spend the summer in a run-down California mansion. They take care of the place and deliver meals to the owner's elderly mother, who lives in the attic and is never to be seen or disturbed; but as various incidents disturb the peace, the house seems to regenerate, and Marian's behaviour changes, as if she were slowly possessed by the spirit of the abode. For anyone keen to watch Reed and Black do chores, **Dark Shadows** creator Dan Curtis's creeper delivers in spades. Yet the slow pace is punctuated by chilling moments, such as Ben's recurring nightmares of a hearse and its ghoulish driver, and the third act delivers plenty of shocks, climaxing in a bloody, **Psycho**-inspired finale. Largely ignored upon release, **Burnt Offerings** however helped shape one of the decade's biggest horror hits, **The Amityville Horror**: another tale of a family slowly torn apart by a malevolent house. Its location, California's famed Dunsmuir House, later featured in the likes of **Phantasm** (1979) and **A View to a Kill** (1985).

Up the ancient stairs, down the twisting corridor, behind the locked door, something lives, something strange, something evil, something from which no one has ever returned.
BURNT OFFERINGS
P.E.A. FILMS, INC. presents A Film by DAN CURTIS
KAREN BLACK · OLIVER REED in "BURNT OFFERINGS" co-starring BURGESS MEREDITH
EILEEN HECKART · LEE MONTGOMERY · DUB TAYLOR · BETTE DAVIS as Aunt Elizabeth
Screenplay by WILLIAM F. NOLAN and DAN CURTIS · Based on the novel by ROBERT MARASCO · Produced and Directed by DAN CURTIS
Produced in Association with DAN CURTIS PRODUCTIONS, INC. · Production Services by THE CASA COMPANY
United Artists
A Transamerica Company
PG PARENTAL GUIDANCE SUGGESTED
Copyright © MCMLXXVI United Artists Corporation. All Rights Reserved.

## THE SIGNALMAN

UK, 1976
Director: Lawrence Gordon Clark.
Producer: Rosemary Hill.
Screenplay: Andrew Davies.
Music: Stephen Deutsch.
Cinematography: David Whitson.
Cast: Denholm Elliott, Bernard Lloyd, Reginald Jessup, Carina Wyeth.

The first instalment in the BBC's **Ghost Story for Christmas** series not to be adapted from the works of M.R. James, **The Signalman**, based on an 1866 short story by Charles Dickens, is arguably the most atmospheric, mist-shrouded, spooky tale in the show's original run (1971 to 1978). Written by Andrew Davies (**House of Cards**, 1990) and directed by Lawrence Gordon Clark, who helmed all but the last in the series, this short piece is essentially a two-hander in which the signalman (Denholm Elliott, best known today as Marcus Brody in the Indiana Jones saga; at the time also the star of a couple of Amicus productions) of a countryside train station tells an unnamed traveller (Bernard Lloyd) of the chilling, premonitory apparition he has spotted by the tracks, warning him of impending train accidents. Dickens penned the original story a few months after being involved in the Staplehurst rail crash that killed ten in June 1865; the tragedy left a lasting impression on the author and on his work. Interior scenes were shot inside the actual signal box at Highley station, in Shropshire; the exterior however was built for the shoot, on the side of the railway tunnel in Bewdley.

## FULL CIRCLE

UK/Canada, 1977
Director:
Richard Loncraine.
Producers:
Peter Fetterman,
Alfred Pariser.
Screenplay:
Dave Humphries, Harry
Bromley Davenport.
Music: Colin Towns.
Cinematography:
Peter Hannan.
Cast: Mia Farrow,
Keir Dullea, Tom Conti,
Jill Bennett,
Robin Gammell,
Cathleen Nesbitt.

Frail, diaphanous Mia Farrow is the very picture of grief in the titular role of this 1977 adaptation of a 1975 Peter Straub novel. After her young daughter Kate chokes to death in front of her, Julia Lofting (Farrow) leaves her husband (Keir Dullea) and moves into a fully furnished house. She feels Kate's presence everywhere, and brings in a medium to make contact. The woman reveals terrible things have happened in Julia's new dwellings, and that she should leave immediately. With long, creeping shots of its location, and entire scenes devoid of dialogue, focusing on Julia's fragile psyche, Richard Loncraine's **Full Circle** isn't a movie for the ADHD crowd. For all its melancholy cinematography, haunting score, and ghostly happenings, its strength lies not in the rare scenes of supernatural occurrences (**The Changeling** would cover similar ground a few years later with more success) but in simple character moments, such as the horrifying reveal of the personality of Olivia — the little girl who once lived in Julia's hideaway — or Olivia's mother's chilling admission. A huge flop in the UK, where it originated, **Full Circle** didn't come out in the U.S. until 1981, rebranded as **The Haunting of Julia**.

## HOUSE

Japan, 1977
Director: Nobuhiko Ôbayashi.
Producers: Tomoyuki Tanaka, Yorihiko Yamada, Nobuhiko Ôbayashi. Screenplay: Chiho Katsura. Music: Asei Kobayashi, Mickie Yoshino. Cinematography: Yoshitaka Sakamoto.
Cast: Kimiko Ikegami, Kiyohiko Ozaki, Kumiko Ohba, Ai Matsubara, Miki Jinbo, Mieko Satô.

A group of schoolgirls are plagued by supernatural occurrences on a summer trip to an old aunt's countryside manor. The premise may sound familiar, but trust 1970s Japan to produce the most bizarre and unconventional haunted house ever made on the most banal concept. Commissioned by legendary company Toho Studios to write a script which would rival the spectacle and appeal of **Jaws**, Hiroshima-born painter, musician and commercial director Nobuhiko Ōbayashi asked his eleven-year-old daughter, who gets original story credit on the movie, what scared her, and compiled her thoughts into a surreal tale. Toho greenlit the project, but couldn't find any filmmakers to tackle it, and eventually offered it to Ōbayashi to helm. And truly, who else could have handled this psychedelic blend of ghost cats, floating heads, swinging soundtrack (composed before production), bright colours, deliberately artificial-looking backgrounds and effects, people-eating house, and piano-playing severed fingers? He experiments with every camera and editing trick in the book, and with a cast mostly comprising amateurs, mixing high school clichés and childhood fears with traditional spooks such as the *kaibyo* (or supernatural cat): a creature so popular it inspired an entire sub-genre of Japanese horror cinema.

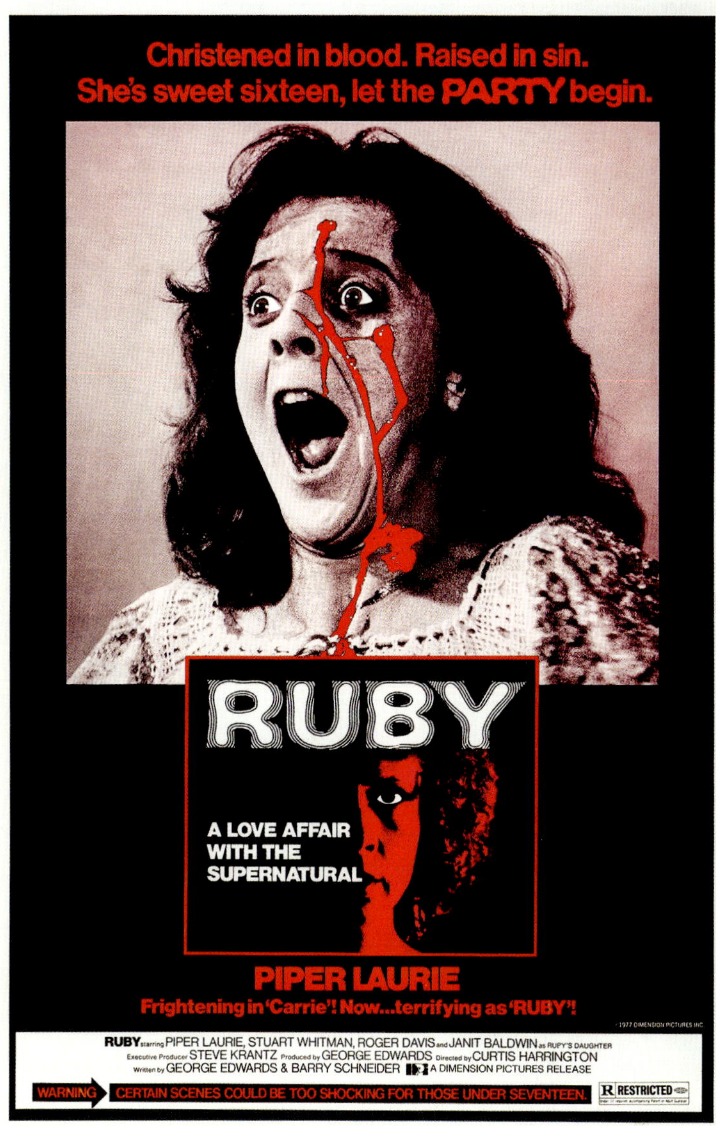

## RUBY

USA, 1977
Director: Curtis Harrington.
Producer: George Edwards.
Screenplay: George Edwards, Barry Schneider.
Music: Don Ellis.
Cinematography: William Mendenhall.
Cast: Piper Laurie, Stuart Whitman, Roger Davis, Janit Baldwin, Crystin Sinclaire, Paul Kent.

Hot on the heels of **The Exorcist** and **Carrie** came **Ruby**, a low-budget shocker that capitalized on the success of recent supernatural/possession flicks. The titular character, played by **Carrie**'s Piper Laurie, is a woman whose deaf daughter (Janit Baldwin), on her sixteenth birthday, starts talking in the voice of her late father, a lowlife mobster who died before the girl's birth. Levitation, back bends, and creepy daughter-to-mother aggressive sexual behaviour ensue. Cinephile and consummate horror fan Curtis Harrington (**Night Tide**, 1961; **Queen of Blood**, 1966) directed, yet the experience left a sour taste due to constant interference from producer Steve Krantz. Post production was particularly nightmarish, with Harrington's original ending, which saw Ruby and her dead lover walk into the lake, replaced by an abrupt, **Carrie**-style jolt. The picture was further maimed for its television broadcast: to conform with CBS's Standards and Practices, scenes of violence were excised; another director, cult/exploitation filmmaker Stephanie Rothman, was then hired to boost the 70-minute running time with new dialogue scenes. This version, released under the Alan Smithee pseudonym, somehow also made its way to video, further harming the movie's reputation. The latest release rights this wrong, but Harrington's romantic ending is by all accounts forever lost.

## THE SENTINEL

USA, 1977
Director: Michael Winner. Producers: Michael Winner, Jeffrey Konvitz.
Screenplay: Michael Winner, Jeffrey Konvitz. Music: Gil Melle.
Cinematography: Dick Kratina.
Cast: Cristina Raines, Martin Balsam, Chris Sarandon, John Carradine, José Ferrer, Ava Gardner.

After a couple of suicide attempts, NYC model Alison (Cristina Raines, daughter of Claude **The Invisible Man** Raines) moves into an old apartment, away from her boyfriend (Chris Sarandon), to learn to stand on her own feet. Before long, she's invited to meet her neighbours, a disquieting mix of oddballs, only to learn the next day than she and a blind priest on the top floor are the building's only (living) inhabitants. When her dead father appears running around the brownstone in his underwear, Alison really starts doubting her sanity. Coming at the tail end of the seventies' wave of religious horrors, Michael Winner's **The Sentinel** may strongly echo **Rosemary's Baby**, but it is undeniably the strangest, most subversive of them all, loaded with nightmarish and transgressive imagery (Beverly D'Angelo as a masturbating ballerina is a sight to behold), and presenting the Catholic Church as a rigid institution offering little comfort. It surrounds its damaged heroine with controlling men, from priests and neighbours to employers and photographers, who grab, patronize, and manipulate her. **The Sentinel** was noted for its intense gore, courtesy of FX master Dick Smith, yet it was Winner's decision to cast extras with actual deformities as souls of the damned in its hellish, surreal climax, that drew the ire of critics at the time.

The year's most bizarre Best-Seller.

THE SENTINEL

"THE SENTINEL"
A MICHAEL WINNER FILM
CHRIS SARANDON · CRISTINA RAINES
MARTIN BALSAM · JOHN CARRADINE · JOSE FERRER
AVA GARDNER · ARTHUR KENNEDY · BURGESS MEREDITH · SYLVIA MILES · DEBORAH RAFFIN · ELI WALLACH
Screenplay by MICHAEL WINNER · Based on the novel by JEFFREY KONVITZ · Music by GIL MELLÉ · Directed by MICHAEL WINNER · Produced by MICHAEL WINNER and JEFFREY KONVITZ · A UNIVERSAL PICTURE · TECHNICOLOR®

## SHOCK

Italy, 1977
Director: Mario Bava. Producer: Turi Vasile.
Screenplay: Lamberto Bava, Francesco Barbieri, Paolo Brigenti, Dardano Sacchetti.
Music: I Libra. Cinematography: Alberto Spagnoli.
Cast: Daria Nicolodi, John Steiner, David Collin Jr., Ivan Rassimov, Nicola Salerno, Paul Costello.

Mario Bava's last theatrical feature before his passing in 1980, **Shock** stands apart in the maestro's filmography as a contained, sober ghost story, far from the colourful excesses of the giallo genre and the Gothic scares he is best remembered for. Imagined by Bava's son Lamberto to get his father back on track after the traumatic production of **Rabid Dogs** (1974), it follows the typical seventies plot, halfway between **Full Circle** and **Ruby**. Dario Argento muse Daria Nicolodi plays Dora, the requisite woman-on-the-brink-of-madness who, after a stay in a mental hospital, moves with her family into the home she once shared with her late husband. Haunted by memories of the past, she soon believes her son to be possessed by her husband's spirit. Partially directed by Lamberto, **Shock** may be amongst Bava's more conventional works, yet Dora's nightmares and hallucinations contain moments of genuine fright, evidencing the filmmaker's technical genius; one of its most effective scares, where a child unexpectedly turns into an adult, was re-used to great effect in **The Conjuring** spin-off **Annabelle** (2014). In the U.S., **Shock** was released as **Beyond the Door II**, promoted as a sequel to Ovidio Assonitis's unrelated 1974 movie about a pregnant woman possessed by a demonic entity.

## AAYIRAM JENMANGAL

India, 1978
Director: Durai. Producer: M. Muthuraman.
Screenplay: S.L. Puram Sadanandan.
Music: M.S. Viswanathan. Cinematography: V. Ranga.
Cast: Rajinikanth, Vijayakumar, Latha, Kannan,
Suruli Rajan, Manorama.

Inspired by the 1976 Indian Malayalam film **Yakshagaanam**, starring and directed by popular actress Sheela and remade in Telugu the same year, **Aayiram Jenmangal** (translated literally, 'A Thousand Generations' or 'A Thousand Incarnations'), one of the earliest examples of Tamil horror movies, tells the all-singing story of Savitri (Latha Sethupathy), a woman possessed by the spirit of her husband's late fiancée who wants to reunite with her former flame. Although India's first horror, Kamal Amrohi's major hit **Mahal**, came out as early as 1949, the genre wouldn't hit its stride in the country until the 1970s, before exploding in the last twenty years. Tamil scary movies in particular often explore themes of social injustice, and contrast the traditions and superstitions of old with the contemporary way of life. In the '70s, they were sometimes used as a means to promote a return to Hindu values; in **Aayiram Jenmangal**, the invasive soul is destroyed after being trapped in a temple. Their focus is generally ghosts or demons and possessions, as opposed to monsters, zombies or vampires; horror movies are referred to as *pey padam* — literally 'ghost films' — in the Tamil language. In 2014, producer Muthuraman filed a lawsuit against the makers of hit horror comedy **Aranmanai** (2014), which he argued held so many similarities with the thriller classic as to constitute copyright infringement. The case was settled out of court.

## THE AMITYVILLE HORROR

USA, 1979
Director: Stuart Rosenberg. Producers: Ronald Saland,
Elliot Geisinger. Screenplay: Sandor Stern.
Music: Lalo Schifrin. Cinematography: Fred J. Koenekamp.
Cast: James Brolin, Margot Kidder, Rod Steiger,
Don Stroud, Murray Hamilton, John Larch.

Rarely have the words 'based on a true story' been more controversial than in the case of the Amityville franchise. Adapted from a 1977 book by Jay Anson relating the paranormal experiences of the Lutz family in the infamous Long Island murder house, Stuart Rosenberg's **The Amityville Horror** benefitted from both the public appetite for supernatural fare after the success of **The Exorcist**, and the curiosity surrounding the allegedly real events which inspired it. James Brolin and Margot Kidder star as George and Kathy Lutz, who move with their three children into a home where the year before, Ronald DeFeo Jr. shot his parents and four siblings in their sleep. The Lutzes ask Father Delaney (Rod Steiger) to bless the house, but sudden sickness and a swarm of flies force him away. Various incidents, combined with George's unexplainable mood swings, soon convince them that their new home is haunted. In his 1981 book *Danse Macabre*, Stephen King aptly described the appeal of **The Amityville Horror** as 'financial horror', saying it 'might as well have been subtitled the horror of the shrinking bank account'. Indeed, the movie starts off slow, with what could be best described as minor annoyances — a window slides on a kid's finger, a babysitter is locked is a closet, a little girl spends too much time with her invisible friend — in lieu of scares, before going all out and destroying the property in a Grand Guignol finale. A huge hit upon release, it not only influenced filmmakers to come, but also launched a franchise on-going to this day.

"FOR GOD'S SAKE, GET OUT!"
THE AMITYVILLE HORROR
From the bestseller that made millions believe in the unbelievable.
SAMUEL Z. ARKOFF PRESENTS
A PROFESSIONAL FILMS, INC. PRODUCTION
JAMES BROLIN, MARGOT KIDDER and ROD STEIGER
In
"THE AMITYVILLE HORROR"
READ THE BANTAM PAPERBACK
Also Starring MURRAY HAMILTON Music by LALO SCHIFRIN Executive in Charge of Production JERE HENSHAW
Executive Producer SAMUEL Z. ARKOFF Screenplay by SANDOR STERN Based on the Book by JAY ANSON
Produced by RONALD SALAND and ELLIOT GEISINGER Directed by STUART ROSENBERG
R RESTRICTED
UNDER 17 REQUIRES ACCOMPANYING PARENT OR ADULT GUARDIAN
Color by MOVIELAB AN AMERICAN INTERNATIONAL PICTURE A CINEMA 77 FILM
COPYRIGHT ©1979 AMERICAN INTERNATIONAL PICTURES, INC.

## SCREAMS OF A WINTER NIGHT

USA, 1979
Director: James L. Wilson. Producers: Richard H. Wadsack, James L. Wilson. Screenplay: Richard H. Wadsack. Music: Don Zimmers. Cinematography: Robert E. Rogers. Cast: Matt Borel, Gil Glascow, Mary Agen Cox, Patrick Byers, Robin Bradley, Ray Gaspard.

Existing at the crossroads between the drive-in and VHS ages, **Screams of a Winter Night**, from director-producer James L. Wilson (whose only other credits, intriguingly, are as an actor playing Santa Claus in a couple of Disney television productions), starts off as a **Texas Chain Saw Massacre** or **Hills Have Eyes** wannabe, when a group of friends stop at a gas station on their way to the cabin they will be spending the night at, on haunted Indian grounds; before turning into an anthology of three tales based on urban legends, told by the protagonists at the cabin that night. While the other two stories present very human killers, the middle one, 'The Green Light', concerns the spooky happenings awaiting three pledges at a supposedly haunted abandoned hotel. Distributed by Dimension Pictures, already responsible for **Ruby** and **Return to Boggy Creek** (both 1977), **Screams of a Winter Night** feels like the work of a group of local amateurs, shot as it was in 16mm on a non-existent budget in Louisiana. This arguably lends this otherwise rather lifeless family-friendly picture a certainly nostalgic charm, enhanced by the fact that it can only nowadays be seen on old VHS tapes.

© U.T.A.
THEATRICAL ACCESSORIES DISTRIBUTION
1658 CORDOVA ST., L.A. CAL. 90007 • (213) 734-9178

SCREAMS OF A WINTER NIGHT
©1979 DIMENSION PICTURES INC
A DIMENSION PICTURES RELEASE
PG PARENTAL GUIDANCE SUGGESTED
SOME MATERIAL MAY NOT BE SUITABLE FOR CHILDREN

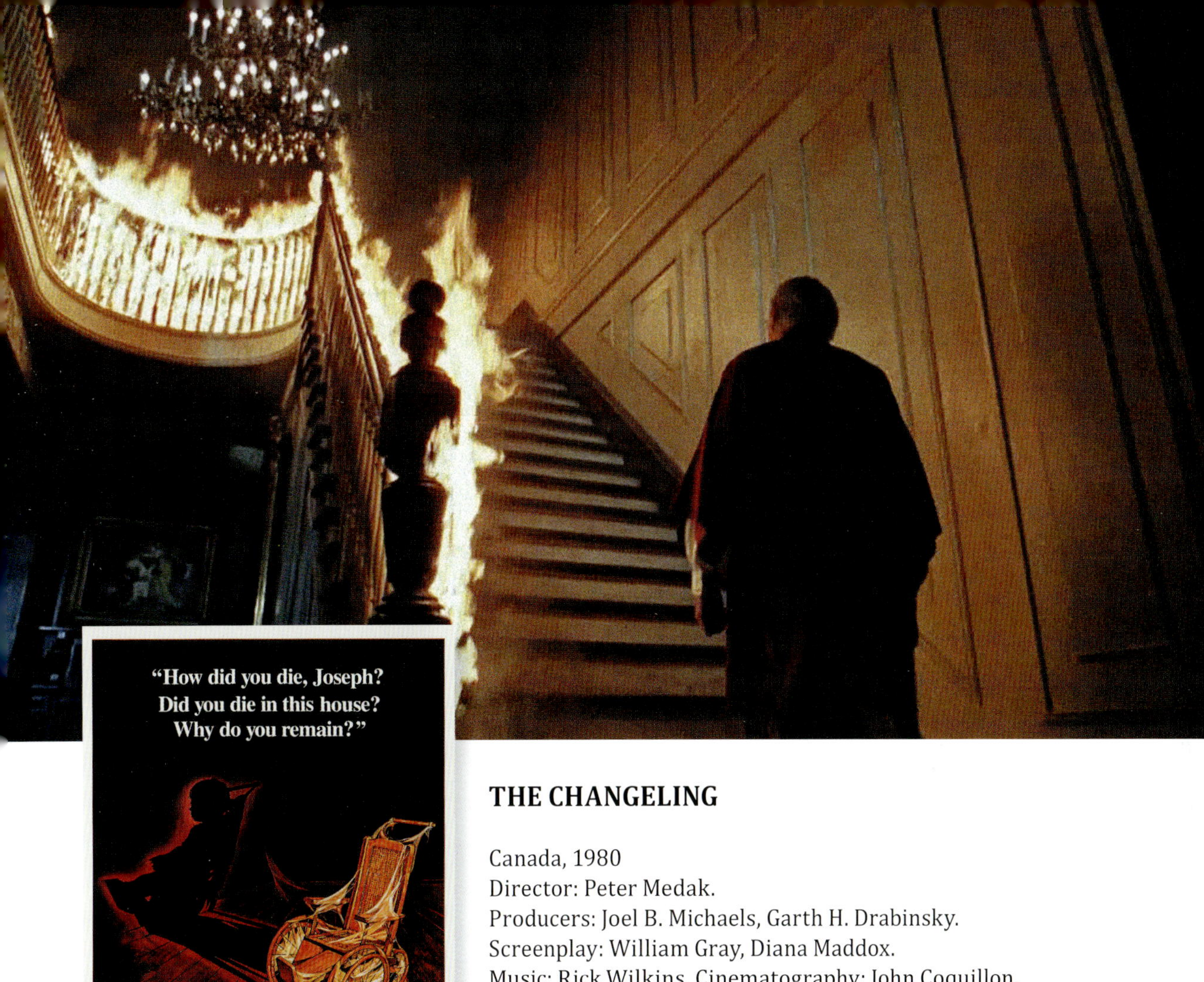

## THE CHANGELING

Canada, 1980
Director: Peter Medak.
Producers: Joel B. Michaels, Garth H. Drabinsky.
Screenplay: William Gray, Diana Maddox.
Music: Rick Wilkins. Cinematography: John Coquillon.
Cast: George C. Scott, Trish Van Devere, Melvyn Douglas, Jean Marsh, Barry Morse, Bernard Behrens.

Ghost stories tend to feature protagonists, generally young and female, whose perceived frailty of mind and body makes them easy victims to empathize with. Not so with **The Changeling**, which stars burly, stern, fifty-two-year-old George C. Scott (**The Exorcist III**) as John Russell, a recently widowed composer whose new abode, a mansion on the outskirts of Seattle, appears haunted by the spirit of a child killed on the grounds. Looking into the history of the property, Russell brings to light sordid and sad events regarding the previous owner's family. The story is based on inexplicable phenomena music composer and co-writer Russell Hunter experienced while living in an old home near Cheesman Park, Colorado, in 1969. While the previous filmmakers attached to the movie (Donald Cammell and Tony Richardson) had favoured a little house as the main location, director Peter Medak insisted on setting the story in a gothic, classical haunted mansion. An exterior facade was built for the picture in Victoria, Canada; interiors were filmed in a Vancouver soundstage. A masterpiece of understatement, using music and effects sparingly, instead focusing on terrific performances from Scott and frequent co-star and real-life wife Trish Van Devere (**The Hearse**), **The Changeling** offers truly chilling moments, and its influence on the horror genre is still felt today. The bouncing ball gag, perfectly executed, has been riffed on in everything from **The Awakening** and **The Conjuring**, to **Scary Movie 2** and **Crimson Peak**.

## DEATH SHIP

Canada/UK, 1980
Director: Alvin Rakoff.
Producers: Derek Gibson, Harold Greenberg.
Screenplay: John Robins. Music: Ivor Slaney.
Cinematography: René Verzier.
Cast: George Kennedy, Richard Crenna, Nick Mancuso,
Sally Ann Howes, Kate Reid, Saul Rubinek.

**The Fog** wasn't the only film to feature ghostly sailors on misty seas in 1980. Written by Jack Hill and John Robins, and directed by Alvin Rakoff, **Death Ship** (not to be confused with **Ghost Ship**, 2002) sees the survivors of a cruise liner sunken by an ancient Nazi freighter find refuge on board the mysterious vessel. Partly filmed in the Gulf of Mexico, where the unit was reportedly plagued by hurricanes and electrical storms, the British-Canadian movie stars George Kennedy, Nick Mancuso and Sally Ann Howes (**Dead of Night**, 1945) alongside the 'Maurine K', a 2,080-ton single deck lumber freighter built originally used on the Amazon river and the South American coast. Interiors were filmed in Quebec City, and shots from 1960's **The Last Voyage** were used to boost the sinkage scene. Despite plot holes, improbable character reactions, and some of the most random slow-motion shots in recent history, **Death Ship** offers a number of memorable set pieces (including a blood shower scene) in an unusual, spooky setting, but is perhaps best remembered today for its fantastic VHS art, where the ghostly craft, anchor holes and rust stains looking like a giant skull, comes out of the fog to attack a row boat.

## ENCOUNTERS OF THE SPOOKY KIND

Hong Kong, 1980
Director: Sammo Hung.
Producers: Chan Pui-wah, Raymond Chow, Lau Chi-chong. Screenplay: Sammo Hung, Huang Ying. Music: Frankie Chan.
Cinematography: Lee Yau-tong, Ng Cho-wah.
Cast: Sammo Hung, Chung Fat, Chan Long, Lam Ching-ying, Wong Ha, Wu Ma.

So inventive and entertaining is Sammo Hung's kung fu horror comedy **Encounters of the Spooky Kind** (original title **Gwai daa gwai** — literally 'Ghost Fights Ghost'), that it single-handedly launched a new sub-genre of Hong Kong cinema. Hung plays Bold Cheung, who on a dare agrees to stay overnight in a haunted mausoleum, unaware that his boss, who is having an affair with his wife, has hired an evil necromancer (Lung Chan) to raise the dead and get rid of him. Genuinely funny — Hung's comedic timing is impeccable — but also featuring truly effective supernatural gags, **Encounters** is perhaps most memorable for its relentless energy, comparable in the U.S. to Sam Raimi's subsequent **Evil Dead II**, and its inventive kung fu scenes. It also introduced a new generation of international viewers to Chinese/Hong Kong mythology: a world of spells, talismans, sticky rice, Taoist priests, and the famous *jiangshi* or hopping vampires. Presumably derived from the ancient practice of tying a corpse's arms to bamboo sticks and carrying it at night to repatriate it, which to onlookers would seem like the body was bouncing with arms outstretched, the hopping vampire isn't a bloodsucker; the line between vampires, zombies and ghosts perhaps wasn't as clearly defined as it is in Western cinema.

## THE FOG

USA, 1980
Director: John Carpenter. Producer: Debra Hill.
Screenplay: John Carpenter, Debra Hill.
Music: John Carpenter.
Cinematography: Dean Cundey.
Cast: Adrienne Barbeau, Hal Holbrook, Janet Leigh, Jamie Lee Curtis, John Houseman, Tom Atkins.

Part of a two-picture deal John Carpenter signed with AVCO-Embassy after the success of 1978's **Halloween**, **The Fog** is a straightforward, old-fashioned campfire ghost story with occasional nods and winks to Hitchcock, evidencing the filmmaker's will to explore all facets of the genre. Inspired by a trip to Stonehenge with co-writer and producer Debra Hill, **The Fog** takes place in the fictional town of Antonio Bay, whose inhabitants (including Adrienne Barbeau, Tom Atkins and Janet Leigh, plus hitchhiker Jamie Lee Curtis) are threatened, on the eve of its 100th anniversary, by a mysterious fog bank moving against the wind and leaving a trail of bodies in its wake. The fog itself was achieved through a combination of dry ice vapours, optical effects, fog machines and natural mist; Point Reyes, where the bulk of the shoot took place, being one of the foggiest places in America. FX artist Rob Bottin, who would later work on **The Thing**, appears as lead ghost Blake, in addition to creating the red eye mask, and a ghost for the top of the lighthouse scene. Although production went smoothly, Carpenter decided during post — a mere three months from release — to re-cut, re-shoot and re-structure most of the picture, as he felt the story and chills fell flat. Adding mood and scares throughout, he also re-imagined the music and sound effects. The result is a terrific, atmospheric movie. graced by one of Carpenter's best soundtracks.

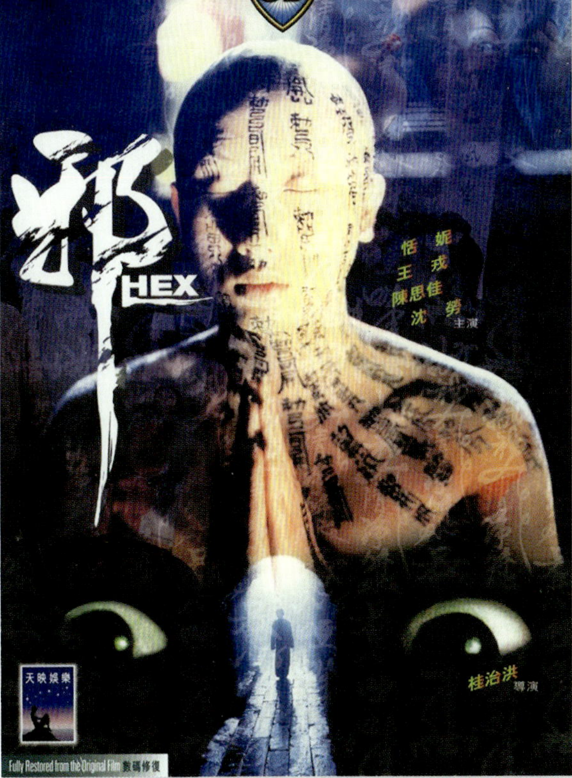

## HEX

Hong Kong, 1980
Director: Kuei Chih-hung. Producer: Runme Shaw.
Screenplay: Kuei Chih-hung, Tan Chin-hua.
Music: Eddie Wang. Cinematography: Li Hsin-yeh.
Cast: Tien Ni, Wang Jung, Chen Szu-chia,
Hon Kwok-choi, Yu Tsui-ling, Shen Lao.

Chinese writer-director Kuei Chih-hung helmed nearly forty movies for Shaw Brothers Studios over the course of his twenty-year career, ranging from crime thrillers and martial arts epics, to romantic comedies. In the early eighties, he turned his attention to the supernatural horror genre: **Hex** (**Xie**) is his most memorable attempt. The storyline reads like Hong Kong's answer to Henri-Georges Clouzot's 1955 **Les diaboliques**. A frail, ill woman (Tien Ni) kills her cruel, abusive husband (Yung Wang) with the help of her new servant, only to see the corpse return to persecute her. Yet its frequent plot twists and tonal shifts, over-the-top sequences mixing slapstick humour and special effects (including an aggressive severed hand) and varied apparitions place it in a league of its own. The movie culminates in a long, absolutely demented conjuring and exorcism sequence somehow involving painted symbols and nude ritualistic dancing. Parallels could be drawn with Sammo Hung's more successful **Encounters of the Spooky Kind**, released the same year, though **Hex** is overall darker in tone. **Hex** is the first entry in a loose trilogy comprised of the more comedic, modern-day **Hex Vs Witchcraft** (1980) and **Hex After Hex** (1982), both signed by Kuei.

## THE SHINING

UK/USA, 1980
Director: Stanley Kubrick.
Producer: Stanley Kubrick.
Screenplay: Stanley Kubrick, Diane Johnson.
Music: Wendy Carlos, Rachel Elkind. Cinematography: John Alcott.
Cast: Jack Nicholson, Shelley Duvall, Danny Lloyd, Scatman Crothers, Barry Nelson, Philip Stone.

Stanley Kubrick's adaptation of Stephen King's 1977 novel is a landmark in the evolution of horror and the history of cinema. Largely considered one of the most terrifying pictures ever made, it also stands out for its incredible technical ingenuity, and was amongst the first features to use a Steadicam for its long, elaborate shots down the hallways and gardens of the haunted Overlook hotel, where psychically gifted child Danny Torrance (Danny Lloyd) is chased by various apparitions and eventually by his own father, Jack (Jack Nicholson). The Timberline Lodge in Oregon was used as the outside of the Overlook, while interiors were built on soundstages at Elstree Studios outside London, their designs picked from hundreds of pictures of existing hotel rooms. While the worst of the haunting takes place in room 217 in the book, it's room 237 — a number which doesn't exist in the actual location — that's referred to in the screen version, at the request of the Timberline Lodge managers who feared no one would want to stay in 217 after the release of the picture. Filming went on for over a year, and Kubrick's famously obsessive methods, prodding actors and demanding dozens of takes, led to some brilliant results — Torrance's famous line, 'Here's Johnny!' was ad-libbed by Nicholson, who used Ed McMahon's catchphrase from *The Tonight Show Starring Johnny Carson* — but also made working conditions hellish for some of his cast. Bullied, isolated, and pushed to her limits by the director to get the performance he wanted, Duvall was made ill by the stress of production. To this day, King is vocal about his dissatisfaction with Kubrick's version, citing Duvall's depiction of Wendy, which he sees as weak and misogynistic, and Nicholson's Jack Torrance, who he says has no arc. The author prefers Mick Garris's 1997 ABC mini-series, filmed at the Stanley Hotel, Colorado, which inspired the book. Also of note is Rodney Ascher's 2012 documentary **Room 237**, which reveals the many conspiracy theories and intricate analyses **The Shining** has lent itself to over the years.

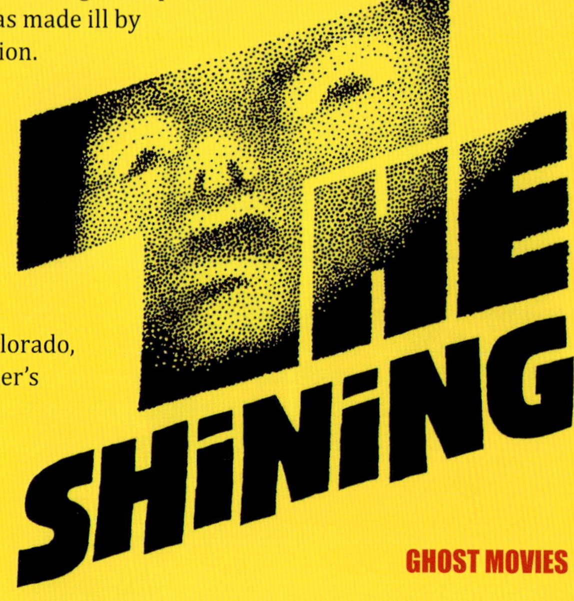

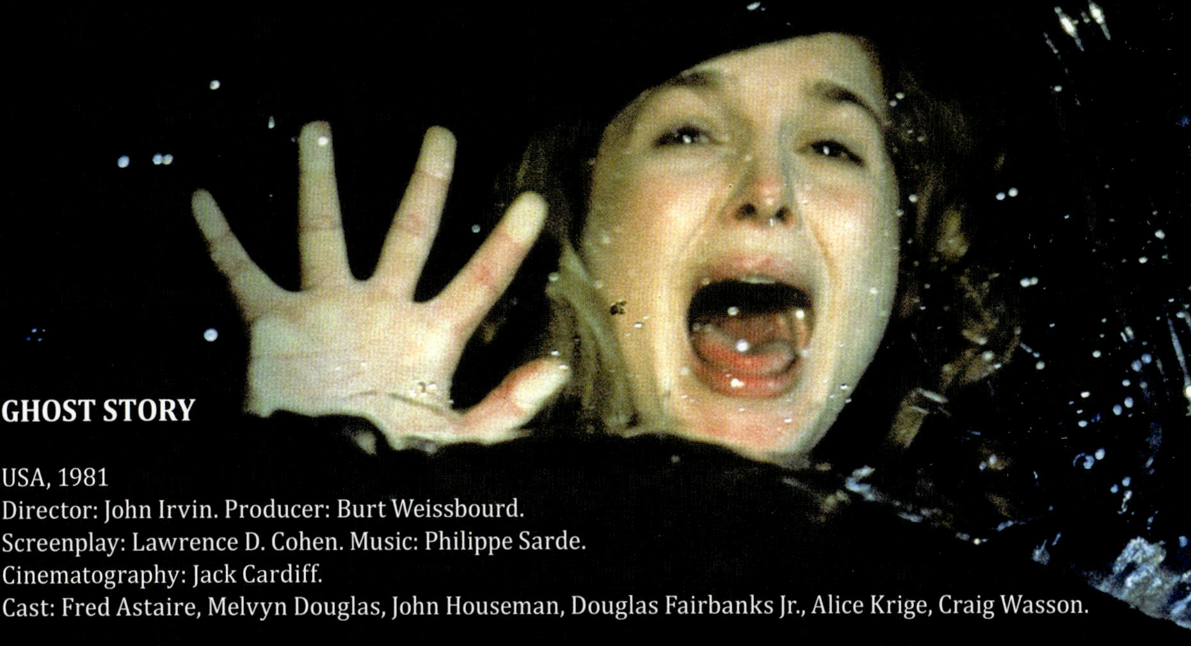

## GHOST STORY

USA, 1981
Director: John Irvin. Producer: Burt Weissbourd.
Screenplay: Lawrence D. Cohen. Music: Philippe Sarde.
Cinematography: Jack Cardiff.
Cast: Fred Astaire, Melvyn Douglas, John Houseman, Douglas Fairbanks Jr., Alice Krige, Craig Wasson.

Turning novels into feature films typically necessitates dropping a number of details and nuances to fit the running time, with more of less minor consequences, but in the case of **Ghost Story**, adapted from Peter Straub's 1979 novel of the same name, the subtleties left out of the plot changed the villain's very nature. Spoiler alert: In Straub's work — reportedly inspired by the atmosphere of Stephen King's Salem's Lot — Eva Galli, the woman who returns from the grave to torment the protagonists throughout their lives, turns out to be an ancient shape-shifting creature: a manitou, who lives much longer than humans and tortures them for its own entertainment. Screenwriter Lawrence D. Cohen (**Carrie**, 1976) and British film and television director John Irvin (**Raw Deal**, 1986) dropped this revelation from the finale, in effect turning Eva (played by an unforgettable Alice Krige) into a ghost haunting the members of the Chowder Society for revenge, a constant reminder of their guilt after they accidentally caused her death. Best known for marking Fred Astaire's and Douglas Fairbanks Jr.'s last appearances on screen, **Ghost Story** also stars John Houseman and Melvyn Douglas, and was lensed by legendary cinematographer Jack Cardiff (**Black Narcissus**, **The Red Shoes**).

The time has come to tell the tale.

BASED ON THE TERRIFYING BEST-SELLING NOVEL BY PETER STRAUB

FRED ASTAIRE MELVYN DOUGLAS
DOUGLAS FAIRBANKS, JR. JOHN HOUSEMAN
CRAIG WASSON
PATRICIA NEAL ALICE KRIGE
IN A BURT WEISSBOURD PRODUCTION OF A JOHN IRVIN FILM
SCREENPLAY BY LAWRENCE D. COHEN MUSIC BY PHILIPPE SARDE
DIRECTOR OF PHOTOGRAPHY JACK CARDIFF, B.S.C. CO-PRODUCER DOUG GREEN
PRODUCED BY BURT WEISSBOURD DIRECTED BY JOHN IRVIN A UNIVERSAL PICTURE
© 1981 by UNIVERSAL CITY STUDIOS, INC.
READ THE PAPERBACK FROM POCKET BOOKS
R RESTRICTED UNDER 17 REQUIRES ACCOMPANYING PARENT OR ADULT GUARDIAN

## THE ENTITY

USA, 1982
Director: Sidney J. Furie. Producer: Harold Schneider.
Screenplay: Frank De Felitta. Music: Charles Bernstein.
Cinematography: Stephen H. Burum.
Cast: Barbara Hershey, Ron Silver, David Labiosa,
George Coe, Margaret Blye, Jacqueline Brooks.

In the early 1980s, real-life hauntings became hot property for producers hoping to capitalize on the success of **The Amityville Horror**. And so it wouldn't be long before Frank De Felitta's 1978 book *The Entity* would be adapted for the screen. At the polar opposite of **Poltergeist**, **The Entity** — both book and movie — is based on the infamous story of Doris Bither, a single mother of four who claimed to be repeatedly molested by the ghosts of three Asian men at her home in Culver City, California. The attacks happened frequently, sometimes in front of witnesses (mainly Bither's children, but also a team of doctoral researchers from the University of California), and grew increasingly violent. Classified as poltergeist activity, its spectrophilia elements highly controverted, the case saw its victim's reputation quickly sullied.

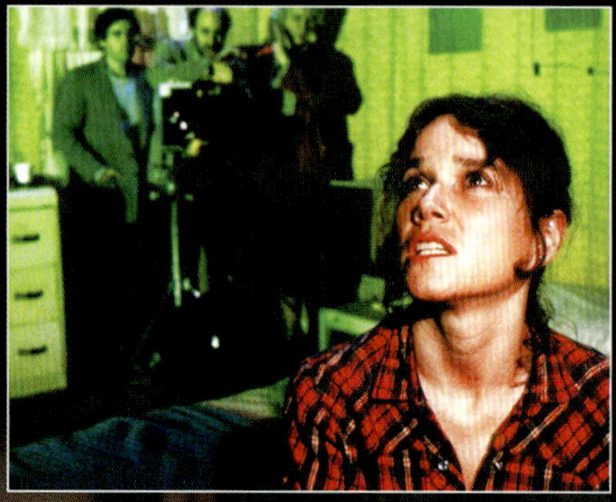

Director Sidney J. Furie (**The Ipcress File**) and star Barbara Hershey did not meet with Bither before the shoot, and limited their research into the facts to a strict minimum, preferring to present their own fictionalized interpretation. The resulting movie was considered so racy that its release was pushed back a year, and some of its more shocking scenes — including a sequence in which the entity forces their victim to have incestuous thoughts — excised. After the events described in the movie, Doris Bither moved away from her house, first to Carson, CA, then to Texas, then back to California. Her spectral tormentors followed her every time. She died of multiple organ failure in 1999; the cause was never determined.

## THE HOUSE WHERE EVIL DWELLS

USA/Japan, 1982
Director: Kevin Connor. Producer: Martin B. Cohen. Screenplay: Robert Suhosky.
Music: Ken Thorne. Cinematography: Jacques Haitkin.
Cast: Edward Albert, Susan George, Doug McClure, Amy Barrett, Mako Hattori, Toshiyuki Sasaki.

U.S. ex-pats (**Galaxy of Terror**'s Edward Albert and **Straw Dogs**' Susan George) and their daughter rent a traditional Japanese house which turns out to be haunted by the souls of a samurai and the adulterous lovers he murdered before killing himself. In a similar vein as its American contemporaries, but with added **Kwaidan** flavour, **The House Where Evil Dwells**, a Japanese-American co-production shot in Tokyo with a largely Japanese crew, is based on a novel by James Hardiman and plays like a schlocky domestic drama, where the ghosts use every trick — from physical possession to appearing in the young daughter's bowl of soup — to see the protagonists' marriage dissolve. Amusingly, the spooks appear see-through and blue; they are filmed through an old-school theatre illusion technique called Pepper's ghost, which uses reflections in panes of glass (the same method applied in Disneyland's Haunted Mansion). Director Kevin Connor (**Motel Hell**) has since complained about the movie not reflecting his vision, and being recut by the producers to remove much of the character development scenes. Nonetheless, **The House Where Evil Dwells**, released more than two decades before the remake of **The Grudge**, and years before Asian horror found favour with Western audiences, is a precursor of sorts.

## POLTERGEIST

USA, 1982
Director: Tobe Hooper. Producers: Steven Spielberg, Frank Marshall.
Screenplay: Steven Spielberg, Michael Grais, Mark Victor.
Music: Jerry Goldsmith. Cinematography: Matthew F. Leonetti.
Cast: Craig T. Nelson, JoBeth Williams, Beatrice Straight, Dominique Dunne, Oliver Robins, Heather O'Rourke.

The ultimate family-friendly horror movie, **Poltergeist** was a gateway into the genre for an entire generation. The story of a likable, typical American family who discover their new home is a hub of paranormal activity, it mixes genuine scares with real heart, and introduced the world to groundbreaking visual effects, while popularizing the concept of poltergeist (literally 'loud ghost'), a type of spirit causing physical disturbances and generally attached to a person, rather than a place. Contractually prevented from directing while prepping **E.T.** (which came out a week after **Poltergeist**, leading some to dub June 1982 'the Summer of Spielberg'), producer Steven Spielberg, who originated the story, hired Tobe Hooper to helm, yet remained heavily involved on set, leading to a controversy raging on to this day as to who truly called the shots. Two sequels revolve around the character of Reverend Henry Kane, the entity which appeared in the Freeling house as the Beast in the first movie. **Poltergeist II: The Other Side** (1986) explores darker territory — the scene where Kane possesses Steven, who then attempts to rape his wife, is terrifying — and benefits from a great villain (Julian Beck). **Poltergeist III** (1988) moves the story to a Chicago skyscraper. Twelve-year-old star Heather O'Rourke tragically passed away during post-production; reshoots of the ending involved a double. Over the years, **Poltergeist** gained the reputation of being a cursed franchise due to the untimely death of several of its cast members (including the murder of twenty-two-year-old Dominique Dunne, shortly after the release of the first movie). A long-mooted (and critically panned) remake starring Sam Rockwell and Rosemarie DeWitt came out in 2015.

*"They're here."*

POLTERGEIST

*It knows what scares you.*

## SUPERSTITION

USA, 1982
Director: James W. Roberson. Producer: Ed Carlin.
Screenplay: Donald G. Thompson. Music: David Gibney.
Cinematography: Leon Blank.
Cast: James Houghton, Albert Salmi, Larry Pennell, Lynn Carlin, Maylo McCaslin, Joshua Cadman.

Filmed under the decidedly more appropriate title **The Witch** in 1981, **Superstition**, directed by James W. Roberson (best known as a cinematographer: **The Town That Dreaded Sundown**, 1976), subjects an ill-fated family of five to the wrath of the merciless spirit of a witch executed on the grounds their new home was built on. Closer in tone to the likes of **Friday the 13th** than to its immediate haunted house predecessor **The Amityville Horror**, **Superstition** wastes no time establishing complex characters, instead dispatching them quickly in increasingly gruesome ways, including an exploding head in a microwave and a death by wine press. Halfway between slasher and giallo, the movie keeps its ghostly killer for the most part off screen, occasionally revealing a black, long-nailed hand. Reminiscent in tone of Lucio Fulci's **The House by the Cemetery** (1981), the movie has a decidedly European feel, and makes ample use of Berlioz's Symphonie Fantastique, a year after it became indelibly linked to **The Shining** in the minds of horror fans. Oddly enough, Italian movie **Streghe** (also known as **Witch Story**, 1989) was released as a sequel — **Superstition 2** — in the United States, despite the first one having been shelved in its homeland until 1985. It didn't fare much better in the UK, where it was added to the video nasties list, making tapes liable for seizure by the authorities.

HOW DO YOU KILL SOMETHING THAT CAN'T POSSIBLY BE ALIVE?

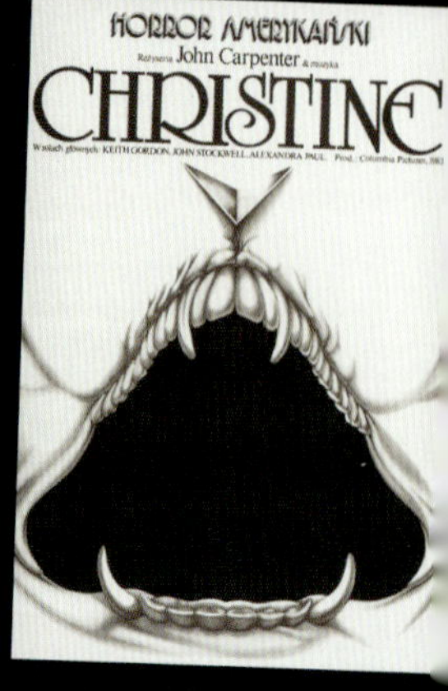


## CHRISTINE

USA, 1983
Director: John Carpenter.
Producer: Richard Kobritz.
Screenplay: Bill Phillips. Music: John Carpenter, Alan Howarth. Cinematography: Donald M. Morgan.
Cast: Keith Gordon, John Stockwell, Alexandra Paul, Robert Prosky, Harry Dean Stanton, Christine Belford.

In the midst of Stephen King mania, John Carpenter, badly in need of a job after the commercial failure of **The Thing** (1982) and his subsequent dismissal from **Firestarter**, returns to the ghost sub-genre with this adaptation of *Christine*, the story of a teenage boy and the eponymous 1958 Plymouth Fury who loves him. Filmed from low angles, gleaming, fire-engine red and practically sexualized (the sequence where she regenerates after being vandalized is filmed like a strip-tease), Christine is, rightfully, the main attraction of the picture. While King's novel had her possessed by the spirit of her previous owner, Carpenter's car is sentient from her very creation, as suggested by the opening credits. As is always the case in the filmmaker's works, the soundtrack is particularly note-worthy: both the atmospheric, pulse-pounding score by Carpenter and Alan Howarth, and the accompanying selection of 1950s songs, which, beyond their **American Graffiti**-style nostalgic appeal, take on a creepy dimension in the context of the movie. If Carpenter took on the project purely as a job, it never shows on screen. The director repeatedly admitted being dissatisfied with the result, which he says he never found scary. A generation of moviegoers disagree.

## GHOSTBUSTERS

USA, 1984
Director: Ivan Reitman. Producer: Ivan Reitman.
Screenplay: Dan Aykroyd, Harold Ramis.
Music: Elmer Bernstein. Cinematography: László Kovács.
Cast: Bill Murray, Dan Aykroyd, Harold Ramis, Sigourney Weaver, Rick Moranis, Annie Potts.

Who you gonna call?
So enduring is the appeal of 1984's generation-defining **Ghostbusters**, that its iconic lines are still widely known and quoted nearly 35 years after its release. Originally conceived by Dan Aykroyd as a vehicle for fellow *Saturday Night Live* star John Belushi, who based it around the idea of a ghost-hunting enterprise taking an ad in the Yellow Pages, this comedy about a group of bumbling parapsychologists launching a business was inspired by Aykroyd's own belief and fascination for the paranormal. His father's tales of apparitions and home séances regaled him from a young age; Peter H. Aykroyd's own interest in the subject matter culminated in the 2009 publication of a non-fiction book, *A History of Ghosts: The True Story of Séances, Mediums, Ghosts and Ghostbusters*. Combining this background with influences such as Disney's 1937 cartoon **Lonesome Ghosts** and the Bowery Boys' 1946 **Spook Busters**, and reimagined for Bill Murray and Harold Ramis after Belushi's untimely passing, **Ghostbusters** was filmed in Manhattan, on the Warner Bros. lot in Burbank, as well as in a handful of Los Angeles locations. Nominated for two Academy Awards (Best Visual Effects and Best Original Song), the movie generated a 1989 sequel, two animated series, and a 2016 remake.

## HAUNTED HONEYMOON

USA, 1986
Director: Gene Wilder. Producer: Susan Ruskin.
Screenplay: Gene Wilder, Terence Marsh.
Music: John Morris. Cinematography: Fred Schuler.
Cast: Gene Wilder, Gilda Radner, Paul L. Smith,
Dom DeLuise, Jonathan Pryce, Peter Vaughan.

The success of **Ghostbusters** led to a mini-revival of the haunted house comedy in the second half of the eighties, with titles such as **Beetlejuice**, **High Spirits** (both 1988), and **Haunted Honeymoon**, a Gene Wilder vehicle in which a radio presenter with a speech impediment finds himself in a real-life murder mystery when his uncle turns his wedding trip to his family castle into shock therapy. Wilder, off the success of previous directorial effort **The Woman in Red** (1984), directs from a script co-written with famed production designer Terence Marsh. Wilder often hinted at the difficulties of both directing and starring in the movie, which would mark the last time he would work behind the camera. Co-star and real-life wife Gilda Radner, a regular on *Saturday Night Live* who had already acted opposite him in **Hanky Panky** (1982) and **The Woman in Red**, was diagnosed with ovarian cancer in October of the same year, and this would be her last big screen role before passing away in 1989. Sadly, **Haunted Honeymoon** was a calamitous flop. Yet the picture, an homage to the comedy chillers he grew up watching, is light and entertaining, and although not on par with **Young Frankenstein**, essential viewing for Wilder fans.

## WITCHBOARD

USA, 1986
Director: Kevin S. Tenney. Producer: Gerald Geoffray. Screenplay: Kevin S. Tenney. Music: Dennis Michael Tenney. Cinematography: Roy H. Wagner.
Cast: Todd Allen, Tawny Kitaen, Stephen Nichols, Kathleen Wilhoite, Burke Byrnes, James W. Quinn.

For his first feature as writer-director, Kevin Tenney (**Night of the Demons**, 1988) draws inspiration from a party where a friend of his had brought a Ouija board during his time at USC. Researching the phenomenon of planchette and spirit communication, he developed this story of a group of pals (Todd Allen, Tawny Kitaen and Stephen Nichols) haunted by what they believe to be the ghost of a lonely ten-year-old boy. Much of the movie focuses on the relationships between the trio of characters, and the slow possession of one of them. Tenney originally planned to title the movie 'Ouija' before realizing Parker Brothers had copyrighted the name, which explains how he ended up with **Witchboard** despite a flagrant absence of witch in the story. They also weren't allowed to use officially licensed boards, though some footage filmed before film attorneys highlighted the issue found its way into the final edit. A success at the time with healthy box office returns and over 80,000 videotapes sold, **Witchboard** has since developed a cult following and received two loosely related, inferior sequels: **Witchboard 2: The Devil's Doorway** (1993), also written and directed by Tenney, and **Witchboard 3: The Possession** (1995).

Gene
WILDER
Gilda
RADNER
Dom
DeLUISE
in
HAUNTED
HONEYMOON
...A COMEDY CHILLER
"HAUNTED HONEYMOON"
Also Starring JONATHAN PRYCE · PAUL L. SMITH Music by JOHN MORRIS
Production Designer TERENCE MARSH Costume Designer RUTH MYERS Edited by CHRIS GREENBURY
Director of Photography FRED SCHULER Written by GENE WILDER & TERENCE MARSH
Produced by SUSAN RUSKIN Directed by GENE WILDER Prints by DE LUXE®
DOLBY STEREO®
IN SELECTED THEATRES
An ORION PICTURES Release
©1986 Orion Pictures Corporation. All Rights Reserved.
PG PARENTAL GUIDANCE SUGGESTED
SOME MATERIAL MAY NOT BE SUITABLE FOR CHILDREN
PRINTED IN U.S.A.
NSS 860074

# THE WRAITH

USA, 1986
Director: Mike Marvin. Producer: John Kemeny. Screenplay: Mike Marvin. Music: Michael Hoenig, J. Peter Robinson. Cinematography: Reed Smoot. Cast: Charlie Sheen, Nick Cassavetes, Randy Quaid, Sherilyn Fenn, Griffin O'Neal, David Sherrill.

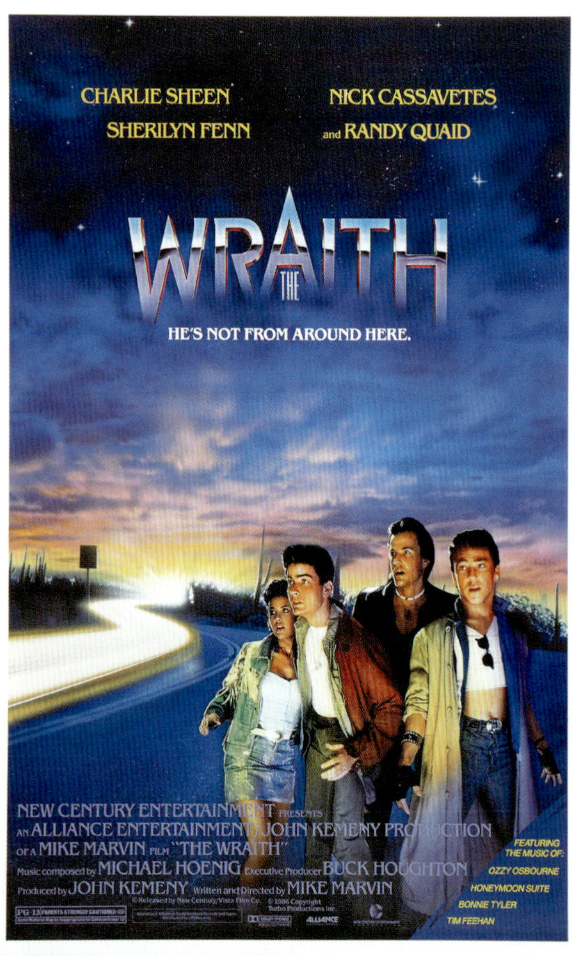


A murdered teen (Charlie Sheen) returns from the dead in a one of a kind Dodge M4S Turbo Interceptor, to take out a gang of car thieves ruled by Packard Walsh (Nick Cassavetes), and free former flame Keri (Sherilyn Fenn), whom Packard has bullied into becoming his property. Could **The Wraith** be the quintessential eighties movie? Mike Marvin's cult supernatural actioner is as much loved for its terrible acting (worsened by the occasional ADR line), awkward dialogue ('roadblocks won't stop something that can't be stopped') and premise halfway between **High Plains Drifter** and **The Road Warrior**, as it is for its fantastic cars, exciting chases scenes, colourful costumes, and a soundtrack blending synth music and rock classics — all wonderfully of its time. The Wraith itself, of course, is pure eighties legend. A concept from Chrysler and PPG Industries used as a pace car for the Indianapolis 500, it never made it to production; six copies were created for the movie, only two of which were drivable. The original can be seen in some close-ups. The action sequences for which the movie is famed were initially scheduled to be filmed over three weeks, but ended up compressed to eight days after the accidental crash of one of the cars into a mountain, tragically killing camera operator Bruce Ingram and leaving another crew member paraplegic. The movie is dedicated to Ingram's memory.

## A CHINESE GHOST STORY

Hong Kong, 1987
Director: Ching Siu-tung. Producer: Tsui Hark.
Screenplay: Yuen Kai-chi. Music: Romeo Díaz, James Wong.
Cinematography: Poon Hang-sang, Sander Lee Kar-ko, Tom Lau Moon-tong, Wong Wing-hang.
Cast: Leslie Cheung, Joey Wong, Wu Ma, Lau Siu-ming, Lin Wei, Sit Chi-lun.

A classic supernatural tale told with peak eighties kinetic energy, **A Chinese Ghost Story**, about a debt collector who falls in love with a ghost and battles a demon to free her soul, is rightfully regarded as one of the best of its kind. Producer Tsui Hark, the superstar filmmaker who brought big spectacle supernatural adventures back to the forefront of Hong Kong cinema with **The Butterfly Murders** (1979) and **Zu: Warriors from the Magic Mountain** (1983), had originally envisioned the Qing Dynasty-era legend the movie is derived from as the basis for a television series. Having failed to raise the interest of networks, he reimagined it as a feature, in the style of the pictures he loved as a child, such as Lee Han-hsiang's 1960 **The Enchanting Shadow**. Hark enlisted action director and accomplished martial artist and fight choreographer Ching Siu-tung yet remained heavily involved, visiting the set every day. This mix of sensibilities resulted in a highly entertaining blend of kung fu, pop music, classical imagery, stop-motion cadavers, goofy humour and tragedy. Also key to **Ghost Story**'s success is the chemistry between Cantopop star Leslie Cheung, fresh off the success of John Woo's 1986 **A Better Tomorrow**, and Joey Wong, whom the movie propelled to stardom throughout Asia. Supporting actor Wu Ma (**Encounters of the Spooky Kind**, **Mr. Vampire**) as the Taoist priest is a highlight, especially for his odd rap number 'Tao'. **A Chinese Ghost Story II** (1990) reunited Cheung and Wong; its 1991 sequel paired Wong with Tony Leung Chiu-Wai. A 1997 animated movie and a 2011 remake also followed.

## PRISON

USA, 1987
Director: Renny Harlin. Producer: Irwin Yablans.
Screenplay: C. Courtney Joyner, Renny Harlin [uncredited].
Music: Richard Band, Christopher L. Stone. Cinematography: Mac Ahlberg.
Cast: Viggo Mortensen, Chelsea Field, Lane Smith, Lincoln Kilpatrick, Tom Everett, Ivan Kane.

Part of a mini wave of electric chair slashers alongside **Shocker** (1989) and **The Horror Show** (aka **House III**, 1989), **Prison** takes place in a different type of haunted house, where the guards and inmates of fictional penitentiary Creedmore are picked one by one by the vengeful soul of Charlie Forsythe (Kane Hodder, doubling as stunt coordinator), executed over twenty years earlier for a murder he did not commit. For their first co-producing venture, Irwin Yablans (the first three **Halloween** films) and Charles Band (**From Beyond**) offered Finnish director Renny Harlin, who had impressed them with his English-language movie **Born American** (1986) and at the time lived in his car in Los Angeles, his first American feature. Showing remarkable flair, the team cast Viggo Mortensen in his first leading role, while many of the secondary parts were played by real-life inmates, as the movie was shot on location at Wyoming State Penitentiary in Rawlins. The electric chair was built in the prison's actual gas chamber; armed guards kept the set secure and the extras well-behaved. Despite the challenges presented by the location (and the high altitude sun causing countless sunburns), **Prison**'s elaborate, gory deaths caught the eye of New Line CEO Bob Shaye, who offered Harlin the fourth instalment in the **Nightmare on Elm Street** franchise, **The Dream Master**.

## BEETLEJUICE

USA, 1988
Director: Tim Burton. Producers: Michael Bender, Larry Wilson, Richard Hashimoto.
Screenplay: Michael McDowell, Warren Skaaren. Music: Danny Elfman. Cinematography: Thomas E. Ackerman.
Cast: Michael Keaton, Alec Baldwin, Geena Davis, Jeffrey Jones, Catherine O'Hara, Winona Ryder.

'A feel-good movie about death', as screenwriter Michael McDowell describes it, Tim Burton's **Beetlejuice** arguably represents the peak of the brief 1980s comedy ghost story. A haunted house movie from the point of view of the dead, it stars Alec Baldwin and Geena Davis as the recently deceased couple hiring self-proclaimed bio-exorcist Betelgeuse (Michael Keaton) to rid them of the obnoxious family now inhabiting their home. McDowell's original drafts were much darker, more graphic than the wonderfully odd and humorous final product, with the title character presented as a winged demon who could shape shift into a human (for whom the director originally planned to cast Sammy Davis Jr. — Keaton was producer David Geffen's suggestion). Burton then brought in script doctor Warren Skaaren to introduce a lighter tone, and worked with Keaton on improvising some gags, and production designer Bo Welch to develop his vision of the afterlife. So successful were those afterlife scenes in test screenings that an ending, in which Beetlejuice gets his head shrunk by a witch doctor, was added at the last minute. A joyous, offbeat ode to life, imagination and Harry Belafonte, **Beetlejuice** to this day hasn't received its oft-discussed sequel. Nevertheless, it spawned an animated series (1989-1992), a Universal Studios show (*Beetlejuice's Rock and Roll Graveyard Revue*), lunch boxes, toys, and an endless supply of Halloween costumes.

## HIGH SPIRITS

UK/USA, 1988
Director: Neil Jordan. Producers: Stephen Woolley, David Saunders. Screenplay: Neil Jordan. Music: George Fenton. Cinematography: Alex Thomson. Cast: Daryl Hannah, Peter O'Toole, Steve Guttenberg, Beverly D'Angelo, Jennifer Tilly, Liam Neeson.

By the late eighties, the comedic ghost trend was slowly dying. Amongst its last croaks is a movie surprisingly co-written (with **Beetlejuice**'s Michael McDowell) and directed by one of the era's most brilliant young authors: Neil Jordan, best known then for highly acclaimed, personal efforts **The Company of Wolves** (1984) and **Mona Lisa** (1986). With an all-star cast led by Steve Guttenberg, Daryl Hannah and Peter O'Toole, **High Spirits** saw a bankrupt aristocrat converting his castle into a haunted house attraction, complete with servants in medieval armours and banshees floating about on pulleys. Ironically perhaps for a movie about an Irishman whose business depends on the financial contribution of an American set to sabotage him, Jordan's first Hollywood studio movie, with Tri Star Pictures on a $16 million budget, turned out to be an unhappy collaboration, with the filmmaker reportedly finding himself shut out of the editing room. Mixing screwball comedy with contrived romance and histrionics from an unbridled O'Toole, **High Spirits** nonetheless looks beautiful, thanks to Anton Furst's art direction, and contains just enough moments of Jordan's poetry — Guttenberg barging in on Hannah and Liam Neeson's murder re-enactment, or finding himself in bed with a gooey corpse — to marvel at what could have been.

## LADY IN WHITE

USA, 1988
Director: Frank LaLoggia. Producers: Andrew G. La Marca, Frank LaLoggia.
Screenplay: Frank LaLoggia.
Music: Frank LaLoggia.
Cinematography: Russell Carpenter.
Cast: Lukas Haas, Len Cariou, Alex Rocco, Katherine Helmond, Jason Presson, Jared Rushton.

Part of a 1980s slew of family-friendly scary movies, alongside Joe Dante's **Gremlins** (1984) or John Hough's **The Watcher in the Woods** (1980), **Lady in White** stars Lukas Haas, already a star at age eleven for his turn in **Witness** (1985), as a small-town boy who sees the ghost of a little girl murdered by a serial killer still on the loose. Quadruple threat writer-director-producer-composer Frank LaLoggia (**Fear No Evil**, 1981) loosely based the story around early childhood memories, drawing inspiration from parents and siblings for his portrayal of an Italian-American family, as well as on the legend of the White Lady (or Lady of the Lake), a melancholy apparition haunting LaLoggia's native city of Rochester, New York. Producing alongside Andrew G. La Marca, LaLoggia raised nearly $5 million independently; regrettably, its distributor, New Century, lacked funds to advertise its release (the company went bankrupt within the year), and this nostalgic and poetic coming-of-age ghost story, although generally positively reviewed, didn't get the reception it deserved. Although he was hired to write a draft of **Spider-Man** for then-attached director James Cameron, LaLoggia would have to wait seven years to direct another picture, direct-to-video thriller **Mother**, starring Diane Ladd.

## THE WOMAN IN BLACK

UK, 1989
Director: Herbert Wise.
Producer: Chris Burt.
Screenplay: Nigel Kneale.
Music: Rachel Portman.
Cinematography: Michael Davis.
Cast: Adrian Rawlins, Bernard Hepton, David Daker, Pauline Moran, David Ryall, Clare Holman.

A walk down a Suffolk marsh inspired author Susan Hill to write her 1982 novel *The Woman in Black*, one of the most beloved and influential ghost stories of the twentieth century. Five years later, it would be adapted into a highly successful and chilling stage play, first in Scarborough, then in London's West End, where it would become the second longest-running non-musical in local history. And on Christmas Eve 1989, this television version premiered on British network ITV. A young solicitor, Arthur Kidd (Kipps in the novel; played by Adrian Rawlins) is tasked with attending the funeral of a client, Mrs. Drablow, in a small coastal village, and sorting papers to prepare her property for sale. Upon leaving the church, he notices a woman in mourning attire, staring at him from across the graveyard. The ominous silhouette turns up again outside Eel Marsh House, the late Mrs. Drablow's home, where Kidd foolishly decided to spend the night… Screenwriter Nigel Kneale (a familiar name to horror fans after **The Stone Tape** and several collaborations with Hammer Films) and director Herbert Wise stuck fairly close to the source material, though the handful of changes they made notoriously infuriated Hill. Favouring a low-key approach, Wise created an eerie, gloomy atmosphere, through wonderfully morose locations, de-saturated photography, and a special attention to sound. Particularly remarkable is the chilling stillness of Drablow's appearances, framed wide in broad daylight, oozing malevolence. Critically acclaimed, Wise's **The Woman in Black** would receive four BAFTA nominations.

## GHOST

USA, 1990
Director: Jerry Zucker. Producer: Lisa Weinstein.
Screenplay: Bruce Joel Rubin. Music: Maurice Jarre.
Cinematography: Adam Greenberg.
Cast: Patrick Swayze, Demi Moore, Whoopi Goldberg,
Tony Goldwyn, Rick Aviles, Vincent Schiavelli.

The most popular ghostly romance of the past fifty years, and one of the highest-grossing movies of all time, genre-bending love story **Ghost** follows dead protagonist Sam (Patrick Swayze) as he tries to solve his own murder, and protect his girlfriend (Demi Moore) from undergoing the same fate. Bruce Joel Rubin's script was at first set to be directed by Frank Oz (**Scrooged**), but his choices — including deleting Sam's shadow from every shot — proved too expensive for the producers, who settled on Jerry Zucker (**Airplane!**), to Rubin's initial dismay. The filmmaker requested extensive rewrites before slowly bringing the story back to its original shape. Casting went through similar adjustments: Moore's then husband Bruce Willis was the first of many stars to turn down the lead, which eventually devolved to Swayze, who had been typecast in lacklustre B-movies after **Dirty Dancing**. Swayze, in turn, is said to have filmed Whoopi Goldberg's audition tape, which convinced the studio to hire her. The Righteous Brothers' Unchained Melody, a song forever associated with the picture, was originally written for 1955 prison flick **Unchained**.

Winner of two Academy Awards, for Best Supporting Actress and Best Original Screenplay, **Ghost**, filmed on location in New York City and on the Paramount lot in Los Angeles, was remade in Japan in 2010 under the title **Ghost: In Your Arms Again** (2010); and was adapted for the stage with *Ghost: The Musical* in 2011. Its famous pottery scene has been spoofed in everything from *Saturday Night Live* and **The Naked Gun 2 1/2** to **Glee** and **Wallace & Gromit**.

## TRULY MADLY DEEPLY

UK, 1990
Director: Anthony Minghella. Producer: Robert Cooper.
Screenplay: Anthony Minghella. Music: Barrington Pheloung.
Cinematography: Remi Adefarasin.
Cast: Juliet Stevenson, Alan Rickman, Bill Paterson, Michael Maloney, Christopher Rozycki, Keith Bartlett.

The year 1990 was marked by romantic hauntings, as theatre and television director Anthony Minghella (**The English Patient**) made his feature debut with **Truly Madly Deeply**, a sentimental comedy in which depressed widow Nina (Juliet Stevenson) is miraculously visited by her late husband Jamie (Alan Rickman), who decides to stay with her in their apartment. Produced for the BBC's Screen Two anthology series, but successful enough to justify a theatrical release, **Truly Madly Deeply** went on to win a BAFTA for Best Original Screenplay as well as several Evening Standard British Film Awards. Shot over six weeks in Bristol and London (the story is set in Highgate), this powerful love story about closure and moving on can be seen as an understated, relatable version of **Ghost**, anchored in the genuine chemistry of its two leads (Rickman and Stevenson had been friends for years before being cast as a couple.)

Minghella credited Jim Henson's folk tales-based television series **The Storyteller**, which he developed, for cultivating his taste for the fantastic and leading his to write a ghost story. **Truly Madly Deeply** launched Minghella's too-brief career (he passed away in 2008) and has retained a cult following over the years.

## SOMETIMES THEY COME BACK

USA, 1991
Director: Tom McLoughlin. Producer: Michael S. Murphey.
Screenplay: Lawrence Konner, Mark Rosenthal.
Music: Terry Plumeri. Cinematography: Bryan England.
Cast: Tim Matheson, Brooke Adams, Robert Hy Gorman, William Sanderson, Robert Rusler, Bentley Mitchum.

Based on a Stephen King short story originally published in 1974, then popularized in 1978 collection *Night Shift*, **Sometimes They Come Back** was originally envisioned by producer Dino De Laurentiis as a segment for anthology movie **Cat's Eye** (1985). But recognizing its standalone potential, he held off until 1990, when he partnered with CBS for this made-for-television feature. Screenwriter Mark Rosenthal (**The Jewel of the Nile**, **Star Trek VI: The Undiscovered Country**) was hired to adapt this story of a man (Tim Matheson) moving back to his hometown to confront the demons of his past — in this case literally, in the shape of three bullies returned from the grave (one of which was played by Robert Rusler who, for his first major villain role, admitted drawing inspiration from watching Robert Englund get into character in **A Nightmare on Elm Street 2: Freddy's Revenge**). While directing this tale of grief and letting go of the past, Tom McLoughlin (**Friday the 13th Part VI: Jason Lives**) underwent some major life changes, as his father died, and his daughter was born. **Sometimes They Come Back** was followed by two sequels: **Sometimes They Come Back... Again** (1996) and **Sometimes They Come Back... For More** (1998), both released directly to video.

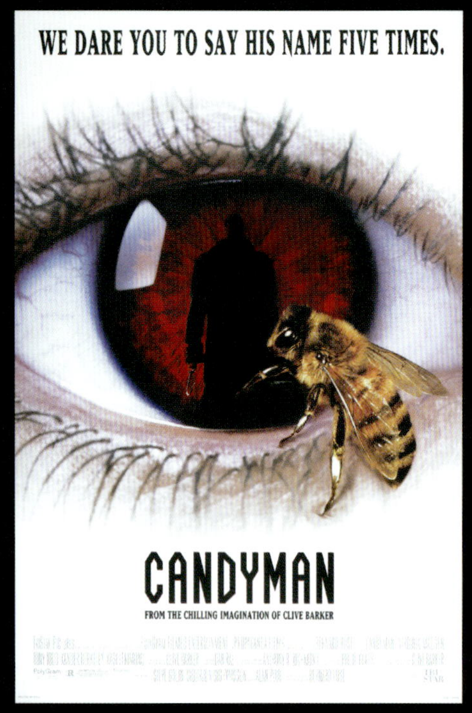

## CANDYMAN

USA, 1992
Director: Bernard Rose.
Producers: Alan Poul, Steve Golin, Sigurjon Sighvatsson.
Screenplay: Bernard Rose. Music: Philip Glass.
Cinematography: Anthony B. Richmond.
Cast: Virginia Madsen, Kasi Lemmons, Xander Berkeley, DeJuan Guy, Tony Todd, Vanessa Williams.

British director Bernard Rose (**Paperhouse**, 1988) transposed the action of Clive Barker's short story *The Forbidden* from Liverpool to Chicago for **Candyman**, about a graduate student (Virginia Madsen) researching the local legend of a mythical killer summoned by saying his name five times while staring in a mirror. The movie, whose titular character is himself a victim of slavery, stalking the grounds of Chicago's newest form of segregation, explores not only the importance of myth, storytelling and urban legends in human nature, but also asks questions of race and social classes. Eddie Murphy was reportedly considered for the part, which eventually devolved to Tony Todd. Rose insisted on shooting in and around the actual Cabrini Green housing project — a place he said inspired genuine fear — where the story is set, and had to cast residents as extras to obtain the filming permit. The last high-rise of the property was demolished in 2011. Philip Glass composed the score, but famously admitted being disappointed with the finished picture, which he saw as a low-grade slasher. Surprising, given **Candyman**'s status as a revered classic; though it did give birth to two largely inferior, formulaic sequels, **Candyman: Farewell to the Flesh** (1995) and **Candyman: Day of the Dead** (1999).

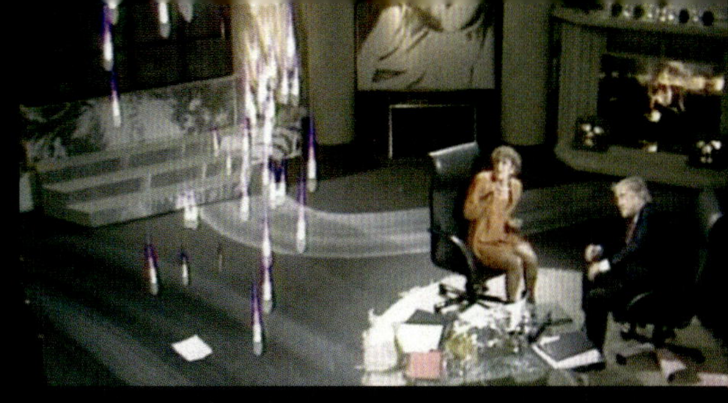

## GHOSTWATCH

UK, 1992
Director: Lesley Manning. Producer: Ruth Baumgarten.
Screenplay: Stephen Volk. Music: Philip Appleby.
Cast: Michael Parkinson, Sarah Greene, Mike Smith,
Craig Charles, Gillian Bevan, Brid Brennan.

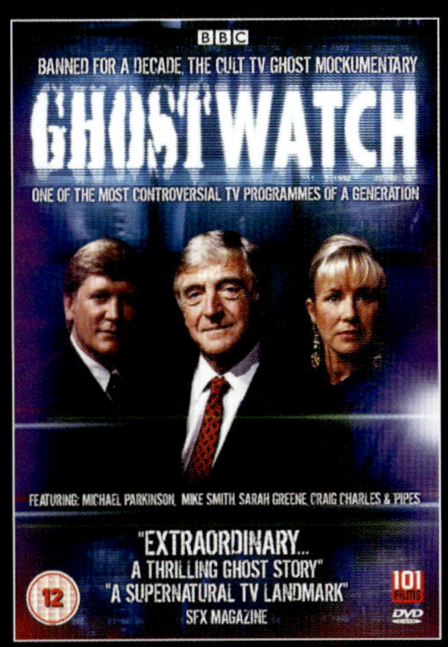


If scary ghost stories were relatively scarce on the big screen in the early nineties, television on the other hand offered at least one terrifying event with the Halloween 1992 'live' broadcast of **Ghostwatch**, a BBC presentation which unexpectedly shocked the United Kingdom, with its team of well-known presenters investigating a haunted house where an apparition called 'Pipes' had been terrorizing the occupants. In truth a feature film scripted by Stephen Volk (who'd originally developed it as a six-parter) and shot documentary style by TV director Lesley Manning as part of BBC Drama's Screen One program, **Ghostwatch** led a surprisingly large amount of its audience to believe that what they were watching was real (much like Orson Welles's 1938 radio play 'War of the Worlds'). The show drew in a record number of complaints, with reports flooding in of viewers suffering from PTSD or soiling themselves; it was even blamed for the death of an eighteen-year-old boy who tragically hanged himself. The Broadcasting Standards Council deliberated on the matter and ruled that the BBC, despite its reputation for reliable and responsible programming, had deliberately 'cultivated a sense of menace' which misled certain viewers. As a result, this groundbreaking work of fiction never aired again on UK television.

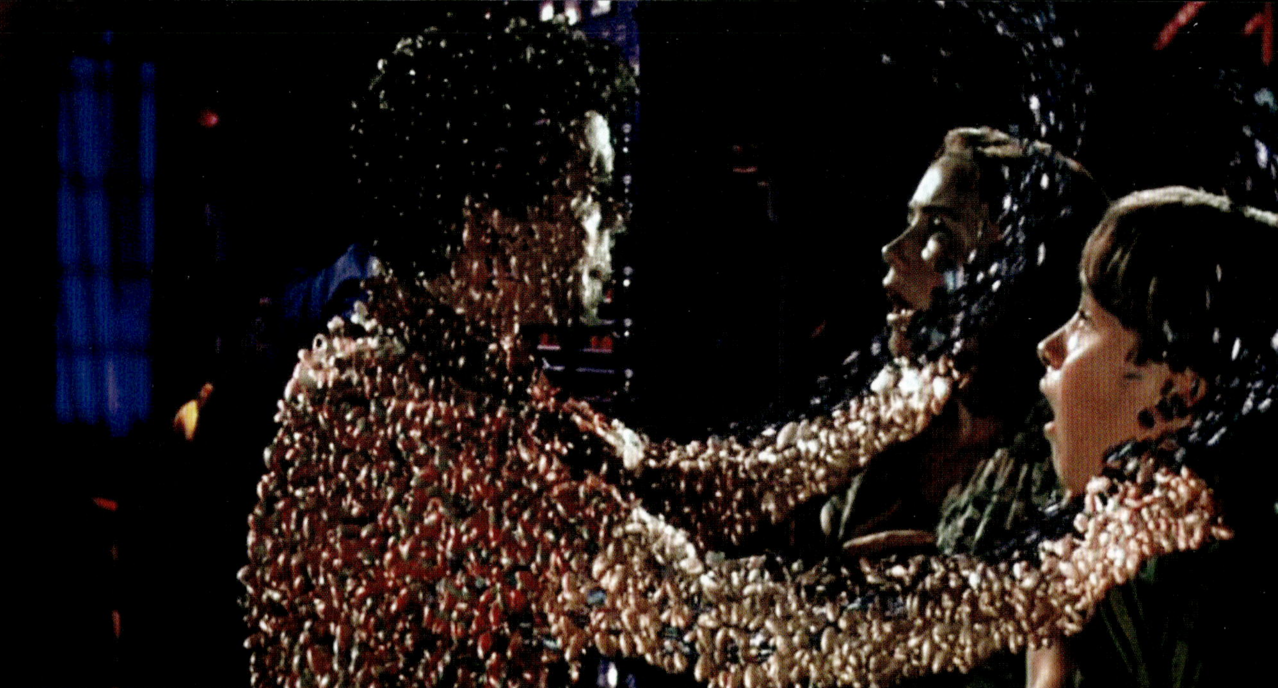

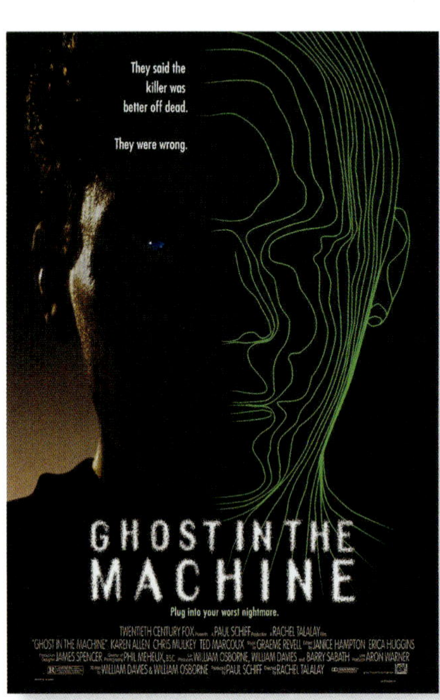

## GHOST IN THE MACHINE

USA, 1993
Director: Rachel Talalay. Producer: Paul Schiff.
Screenplay: William Davies, William Osborne.
Music: Graeme Revell. Cinematography: Philip Meheux.
Cast: Karen Allen, Chris Mulkey, Ted Marcoux, Wil Horneff, Jessica Walter, Brandon Quintin Adams.

The early days of the Internet and home computers ignited the imagination of B-movie writers, giving birth to a slew of thrillers — **The Lawnmower Man** (1992), **The Net** (1995), **Virtuosity** (1995), **Johnny Mnemonic** (1995) — extrapolating on the fears brought on by this brave new world of cyber crime and virtual reality. **Ghost in the Machine**, second feature of **Freddy's Dead: The Final Nightmare** director Rachel Talalay (who started her career working for Bob Shaye and John Waters, and went on to become a prominent television director), follows in the footsteps of Wes Craven's 1989 **Shocker** and sees a single mother (Karen Allen) and her teenage son targeted by a deceased serial killer (Ted Marcoux) whose soul travels through electric currents and computer networks. A similar wave of technophobia would soon take over Japanese horror with movies such as **Ring**, **Kairo**, or **One Missed Call**; but rather than ghosts passing on their curse through a specific medium, **Ghost in the Machine** functions much like a slasher film, with the killer using a variety of weapons to dispatch his victims: Operating at first like a hacker, targeting bank accounts and medical records, he soon moves on to appliances (death by dishwasher! death by microwave!), poorly-designed VR games, and traffic lights.

## HEART AND SOULS

USA, 1993
Director: Ron Underwood.
Producers: Nancy Roberts, Sean Daniel.
Screenplay: S.S. Wilson,
Brent Maddock, Erik Hansen, Gregory Hansen.
Music: Marc Shaiman. Cinematography: Michael W. Watkins.
Cast: Robert Downey Jr., Charles Grodin, Alfre Woodard,
Kyra Sedgwick, Tom Sizemore, Elisabeth Shue.

The early nineties saw a brief revival of the romantic ghost trend, and a few year after the success of **Ghost** and **Truly Madly Deeply** (both 1990) came this feel-good, charming sentimental comedy reuniting director Ron Underwood with his **Tremors** writers Brent Maddock and S.S. Wilson. Set in San Francisco, **Heart and Souls** features an all-star cast (Kyra Sedgwick, Elizabeth Shue, Alfre Woodard, B.B. King, Tom Sizemore) led by Robert Downey Jr. in the role of Thomas, a ruthless businessman mysteriously linked from birth to the souls of four passengers who died in a bus crash, and tasked with helping them cross over into the afterlife. Heartwarming and fantastical, the story uses well-known haunted house movie tropes — body possession, ghosts with unfinished business — but in the context of a comedy, giving them a fresh twist, both amusing and deeply emotional, and a message of finding out what matters in life and not delaying it to the next day. Much of the movie's joy comes from the interactions between the four ghosts, as different from each other as can be but bonded by friendship and a common mission. Years before finding worldwide celebrity with Marvel, Downey lets his incredible talent for physical comedy shine through as his character gets possessed by the spirits, and he impersonates their quirks and behaviours.

## CASPER

USA, 1995
Director: Brad Silberling. Producer: Colin Wilson.
Screenplay: Sherri Stoner, Deanna Oliver. Music: James Horner.
Cinematography: Dean Cundey.
Cast: Christina Ricci, Bill Pullman, Cathy Moriarty, Eric Idle, Garette Ratliff Henson, Jessica Wesson.

A brief return to the light-hearted comedic ghosts of the eighties, **Casper**, liberally adapted from Seymour Reit and Joe Oriolo's comic books and animated series *Casper the Friendly Ghost*, centres on the heart-warming bond between a little girl (Christina Ricci) and a gentle spirit. The plot gave Casper a tragic backstory, effectively putting an end to an old fan controversy regarding whether the character was indeed a dead child, or if ghosts were a separate type of supernatural entities. A young J.J. Abrams was hired by executive producer Steven Spielberg to work on a draft of the script, and television director Brad Silberling, who would go on to several more family-friendly blockbusters (**Lemony Snicket's A Series of Unfortunate Events**, **Land of the Lost**), was offered the chance to helm his first feature when previously hired filmmaker Alex Proyas (**The Crow**) departed the project. Filled with cameos (Clint Eastwood, Mel Gibson, Dan Aykroyd stand out), and followed by two straight-to-video prequels, **Casper** is best remembered for its groundbreaking, fully computer-generated ghosts. With over 350 visual effects shots to integrate, Silberling, whose VFX experience was limited at best, could thankfully rely on the ILM team and on veteran cinematographer Dean Cundey, who had worked extensively with CG-images on **Back to the Future Part II** and **Part III**, **Death Becomes Her** and **Who Framed Roger Rabbit**.

## HAUNTED

UK/USA, 1995
Director: Lewis Gilbert.
Producers: Anthony Andrews, Lewis Gilbert.
Screenplay: Lewis Gilbert, Timothy Prager, Bob Kellett.
Music: Debbie Wiseman.
Cinematography: Tony Pierce-Roberts.
Cast: Aidan Quinn, Kate Beckinsale, Anthony Andrews, John Gielgud, Anna Massey, Alex Lowe.

Period setting, upper class shenanigans, tea and scones in the breakfast room: **Haunted**, adapted from a James Herbert novel, is as close to a Merchant Ivory horror movie as we're ever likely to see. Aidan Quinn stars as David Ash, an American professor in 1920s England, obsessed with exposing fake mediums, who is invited by the Mariell family to investigate a haunting in their countryside manor, Edbrook, where Nanny Tess (Anna Massey) claims to be seeing deceased relatives. Initially dismissive, Ash is nevertheless instantly smitten with Christina (Kate Beckinsale), to the dismay of her jealous brothers. Directed by Lewis Gilbert (**The Spy Who Loved Me**, **Alfie**), **Haunted** is romantic and leisurely paced, light on scares but heavy on atmosphere. Much of its charm comes from the chemistry of its leading duo: Beckinsale, then twenty-two, is at once sweet, childlike, and manipulative, while Quinn carries the weight of the movie with a subtle, multi-layered performance. **Haunted** culminates into a final plot twist which, while not be entirely unpredictable (especially in retrospect, having seen similar endings in several high profiles releases since), can be seen as a fitting metaphor for the end of the old country estate way of life.

## DON'T LOOK UP

Japan, 1996
Director: Hideo Nakata.
Producers: Koji Kobayashi, Takenori Sentô.
Screenplay: Hiroshi Takahashi.
Music: Akifumi Kawamura.
Cinematography: Takeshi Hamada.
Cast: Yûrei Yanagi, Yasuyo Shirashima, Kei Ishibashi, Ren Osugi, Takanori Higuchi, Sabu [Hiroyuki Tanaka].

Best known as the precursor to **Ring** (1998), the watershed movie which revolutionized Japanese scary movies and gave the genre a boost around the world, **Don't Look Up** (*Joyû-rei*, meaning 'Ghost Actress') is the first horror feature (after episodes of television anthology **Curse, Death & Spirit**, 1992) of director Hideo Nakata, who started his career as an assistant director for sex video company Nikkatsu, and took on the job on **Don't Look Up** despite lacking any personal inclination towards the genre, as a way to help finance a documentary project. Bringing the traditional long-haired female ghost back to the forefront of horror, the movie follows a filmmaker (Yūrei Yanagi) whose set is plagued with unexplained disturbances. When the footage appears intercut with scenes from another production, he starts investigating the identity of the woman whose face can be seen out-of-focus on the mysterious reel. Parallels with **Ring** are easy to draw. Both spirits initially manifest through haunted tapes or celluloid, and have a similar look. But while Sadako was used sparingly, appearing only in brief scenes, **Don't Look Up**'s dead actress ghost is much more present, arguably seen too clearly for its own good. In many ways, this is Nakata honing his craft before embarking on his magnum opus. **Don't Look Up** was remade in the U.S. in 2009 by Chinese director Fruit Chan (**Dumplings**).

## THE FRIGHTENERS

New Zealand/USA, 1996
Director: Peter Jackson. Producers: Jamie Selkirk, Peter Jackson. Screenplay: Fran Walsh, Peter Jackson.
Music: Danny Elfman. Cinematography: Alun Bollinger, John Blick.
Cast: Michael J. Fox, Trini Alvarado, Peter Dobson, John Astin, Jeffrey Combs, Dee Wallace Stone.

While prepping his fourth feature **Heavenly Creatures**, Peter Jackson, then best known amongst genre fans for the splatter-tastic **Braindead**, and wife/partner-in-crime Fran Walsh came up with a new story idea, centering around a ghost buster using his ability to communicate with spirits to con the locals into hiring him. A two-page outline ended up on Robert Zemeckis' desk when the famed producer put out a call for feature ideas for **Tales from the Crypt** spin-offs, and the Kiwi duo were soon hired to write a script. Zemeckis found the concept strong enough to stand on its own, separate from the **Crypt** brand, and Universal agreed to finance **The Frighteners** to the tune of $25 million. Thanks to Zemeckis' shepherding of the project, the studio let Jackson shoot in New Zealand — meaning models would be required to make the town look American — and granted him final cut. The decision to shoot such a VFX-heavy film locally allowed the filmmaker to develop his own effects company, Weta Digital, into an entity able to handle the massive workload of Jackson's subsequent **Lord of the Rings** saga. So confident was Universal about **The Frighteners**, that they pulled it up from its Halloween slot to a summer release when their planned tentpole, **Daylight**, was delayed. This may go a long way to explain why the movie, a unique, energetic, well-reviewed **Beetlejuice**-style horror-comedy, was a box office disappointment.

## EVENT HORIZON

USA/UK, 1997
Director: Paul W.S. Anderson.
Producers: Lawrence Gordon, Lloyd Levin, Jeremy Bolt. Screenplay: Philip Eisner.
Music: Michael Kamen, Orbital. Cinematography: Adrian Biddle.
Cast: Laurence Fishburne, Sam Neill, Kathleen Quinlan, Joely Richardson, Richard T. Jones, Jack Noseworthy.

Ghosts in space: how had no one thought of it sooner? Fresh off the success of **Mortal Kombat**, director Paul W.S. Anderson re-imagines Paramount's **Alien** knock-off (whose original draft actually involved tentacular extraterrestrials) as a haunted house spaceship, drawing inspiration from everything from **The Haunting** and **The Shining**, to **2001: A Space Odyssey** and **Hellraiser**. The chilling premise — a spaceship pioneering an experimental gravity drive travels through hell and brings back some of its inhabitants — lends itself to gothic excesses, which Anderson gleefully exploits. The ship itself, modelled on Notre-Dame de Paris, is a visual feast, filled with arches, spikes, columns, and other unlikely outer space architectural flourishes. A troubled production from the start, **Event Horizon** was marred by incidents on set, and further impaired by the studio's last minute decision to bring its release date forward to fill the gap left in their schedule by James Cameron's delayed **Titanic**. Suddenly under summer tentpole scrutiny, Anderson's gory S&M shocker was subjected to drastic cuts, leaving some of its most striking imagery on the cutting room floor. Abandoned footage included extended shots of the previous crew's blood orgy, featuring real-life amputees, rape, and cannibalism, in a sequence inspired by the works of Bosch and Bruegel. The resulting movie is clunky and campy in places, yet gloomy and disturbing, with an original score from electronic band Orbital and a highly enjoyable turn from Sam Neill as the haunted ship's possessed creator.

## TOWER OF TERROR

USA, 1997
Director: D.J. MacHale.
Producer: Iain Paterson.
Screenplay: D.J. MacHale.
Music: Louis Febre.
Cinematography: Stephen McNutt.
Cast: Steve Guttenberg, Kirsten Dunst, Nia Peeples, Michael McShane, Amzie Strickland, Melora Hardin.

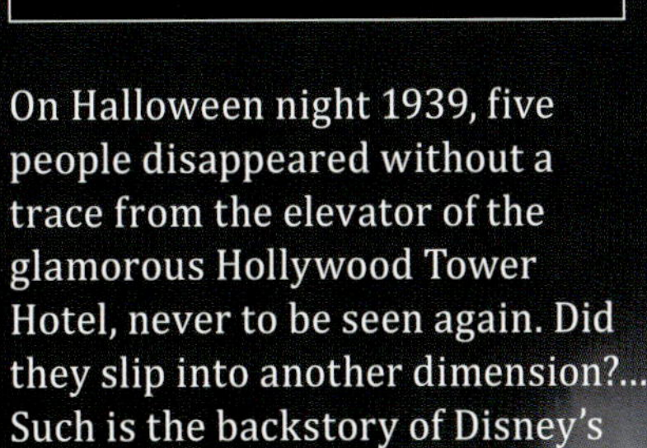

On Halloween night 1939, five people disappeared without a trace from the elevator of the glamorous Hollywood Tower Hotel, never to be seen again. Did they slip into another dimension?... Such is the backstory of Disney's theme park drop ride *The Twilight Zone Tower of Terror*, which opened in 1994 and serves as the basis for this television movie starring Steve Guttenberg as a down on his luck tabloid journalist investigating the story, and Kirsten Dunst as his niece and partner in crime. Unlike the attraction however, this adaptation holds no relation to the *Twilight Zone* TV show. Exteriors as well as many interior scenes were shot in and around the actual theme park ride in Anaheim, California; naturally, the storyline includes a drop mirroring that of the actual attraction. A new version has been in development for some time, with **Big Fish** screenwriter John August hired to pen a draft in 2015. Also worth noting is the fact that **Gremlins** director Joe Dante helmed the two-minute pre-ride video starring Rod Serling, lifted from clips from the November 1961 episode 'It's A Good Life', with a sound-alike voiceover artist (picked by no less than Serling's widow Carol) recording pertinent monologue.

## RING

Japan, 1998
Director: Hideo Nakata. Producers: Takashige Ichise, Shin'ya Kawai, Takenori Sentô.
Screenplay: Hiroshi Takahashi. Music: Kenji Kawai. Cinematography: Jun'ichirô Hayashi.
Cast: Nanako Matsushima, Miki Nakatani, Yûko Takeuchi, Hitomi Satô, Yôichi Numata, Yutaka Matsushige.

To say that Hideo Nakata's **Ring** (the added letter in the often seen title **'Ringu'** is a poor translation of the 'ng' sound in the Japanese alphabet) is one of the most influential horror films of the 20th century isn't an overstatement. The movie that launched countless long-haired ghosts, as well as a Korean reimagining (**The Ring Virus**), a U.S. franchise, two television series, three sequels (including **Spiral / Rasen**, released at the same time in Japan), a crossover with **The Grudge** (**Sadako Vs Kayako**, 2016) and manga and video game adaptations, it is commonly held responsible for the popularity of Hollywood horror remakes, and on a more positive note, the wave of supernatural movies of the late 1990s / early 2000s. Based on the eponymous novel by Koji Suzuki, **Ring** tells the story of a reporter (Nanako Matsushima) investigating the deaths of four teenagers who passed away precisely a week after watching an odd video. Having seen the tape, she traces its origins to Sadako (Rie Inō), a young woman with psychic powers, who disappeared in mysterious circumstances. Despite its apparent focus on technology, the movie is steeped in Japanese folklore; its vengeful ghost being in appearance and essence a classic *yurei*. Appropriately for a film about the viral nature of information and rumours, **Ring**'s success can be largely attributed to word-of-mouth, and to bootleg tapes passed on from fan to fan before its official release. Beyond the hype, it stands as a solid intrigue, capped with a now famous, unforgettable scene in which Sadako, all sharp angles and unnatural moves, crawls out of a television set, making viewers question whether they really are safe in front of their screens.

## WHISPERING CORRIDORS

South Korea, 1998
Director: Park Ki-hyung. Producer: Lee Choon-yeon.
Screenplay: In Jung-ok, Park Ki-hyung.
Music: Moon Sung-heon. Cinematography: Hahm Sung-won.
Cast: Choi Kang-hee, Kim Gyu-ri, Kim Min-jung, Kim Roe-ha, Kim Yu-seok, Lee Mi-yeon.

Released the same year as Japan's **Ring**, South Korean chiller **Whispering Corridors** marks the start of the country's horror boom, launched after a 1996 ruling from the Constitutional Court declared unconstitutional the strict censorship system of the time. A commentary on Korea's oppressive education system, which institutionalises physical punishment and psychological abuse, **Whispering Corridors** is set in a high school haunted by the vengeful ghost of a student who committed suicide. First-time feature filmmaker Park Ki-hyung, who co-wrote the script with In Jung-ok, consulted schoolgirls on their experiences to enhance the story's realism. Shot in two months on a budget of half a million dollars, **Whispering Corridors** builds the foundations for many of the genre's tropes, as well as the slow pace and sense of dread typical of K- and J-horror. As with the majority of Asian ghost movies to follow, the ghost and its victims are female, a consequence of the endemic repression of women, particularly young girls. Four sequels — **Memento Mori** (1999), **Wishing Stairs** (2003), **Voice** (2005) and **A Blood Pledge** (2009) — ensued for this surprise success, all set in all-girls schools, but from different directors and centering on unrelated characters. Park Ki-hyung would dip back into horror with **Acacia** (2003), the tale of a boy with an unnatural attachment to a tree.

## HOUSE ON HAUNTED HILL

USA, 1999
Director: William Malone. Producers: Gilbert Adler, Michael K. Ross, Joel Silver, Robert Zemeckis.
Screenplay: Dick Beebe. Music: Don Davis. Cinematography: Rick Bota.
Cast: Geoffrey Rush, Famke Janssen, Taye Diggs, Peter Gallagher, Chris Kattan, Ali Larter.

A rare example of a ghost story remake which stands on its own merits, William Malone's re-imagining of the 1959 William Castle/Vincent Price classic was the first release from producing outfit Dark Castle Entertainment, the brainchild of Joel Silver, Robert Zemeckis and Gilbert Adler. Starring a John Waters-styled Geoffrey Rush in the Price role, **House on Haunted Hill** sees lifelong horror fan Malone turn the campy original story into a proper scary movie, where ghosts are real and bodies pile up. Amongst the picture's highlights are the opening scene, set in a revolutionarily spooky amusement park, and later sequences where a camcorder allows its viewer to see ghosts re-enacting past events. Both have an old-fashioned, theatrical feel William Castle would not have disavowed, yet inject new and original ideas into the mix. Also of note is the oft-imitated, **Jacob's Ladder**-inspired effect adding a twitching, surreal quality to the movements of the ghosts (most notably Jeffrey Combs's sadistic surgeon). Top-notch special effects make-ups were the works of legendary FX company KNB. In keeping with Castle's spirit, **House on Haunted Hill** was released theatrically with scratch-off vouchers offering audience members the chance to win money, much like the guests of the movie's haunted house.

## SHIKOKU

Japan, 1999
Director: Shunichi Nagasaki. Producers: Masato Hara, Yasushi Tsuge.
Screenplay: Kunimi Manda, Takenori Sentô. Music: Satoshi Kadokura. Cinematography: Noboru Shinoda.
Cast: Yui Natsukawa, Michitaka Tsutsui, Chiaki Kuriyama, Toshie Negishi, Ren Osugi, Makoto Satô.

One of the first movies to be blatantly conceived to cash in on the success of 1998's **Ring**, Shunichi Nagasaki's **Shikoku** features the obligatory long-haired yurei, but is more original and steeped in local culture than its release as part of a double bill with Hideo Nakata's **Ring 2** might suggest. Co-written by **Ring** producer Takenori Sentô from a children's story by award-winning author Masako Bandō, **Shikoku** follows Hinako (Yui Natsukawa) as she returns to her native island of Shikoku to find her childhood friend Sayori (Chiaki Kuriyama, who would later gain roles in **Battle Royale** and **Kill Bill**) has died, and that driven mad with grief, Sayori's mother, a medium and Shinto priestess, started following odd rituals in an attempt to turn the island into the legendary Land of the Dead. Distributed in Japan, like **Ring**, by production company Toho Studios (of **Seven Samurai** and the **Godzilla** series fame), **Shikoku** owes its title to a play on words: the name of the smallest of Japan's four main islands literally means Four Kingdoms, but four being considered an unlucky number throughout Asia, 'Shi' can also be interpreted as death, turning the name into Kingdom of Death.

## THE SIXTH SENSE

USA, 1999
Director: M. Night Shyamalan. Producers: Kathleen Kennedy, Frank Marshall, Barry Mendel.
Screenplay: M. Night Shyamalan. Music: James Newton Howard. Cinematography: Tak Fujimoto.
Cast: Bruce Willis, Haley Joel Osment, Toni Collette, Olivia Williams, Trevor Morgan, Donnie Wahlberg.

Indian-born filmmaker M. Night Shyamalan's third feature **The Sixth Sense**, the story of Cole (then nine-years-old Haley Joel Osment), who sees dead people, and his therapist Malcolm (Bruce Willis), both popularized twist endings — for which the filmmaker remained the poster child — and brought supernatural chills back into the mainstream. The story was long-rumoured to have been inspired by an episode of Canadian anthology series **Are You Afraid of the Dark?** titled **The Tale of the Dream Girl** (1994), but Shyamalan has since denied ever seeing the show; he instead points to an incident he witnessed at a wake, where a grieving little boy spent the night talking to an imaginary friend. The original draft saw Malcolm as a crime scene photographer investigating a serial killer, and understanding his own son could see the killer's victims. Precursors include **Carnival of Souls** (1962) and **Voices** (1973); but beyond the perfectly set up twist, the strength of **The Sixth Sense** lies in its performances and its tragic, touching take on grief, loss, and the meaning of human life. Nominated for six Academy Awards, the movie carefully avoids explicit gore; a scene in which Cole sees dozens of disfigured spirits in a hospital ward was cut, likely to preserve the PG-13 rating Disney required, and leave more to the viewers' imagination.

## SLEEPY HOLLOW

Germany/USA, 1999
Director: Tim Burton. Producers: Scott Rudin, Adam Schroeder.
Screenplay: Andrew Kevin Walker. Music: Danny Elfman.
Cinematography: Emmanuel Lubezki.
Cast: Johnny Depp, Christina Ricci, Miranda Richardson,
Michael Gambon, Casper Van Dien, Jeffrey Jones, Christopher Walken.

After the consecutive commercial failures of **Ed Wood** (1994) and **Mars Attacks!** (1996) and a year spent on the mooted **Superman Lives**, Tim Burton returned to form with **Sleepy Hollow**, a heartfelt and visually stunning homage to Mario Bava and Hammer movies. Based on Washington Irving's 1920 short story *The Legend of Sleepy Hollow*, it follows Ichabod Crane (Johnny Depp), a constable sent from New York City to investigate murders supposedly committed by the ghost of a headless horseman (Christopher Walken). The sixties horror flavour is most palpable in the movie's visuals, each shot steeped in atmospheric mist, autumnal colours and contrasty cinematography. The painstakingly detailed village took production designer Rick Heinrichs and his team four months to build in the English countryside, taking up twenty acres of land; stylized forests made of fiberglass trees and real branches were created on soundstages split between two studios. Christopher Lee cameos as the burgomaster who dispatches Crane to Sleepy Hollow. Dark and moody, yet featuring all the humorous, light touches one can expect from a Tim Burton movie (including subtle references to Disney's version of the tale), **Sleepy Hollow** harkens back to horror classics yet subverts clichés, uses the latest techniques (with visual effects handled by ILM), and adds a layer of reflection on the balance of reason and heart, and the battle between religious fanaticism and scientific progress.

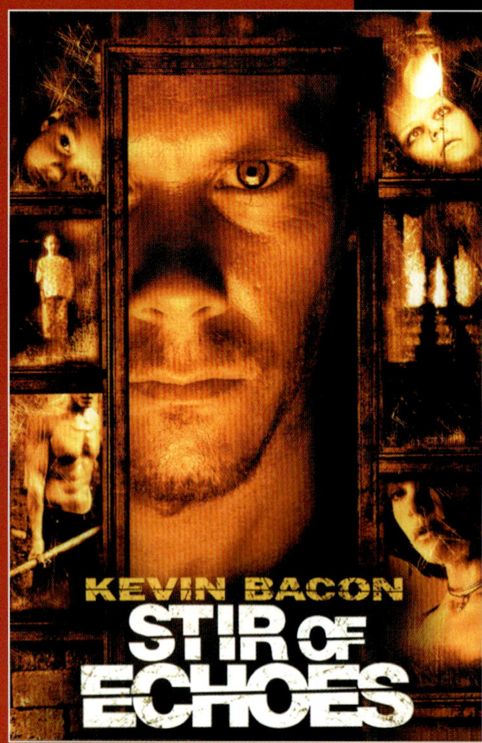

## STIR OF ECHOES

USA, 1999
Director: David Koepp.
Producers: Judy Hofflund, Gavin Polone.
Screenplay: David Koepp. Music: James Newton Howard.
Cinematography: Fred Murphy.
Cast: Zachary David Cope, Kevin Bacon, Kathryn Erbe, Illeana Douglas, Kevin Dunn, Conor O'Farrell.

Based on a 1958 novel by Richard Matheson, David Koepp's **Stir of Echoes** could have staked a claim to the title of best American ghost movie of the nineties, had it not come hot on the heels of superior effort **The Sixth Sense**. Like Shyamalan's mega-hit, its tight supernatural intrigue is steeped in very human drama, where the living turn out to be more dangerous than the dead. Kevin Bacon plays Tom, a telephone lineman living in a blue collar area of Chicago with his pregnant wife Maggie (Kathryn Erbe) and son Jake (Zachary David Cope). After an impromptu hypnosis session with Maggie's sister (Illeana Douglas), he becomes plagued by visions of a missing teenage girl. As the haunting intensifies, Tom grows obsessed with solving the mystery of her disappearance, putting himself and his family at risk in the process. If the neighbourhood conflict is the heart of the story, Koepp treats the supernatural earnestly, building a real sense of dread and peppering it with a couple of effective jump scares. Despite underwhelming numbers, **Stir of Echoes** would be followed eight years later by a television sequel, **Stir of Echoes: The Homecoming**. Koepp himself would return to the spirit world with 2008 Ricky Gervais comedy **Ghost Town**.

## WHAT LIES BENEATH

USA, 2000
Director: Robert Zemeckis.
Producers: Jack Rapke, Steve Starkey, Robert Zemeckis.
Screenplay: Clark Gregg. Music: Alan Silvestri.
Cinematography: Don Burgess.
Cast: Michelle Pfeiffer, Katharine Towne, Miranda Otto, James Rema, Harrison Ford, Victoria Bidewell.

A psychological thriller with A-list pedigree (produced by DreamWorks, directed by Robert Zemeckis and starring Michelle Pfeiffer and Harrison Ford), **What Lies Beneath** could be described as the lovechild of two of 1999's biggest hits, **The Sixth Sense** and **American Beauty**. As its title suggests, the story depicts the cracks under the surface of a perfect marriage. Claire Spencer (Pfeiffer) has a beautiful home, great friends, a successful husband (Ford) and endless supplies of red wine and kombucha tea. But after a car accident and her daughter's departure to college, she starts occupying the long hours her husband spends at work by spying on the couple next door. She soon grows convinced that her neighbour has killed his wife, and that her ghost is now haunting her house. But when the woman turns up alive and well, Claire starts to suspect her own husband may be keeping secrets from her. Filmed during a break in the production of Zemeckis's **Cast Away**, while Tom Hanks lost weight and grew a beard for the second half of the shoot, **What Lies Beneath** is light on supernatural scares, instead focusing on the impact of a buried past and the breakdown of a marriage. The resulting balance between ghost story and Hitchcockian suspense is rather uneasy, yet Pfeiffer's pitch-perfect performance carries the movie, making this a pleasant, rather than thrilling, watch.

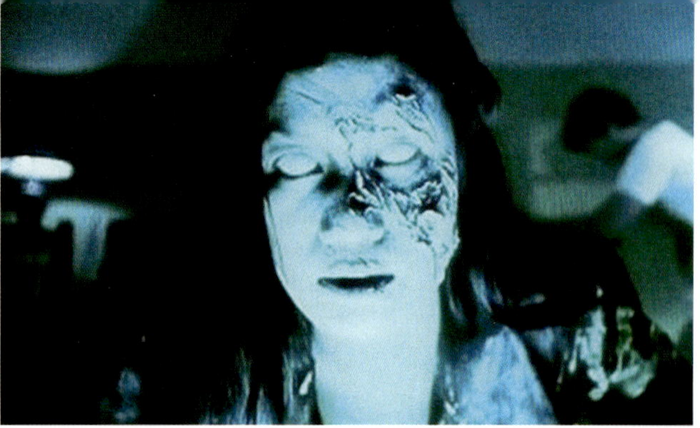

## BANGKOK HAUNTED

Thailand, 2001
Directors: Oxide Pang, Pisut Praesangeam.
Producers: Pisut Praesangeam, Jantima Liawsirikun.
Screenplay: Pisut Praesangeam, Sompop Wetchapipat.
Music: Doctor Head, Orange Music.
Cinematography: Vichien Ruengvichayakun,
Decha Srimunta, Nuttawut Kittikun.
Cast: Pimsiree Pimsee, Pramote Seangsorn, Dawan Singha-wee, Kalyanut Sriboonrueng, Pete Thong-jeur.

**Bangkok Haunted** (original title **Phi sam baht**, which translates as 'Three Baht Ghost', a reference to the average cost of high street comic books in Thailand) is a Thai anthology film compiling three ghost stories told by three women in a Bangkok bar. In 'Legend of the Drum', an antique instrument is possessed by the vengeful spirit of a dancer; in 'Black Magic Woman', an aphrodisiac made from corpses has extreme consequences for the men its user sleeps with; and 'Revenge' follows an investigation into a woman's apparent suicide. The last story not only required extensive research into hanging techniques and two days' filming just for the sequence, but also featured an autopsy scene in an actual morgue, with a real dead body. Clearly made on a small budget, **Bangkok Haunted** is mostly notable for being one of Thailand's first horror hits (on the heels of 1999's **Nang Nak**, also a huge success), and for offering the first scary story from Oxide Pang, who would create a sensation with **The Eye** the following year and become one of the country's most exportable genre filmmakers. Its English title falsely links it to Pang's previous feature **Bangkok Dangerous**, a crime thriller made with his twin brother Danny, and successful enough to warrant both an American remake (with Nicolas Cage, 2008), and an Indian tamil version (**Pattiyal**, 2006). **Bangkok Haunted** is co-directed by actor-writer Pisut Praesangeam, who would never top its success.

## THE BUNKER

UK, 2001
Director: Rob Green.
Producer: Daniel Figuero.
Screenplay: Clive Dawson.
Music: Russell Currie.
Cinematography: John Pardue.
Cast: Jason Flemyng, Andrew Tiernan, Christopher Fairbank, Simon Kunz, Andrew Lee Potts, John Carlisle.

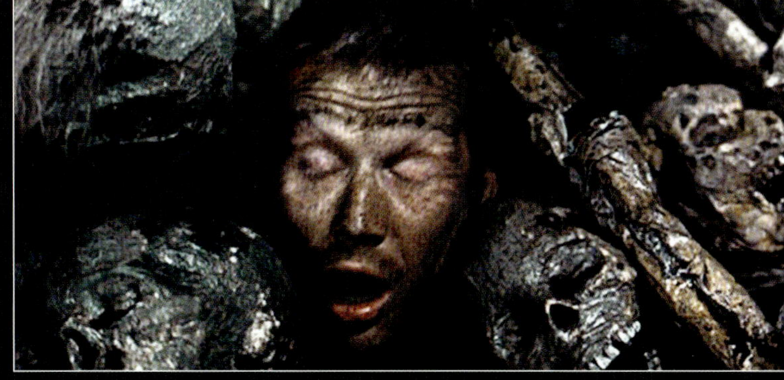

A year before **Dog Soldiers**, **28 Days Later** and **Deathwatch** came **The Bunker**, first in the salve of UK-made soldiers-versus-the-supernatural pictures which marked the beginning of Britain's return to scary movies in the new millennium. Directed by newcomer Rob Green and penned by television writer Clive Dawson, this psychological horror follows the remnants of a German platoon trapped in a bunker at the Belgium-Germany border at the end of World War Two. Fearing they have been surrounded by American troops, the survivors (including Jason Flemyng, who would return to supernatural WWII horrors the following year with David Twohy's **Below**, as well as Jack Davenport and Eddie Marsan) end up in the tunnels underneath their hideout, where greater terrors await. Climbing on the shoulders of Michael Mann's 1983 **The Keep**, and adopting the point of view of Nazi troops like Wolfgang Petersen's 1981 masterpiece **Das Boot**, **The Bunker** plays with ideas of paranoia, guilt, and the psychological consequences of fighting a losing battle. Green was for a while rumoured to be attached to **Fresh Meat**, the long mooted sequel to Neil Marshall's **Dog Soldiers**, as well as **Gladiators Vs Werewolves**, which despite its promising title also failed to see the light of day.

## THE DEVIL'S BACKBONE

Spain/Mexico/France/Argentina, 2001
Director: Guillermo del Toro.
Producers: Agustín Almodóvar, Bertha Navarro.
Screenplay: Guillermo del Toro, Antonio Trashorras, David Muñoz.
Music: Javier Navarrete.
Cinematography: Guillermo Navarro.
Cast: Marisa Paredes, Eduardo Noriega, Federico Luppi, Fernando Tielve, Íñigo Garcés, Irene Visedo.

*'What is a ghost? A tragedy condemned to repeat itself time and again? An instant of pain, perhaps. Something dead which still seems to be alive. An emotion suspended in time. Like a blurred photograph. Like an insect trapped in amber.'*

So starts Guillermo del Toro's **The Devil's Backbone** (aka **El espinazo del diablo**) perfectly encapsulating the sense of nostalgia and human drama permeating this subtle masterpiece. Inspired by the experience at age twelve of hearing ghostly sighs and whispers after a death in the family, the movie is generally considered del Toro's most personal work, along with companion piece **Pan's Labyrinth** (2006). Its story matured in the writer-director's mind for the best part of a decade, from a first draft written just before debut film **Cronos** (1993), through the studio-fighting ordeal of **Mimic** (1997); personal notebooks over the period depict various abandoned ideas, such as an old man with a needle, a three-armed Christ, and a spectral caretaker. The look of the ghost — a little boy named Santi; partly translucent, skin cracking like a broken doll, blood floating up from his fractured skull, rust-coloured tears streaming down his face — is at once sad and disquieting; yet the revenant isn't the movie's villain. Set against the backdrop of the Spanish civil war, a harsh time del Toro believes isn't often enough depicted on screen, **The Devil's Backbone** deals with human monsters and the destruction of innocence, its ghost acting as an undying reminder of past tragedies.

una pelicula de
guillermo del toro
EL ESPINAZO DEL DIABLO
marisa paredes
eduardo noriega
federico luppi

## KAIRO

Japan, 2001
Director: Kiyoshi Kurosawa.
Producers: Ken Inoue, Seiji Okuda, Shun Shimizu, Atsuyuki Shimoda, Hiroshi Yamamoto.
Screenplay: Kiyoshi Kurosawa. Music: Takefumi Haketa.
Cinematography: Jun'ichirô Hayashi.
Cast: Haruhiko Katô, Kumiko Asô, Koyuki, Kurume Arisaka, Masatoshi Matsuo, Shinji Takeda.

The rapid growth of the Internet in the early 2000s was bound to inspire horror stories. Before William Malone's **Feardotcom** (2002) tackled the topic in America, Japanese cult director Kiyoshi Kurosawa released **Kairo** (aka **Pulse**), considered to this day one of the finest films in the J-horror wave. Two storylines develop in parallel: Michi (Kumiko Asô) and a group of fellow students, all reeling from the suicide of a friend, find an old computer disk he worked on; while a tech newbie (Haruhiko Katô) taking his first steps into cyberspace repeatedly ends up on a site inviting him to meet a ghost. Cold, enigmatic and slow-paced, **Kairo** offers some dream-like, subtle scares; greasy stains spread on walls and shadowy figures whisper on computer screens, as the souls of the dead return to our world. A sombre meditation on rampant loneliness in Japanese society, it posits that the web makes users feel more connected, yet actually drives them further apart; and compares net surfers to lonesome ghosts ('Death is eternal loneliness', repeats one of the spirits.) Inevitably, a U.S. remake, helmed by newcomer Jim Sonzero (after both Wes Craven and Kurosawa himself had been rumoured to direct), came out in 2006; it was followed by two sequels.

## THE OTHERS

USA/Spain/France/Italy, 2001
Director: Alejandro Amenábar.
Producers: Fernando Bovaira, José Luis Cuerda, Sunmin Park.
Screenplay: Alejandro Amenábar.
Music: Alejandro Amenábar.
Cinematography: Javier Aguirresarobe.
Cast: Nicole Kidman, Fionnula Flanagan, Christopher Eccleston, Alakina Mann, James Bentley, Eric Sykes.

Writer-director-composer Alejandro Amenábar was only twenty-eight years old when he signed one of the masterpieces of the haunted house sub-genre: **The Others**, an elegant drama in the tradition of M.R. James and *The Turn of the Screw*. Tom Cruise and producing partner Paula Wagner secured remake rights to Amenábar's previous picture **Open Your Eyes** (**Abre los ojos**) after its 1998 Sundance premiere, and after the filmmaker passed on directing, agreed to produce **The Others**. Nicole Kidman, whose nuanced performance carries the movie, came on board shortly after. Mist-shrouded and delicately lit, this tale of darkness and guilt, about a woman awaiting her husband's return from World War II with her two children in her isolated mansion, was originally written in Spanish and set in South America, then eventually translated to English, set on the island of Jersey, and lensed in Spain. The decision to change the language and locale came not only from commercial considerations, but from a sense that the tone and themes of the movie fitted more appropriately into the British ghost story tradition. The ending, which gives this classical feature an entirely new, fresh meaning, was the first part Amenábar penned, letting it inspire and inform the rest of the screenplay.

The movie features post mortem photography, a trend in Victorian times to capture the likeness of loved ones after their passing.

**The Others** won eight Goya awards as well as Golden Globe and BAFTA nominations.

## DARK WATER

Japan, 2002
Director: Hideo Nakata.
Producer: Takashige Ichise.
Screenplay: Ken'ichi Suzuki, Yoshihiro Nakamura, Takashige Ichise [uncredited], Hideo Nakata [uncredited].
Music: Kenji Kawai, Shikao Suga.
Cinematography: Jun'ichirô Hayashi.
Cast: Hitomi Kuroki, Rio Kanno, Mirei Oguchi, Asami Mizukawa, Fumiyo Kohinata, Yu Tokui.

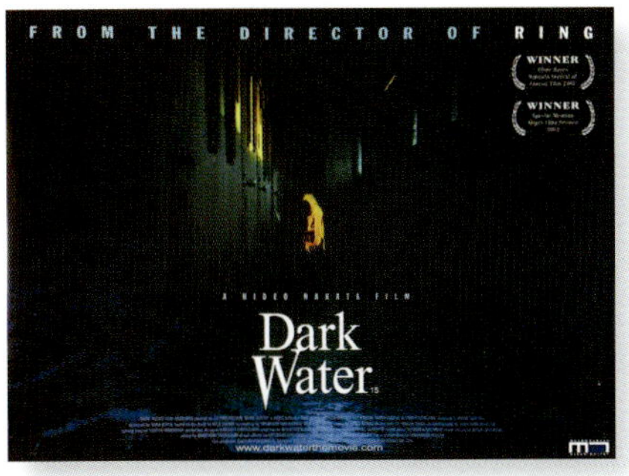


Four years after his worldwide hit, **Ring** director Hideo Nakata returned to dead wet girls with another adaptation of a Koji Suzuki story, and the formula again proved successful. More coherent and character-driven than its predecessor, **Dark Water** follows divorced mother Yoshimi (Hitomi Kuroki) as she rents a new apartment for her and her daughter Ikuko (Rio Kanno) while in the midst of a custody battle. As she investigates a leak in the ceiling, she starts catching glimpses of a little girl in a yellow coat, who looks remarkably like a missing child who disappeared a year earlier. With muted colours, gloomy atmosphere, and very little music, **Dark Water** is a subdued yet multi-layered tale: on the one hand, a chilling ghost story; on the other, a social drama with themes of divorce, housing crisis, and the place of women — specifically single mothers — in Japanese society. Both aspects work in perfect harmony, the spectre herself being a victim of parental neglect; and there are hints that the haunting could be the product of the imagination of a woman pushed to the brink of a nervous breakdown. Walter Salles's 2005 remake took a different approach, eschewing thrills and mystery in favour of grim domestic tragedy.

## DARKNESS

USA/Spain, 2002
Director: Jaume Balagueró.
Producers: Julio Fernández, Brian Yuzna.
Screenplay: Jaume Balagueró, Fernando de Felipe, Miguel Tejada-Flores.
Music: Carles Cases. Cinematography: Xavi Giménez.
Cast: Anna Paquin, Lena Olin, Iain Glen, Giancarlo Giannini, Fele Martínez, Stephan Enquist.

Spanish director Jaume Balagueró made a splash in the independent film world with his award-winning 1999 feature debut **The Nameless** before directing his first English-speaking effort, **Darkness**, three years later. Starring Anna Paquin, Lena Olin and Iain Glen, **Darkness** follows an American family moving into a Spanish countryside house with a dark past. Structured like a haunted house picture, it centres around the occult, and unfinished rituals requiring final sacrifices. **Darkness** was produced by Fantastic Factory, the genre arm of Barcelona-based studio Filmax, shepherded by American horror maestro Brian Yuzna, which released nine films between 2001 and 2006, including Stuart Gordon's Lovecraft-inspired **Dagon** (2001) and the third **Re-Animator** movie, **Beyond Re-Animator** (2003). It marks the start of a golden age of Spanish supernatural flicks, culminating with **The Devil's Backbone** (2001) and **The Orphanage** (2007). Released in its homeland and Europe from October 2002, **Darkness** took two years to come out in the U.S., in a version heavily edited by Miramax in order to receive a PG-13 rating. This pattern would repeat itself for Balagueró's next English-language movie, ghost story **Fragile** (2005), which didn't come out in America until 2010. He achieved international recognition with the **[REC]** saga, also financed by Filmax, from 2007.

## THE EYE

Hong Kong/Singapore, 2002
Directors: Pang Brothers [Danny Pang, Oxide Pang].
Producers: Peter Chan, Lawrence Cheng.
Screenplay: Jojo Hui, Pang Brothers [Danny Pang, Oxide Pang]. Music: Orange Music.
Cinematography: Decha Seementa.
Cast: Angelica Lee, Lawrence Chou, Chutcha Rujinanon, So Yat-lai, Candy Lo, Ko Yin-ping.

Blind from the age of two, Mun (Angelica Lee) regains sight after a cornea transplant. As she learns to adjust and make sense of her new perception of the world, she starts encountering people and shadows no one else seems able to see. Twin brothers Oxide and Danny Pang's biggest hit to date, **The Eye** blends atmosphere with extremely effective scares (the elevator scene and the woman in the calligraphy room are hard to forget) in what undoubtedly stands as one of the best Asian ghost stories of the new millennium. Filmed in Hong Kong and Thailand, two countries the Pang brothers frequently work in, the movie is steeped in Chinese tradition (in particular the myth of ying yang — or ghost-seeing — eyes), and culminates in an impressive and gruesome accident sequence inspired by a 1990 Bangkok gas explosion, and often compared to the climax of **The Mothman Prophecies**, released in the U.S. the same year. The story was inspired by a newspaper report about a young Chinese woman who had committed suicide shortly after undergoing surgery which restored her sight. Not only did **The Eye** spawn the inevitable sequels (**The Eye 2** and **The Eye 10**) and U.S. remake, helmed by French duo David Moreau and Xavier Palud (**Them**, 2006) and starring Jessica Alba; it also inspired an unofficial Bollywood reimagining, **Naina**, in 2005, evidencing the film's pan-Asian appeal.

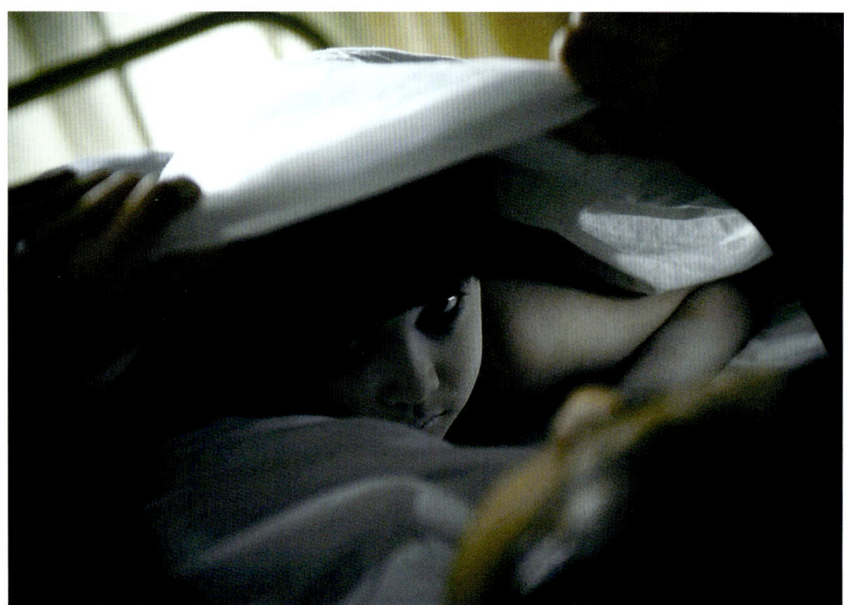

## JU-ON

Japan, 2002
Director: Takashi Shimizu. Producers: Takashige Ichise, Kunio Kawakami, Yoshinori Kumazawa, Hiroki Numata. Screenplay: Takashi Shimizu. Music: Shiro Sato. Cinematography: Tokushô Kikumura. Cast: Megumi Okina, Misaki Itô, Misa Uehara, Yui Ichikawa, Kanji Tsuda, Kayoko Shibata.

'Ju-on: The curse of one who dies in the grip of powerful rage. It gathers and takes effect in the places that person was alive. Those who encounter it die, and a new curse is born.' **Ju-on**, Takashi Shimizu's third standalone movie in the massively popular **Ju-on** saga (after two anthology segments, and two V-cinema — aka straight-to-video — films), opens with an explanation which perfectly encapsulates the concept of the franchise (today comprising a total of twelve full features, as well as the usual novels, comics and video game adaptations). Every instalment indeed presents a series of non-chronological yet linked vignettes revolving around the suburban house where Kayako Saeki and her child Toshio were murdered by Kayako's husband. Their spirits haunt their home, and anyone who comes into contact with them is destined to die and pass on the jinx. Like **Ring**'s killer video, the curse is viral, passed on from victim to victim: a metaphor for the fact that in an overcrowded society such as Japan, everyone is connected, and violence breeds violence. Shimizu's skills lie in the execution of extremely simple, straightforward stories: there may not be much to the script, but his ability to create dread and shocks in bright daylight (a rare fact for ghost movies), relying mostly on clever use of sound effects, is unparalleled.

## THE RING

USA/Japan, 2002
Director: Gore Verbinski. Producers: Laurie MacDonald, Walter F. Parkes.
Screenplay: Ehren Kruger. Music: Hans Zimmer. Cinematography: Bojan Bazelli.
Cast: Naomi Watts, Martin Henderson, David Dorfman, Brian Cox, Jane Alexander, Lindsay Frost.

First in a long line of big budget, A-list J-horror reimaginings engineered by prolific Korean-American producer Roy Lee, **The Ring** sees a pre-**Pirates of the Caribbean** Gore Verbinski, then best known for his 1997 comedy **Mousehunt**, adapt Hideo Nakata's Japanese hit to U.S. tastes. The killer videotape is back, this time threatening to kill Naomi Watts, Martin Henderson and David Dorfman (in a part clearly inspired by **The Sixth Sense**'s Cole Sear); the long-haired spectre's name changed from Sadako to Samara, but the plot sticks closely to the original, and while by the end the curse appears explained and the mystery resolved, the same questions are left unanswered. Aside from a couple of perfectly executed jump-scares and some strikingly graphic Rick Baker-designed make-up on the corpses, this remake shows relative restraint; from script to direction, down to its muted colours and minimalistic soundtrack. A huge success worldwide (including in Japan, where it outperformed **Ring** in less than two weeks), it has so far spawned two sequels: **The Ring Two** (2005), directed by Hideo Nakata himself; and **Rings** (2017), in which the old videotape gets a digital update. Even vengeful spirits have to move with the times.

## A NEW KIND OF HORROR TAKES ROOT...

### BUPPHA RAHTREE

Thailand, 2003
Director: Yuthlert Sippapak.
Producers: Amorn Chanapai, Yuthlert Sippapak.
Screenplay: Yuthlert Sippapak. Music: Kankor Club.
Cinematography: Prapapope Duangpikool.
Cast: Laila Boonyasak, Krit Sripoomseth, Chompunoot Piyapane, Sirisin Siripornsmathikul, Ampon Rattanawong, Somjai Sukjai.

Rich and handsome student Ake (Krit Sripoomseth) sleeps with loner Buppha (Laila Boonyasak) on a dare, then ghosts her. Pregnant from the encounter, Buppha bleeds to death from a botched abortion and soon starts haunting her apartment building, to her neighbours' dismay. **Buppha Rahtree**, from Thai writer-director Yuthlert Sippapak, starts off as a teenage romance then quickly turns to drama, before veering into horror comedy territory. Most of the humor comes from a succession of hapless charlatan shamans and priests trying to exorcise the unfortunate girl's vengeful spirit (including a sequence spoofing **The Exorcist**); but the movie also mixes in jump scares, as well as surprisingly intense material such as sexual assault, amputation (a nod to Takashi Miike's **Audition**), and ghost sex. Buppha's graphic make-up and sharp, fast gestures make her appearance more reminiscent of **Evil Dead** deadites than of the typical Asian *yurei*. A huge hit in its homeland, **Buppha Rahtree** gave birth to a profitable on-going franchise, comprising **Buppha Rahtree Phase 2: Rahtree Returns** (2005), **Buppha Rahtree 3.1: Rahtree Reborn** (2009), **Buppha Rahtree 3.2: Rahtree Revenge** (2009), and **Haunting in Japan** (2016). A soundtrack album of Thai hip hop songs accompanied the release of the original movie.

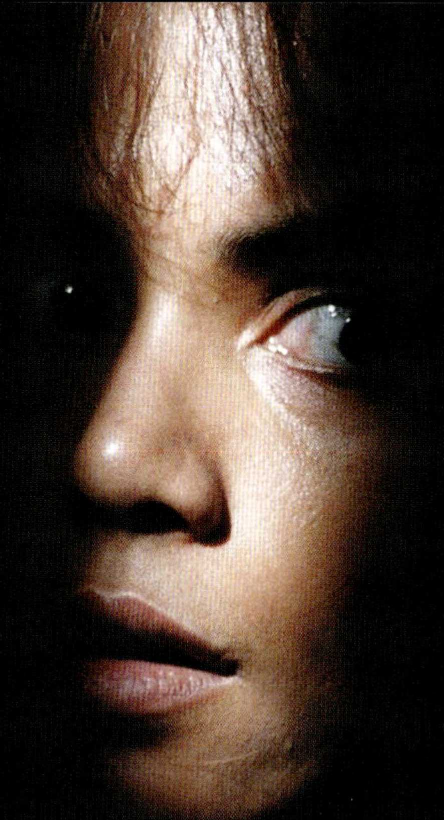

## GOTHIKA

USA, 2003

Director: Mathieu Kassovitz. Producers: Joel Silver, Robert Zemeckis, Susan Levin [Susan Downey]. Screenplay: Sebastian Gutierrez. Music: John Ottman. Cinematography: Matthew Libatique. Cast: Halle Berry, Robert Downey Jr., Charles S. Dutton, John Carroll Lynch, Bernard Hill, Penélope Cruz.

Just as independent horror started soaring with increasingly gory titles such as **House of a Thousand Corpses** (2003) or **Saw** (2004), the mainstream, big budget ghost movie reached a peak of sorts with **Gothika**, a B-movie filled with more A-list talent than one can shake a stick at, on both sides of the camera. Freshly crowned with an Academy Award for 2001's **Monster's Ball**, Halle Berry stars as a psychiatrist to the criminally insane, who wakes up locked in a cell of the hospital she works at, accused of having murdered her husband (Charles S. Dutton), and in the care of a former colleague (Robert Downey Jr.). Penélope Cruz and Bernard Hill round up the rather prestigious cast. Brought on board by Joel Silver and his company Dark Castle Entertainment (**House on Haunted Hill**, **Ghost Ship**, **Thir13en Ghosts**), Berry, who confesses to believing in ghosts and whose mother worked as a nurse in a psychiatric ward, gives the role her all — even accidentally breaking her arm while performing a stunt with Downey, which put production on hold for three weeks. French filmmaker Mathieu Kassovitz (**La haine**, 1995, **The Crimson Rivers**, 2000), who had joined the project relatively late, reportedly took the opportunity to further prep the remaining action scenes.

## THE HAUNTED MANSION

USA, 2003
Director: Rob Minkoff.
Producers: Andrew Gunn, Don Hahn. Screenplay: David Berenbaum.
Music: Mark Mancina. Cinematography: Remi Adefarasin.
Cast: Eddie Murphy, Terence Stamp, Nathaniel Parker,
Marsha Thomason, Jennifer Tilly, Wallace Shawn.

For the 2003 screen adaptation of its famed theme park ride, The Haunted Mansion, Disney re-united the team behind **The Lion King** — director Rob Minkoff and producer Don Hahn — and opted to turn potentially spooky material into a broad Eddie Murphy vehicle, to the dismay of the ride's many die-hard fans. But if chills and atmosphere didn't live up to the material's potential, the movie is however worth singling out for its faithful transposition of the Mansion's world to the screen, with rich production design and costumes, and extraordinary make-ups by legendary artist Rick Baker. **The Haunted Mansion** is littered with familiar figures from the attraction — Madame Leota (Jennifer Tilly, gleeful), Master Gracey, the busts, and fan favourites the Hitchhiking Ghosts, whose originally prominent roles were cut down in later drafts — all brought to life with great attention to detail. The design of the house, built on a Santa Clarita soundstage, mixed elements of the California and Florida versions of the dark ride; the filmmakers drew additional inspiration from movies by Roger Corman and William Castle. Following the success of the **Pirates of the Caribbean** saga, and aware of the ride's massive fan base, Disney announced in 2010 a new, darker adaptation, spearheaded by Guillermo del Toro. It has been in the works ever since.

## INTO THE MIRROR

South Korea, 2003
Director: Kim Sung-ho.
Producer: Kim Eun-young.
Screenplay: Kim Sung-ho.
Music: Mun Dae-hyeon.
Cinematography: Jeong Han-cheol.
Cast: Yu Ji-tae, Kim Myung-min, Kim Hye-na, Gi Ju-bong, Kim Myoeng-su, Lee Yeong-jin.

An ex-cop turned security guard (Yu Ji-tae, **Oldboy**) in a reputedly haunted department store investigates a series of apparent suicides inside the building; all of which seem to have occurred around mirrors. First-time writer-director Kim Sung-ho deftly blends genres in this hybrid of his homeland's two most popular types of movies: detective thriller and supernatural horror. Haunted mirrors have been a relatively popular scary movie device, from Amicus portmanteau **From Beyond the Grave** (1973), John Carpenter's **Prince of Darkness** (1987) and **Poltergeist III** (1988), to 1999 Hong Kong anthology **The Mirror** and Mike Flanagan's 2013 **Oculus**. **Into the Mirror** takes the approach that mirrors are links between two parallel realities, and explores themes of split personalities. The American remake, **Mirrors**, starring Kiefer Sutherland and directed by French filmmaker Alexandre Aja (**The Hills Have Eyes**, 2006), came out in 2008; **Mirrors 2**, by Spanish FX artist-turned-director Víctor García (**Return to House on Haunted Hill**, 2007), went straight to video in 2010. After a brief incursion into family-friendly fare (**How to Steal a Dog**, 2014), Kim himself returned to the subject matter with **The Mirror 3D** (2015), a China-South Korea co-production he co-directed with Danny Pang (**The Eye**) and Thai filmmaker Pakphum Wongjinda.

## ONE MISSED CALL

Japan, 2003
Director: Takashi Miike.
Producers: Yoichi Arishige, Fumio Inoue, Naoki Satô.
Screenplay: Minako Daira. Music: Kôji Endô.
Cinematography: Hideo Yamamoto.
Cast: Ko Shibasaki, Shin'ichi Tsutsumi, Kazue Fukiishi, Anna Nagata, Atsushi Ida, Mariko Tsutsui.

RING... RING... RING... Japanese shock auteur Takashi Miike (then best known internationally for 1999's **Audition** and 2001's **Ichi the Killer**) jumped on the J-horror bandwagon and tapped into the then-new cell phone craze with this uncharacteristically subdued entry, in which college students struggle to escape a seemingly ineluctable fate when they receive phone calls from their future selves, leaving voicemails recording their own deaths. From deadly technology to contamination through a viral curse, Miike borrows heavily from Hideo Nakata, even lifting some of **Ring**'s jump scares. Like several of its predecessors, **One Missed Call** explores themes of child neglect and abuse, and its vengeful spirit, naturally, turns out to be a girl with long hair. Yet despite the familiarity of its set-up and execution, the movie offers some great imagery (the ghost creeping on the ceiling is frankly terrifying) and a couple of neatly executed deaths. A hit in its homeland (and arguably Miike's most mainstream picture), **One Missed Call**, following the now tried-and-true principle of milking a franchise to its last bloody drop, engendered two sequels, a ten-episode television series, and a 2008 U.S. remake from French director Eric Valette (**Maléfique**, 2002), starring Shannyn Sossamon and Ray Wise.

## THE GRUDGE

USA/Japan, 2004
Director: Takashi Shimizu.
Producers: Takashige Ichise, Sam Raimi, Rob Tapert.
Screenplay: Stephen Susco. Music: Christopher Young.
Cinematography: Hideo Yamamoto.
Cast: Sarah Michelle Gellar, Jason Behr,
William Mapother, Clea DuVall,
KaDee Strickland, Grace Zabriskie.

After the success of **The Ring**, producer Roy Lee, eager to bring more Japanese horror to Hollywood, organized a screening of Takashi Shimizu's 2002 hit **Ju-on** for Sam Raimi, who had recently created his own production company, Ghost House. Raimi optioned the rights immediately, and recognizing that the movie's strength lies in its direction more than its script, hired the original helmer. The result, predictably, is a non-chronological succession of scares, some original, some lifted from the previous four **Ju-on** movies, adding on an investigation of the curse. In an unexpected and brilliant move, Raimi allowed Shimizu to shoot in Japan, with American actors (Sarah Michelle Gellar, Bill Pullman, KaDee Strickland) playing expats affected by the curse of the Saeki house. It seems the culture shock depicted on film was also felt off screen, as the American cast struggled to come to grips with Japan's far less regimented filmmaking habits, and Shimizu fought, for the most part successfully, to keep his effects practical, instead of the CGI approach his producers favoured. Chaos however must have somehow benefitted the movie, as audiences worldwide flocked to theatres to enjoy its quick succession of scares. **The Grudge** was followed by two American sequels, with a reboot in the works.

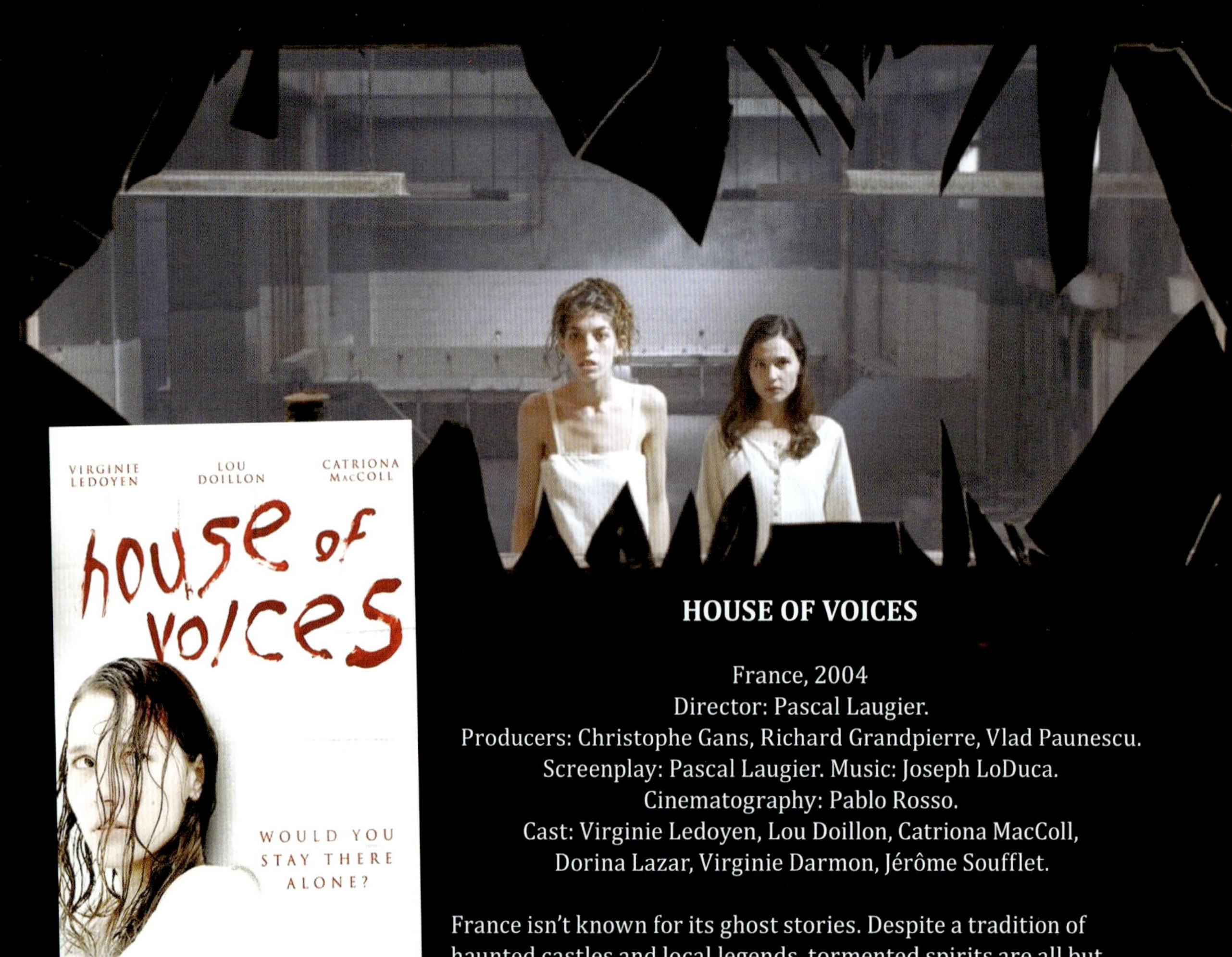


## HOUSE OF VOICES

France, 2004
Director: Pascal Laugier.
Producers: Christophe Gans, Richard Grandpierre, Vlad Paunescu.
Screenplay: Pascal Laugier. Music: Joseph LoDuca.
Cinematography: Pablo Rosso.
Cast: Virginie Ledoyen, Lou Doillon, Catriona MacColl,
Dorina Lazar, Virginie Darmon, Jérôme Soufflet.

France isn't known for its ghost stories. Despite a tradition of haunted castles and local legends, tormented spirits are all but absent from French film and literature. The rare exception to the rule, **House of Voices**, from French writer-director Pascal Laugier, best known for helming 2008 torture shocker **Martyrs**, showcases a gentler, softer side of the filmmaker's talents. Laugier met producer Richard Grandpierre on the set of Christophe Gans's **Brotherhood of the Wolf** (2001), for which he shot the behind-the-scenes featurette. Grandpierre encouraged him to focus on getting his first feature off the ground, and Gans himself offered to lend his name to the picture. Set in 1958, the story follows a pregnant girl (Virginie Ledoyen, **The Beach**) who finds a new home at the old, nearly deserted orphanage of Saint Ange, in the French Alps. Shot in Romania, both in French and in English, with an international audience in mind, **House of Voices** may be set in a location similar to **Fragile** (2005), **The Orphanage** (2007) or **The Awakening** (2011), but unlike its contemporaries, the movies it pays homage to are amongst others the works of Lucio Fulci, whose muse Catriona MacColl cameos as the headmistress.

## R-POINT

South Korea, 2004
Director: Kong Su-chang. Producer: Choi Kang-hyeok.
Screenplay: Kong Su-chang, Pil Yeong-woo.
Music: Dalpalan. Cinematography: Seok Hyeong-jing.
Cast: Kam Woo-seong, Son Byung-ho, Lee Sun-kyun, Park Won-sang, Oh Tae-kyung, Song Jin-ho.

Part of a brief early 2000s mini-trend of troops-against-supernatural movies (along with Britain's **The Bunker**, 2001; **Deathwatch** and **Dog Soldiers**, 2002), Korean entry **R-Point** takes place in 1972 Vietnam, when after receiving a distress call, a South Korean squad head to an area known as Romeo-Point on a rescue mission to find a platoon of soldiers presumed to have died six months prior. For his first feature film as director, screenwriter Kong Su-chang (**The Ring Virus**, 1999) reportedly not only battled the difficulties of a costly shoot in the Cambodian jungle, but also managed pressure from investors leery of the movie's serious tone at a time when lighter efforts fared better at the Korean box office. Yet despite its troubled shoot, **R-Point** is an extremely effective chiller, giving familiar elements (including spooky long-haired girls) a fresh twist by placing them in the new, terrifying setting of an old plantation mansion in the midst of a military conflict. Its use of sound in particular, from ghostly radio transmissions to bells tied to the spirits, serves to build an atmosphere of dread. Kong's second feature **The Guard Post** four years later would see him return to the war horror sub-genre, with less success.

## RIDING THE BULLET

USA/Germany, 2004
Director: Mick Garris. Producers: Mick Garris, Brad Krevoy, David Lancaster, Greg Malcolm, Joel T. Smith, Vicki Sotheran. Screenplay: Mick Garris. Music: Nicholas Pike. Cinematography: Robert C. New. Cast: Jonathan Jackson, David Arquette, Cliff Robertson, Barbara Hershey, Erika Christensen, Barry W. Levy.

The best Stephen King adaptations are the works of filmmakers who give the material a personal interpretation. Frequent King collaborator Mick Garris (**The Stand**, **Sleepwalkers**) truly put his own spin on **Riding the Bullet**, a novella released in 2000 as the world's first mass-market e-book. After a suicide attempt and consequent stay at a hospital, university student Alan Parker (Jonathan Jackson) gets a call informing him that his mother (Barbara Hershey) has suffered a stroke. Fearing the worst, Alan hitchhikes back home and is picked up on the way by George Staub (David Arquette, surprisingly spooky), a ghostly driver who offers him a fateful choice... Drawing from his own experiences of loss and mortality, Garris takes this very simple premise and builds a heartfelt tale on family ties and the value of life, in which Alan, re-imagined as an aspiring artist (whose work on screen was created by the great Bernie Wrightson) fascinated by death, learns to cherish what he has while it lasts. A Halloween Carol in which Arquette plays the Ghost of Halloween Yet To Come, **Riding the Bullet** sits somewhere between horror and drama, neither **The Shining** nor **Stand By Me**. Released at a time when blood and guts were box office gold, the mix proved commercially unsuccessful, but this unjustly overlooked, atypical King story is worth (re)discovering.

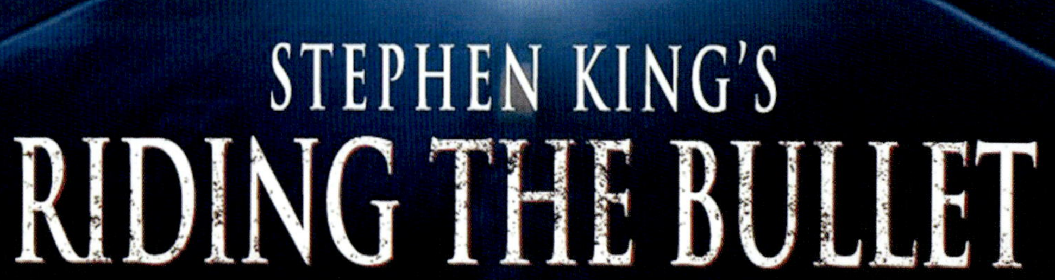

## SHUTTER

Thailand, 2004
Directors: Banjong Pisanthanakun, Parkpoom Wongpoom.
Producer: Yodphet Sudsawad. Screenplay: Parkpoom Wongpoom, Banjong Pisanthanakun, Sophon Sakdaphisit.
Music: Chatchai Pongprapaphan.
Cinematography: Niramon Ross.
Cast: Ananda Everingham, Natthaweeranuch Thongmee, Achita Sikamana, Unnop Chanpaibool, Titikarn Tongprasearth, Sivagorn Muttamara.

**Shutter** marks the debut of writers-directors Banjong Pisanthanakun and college friend Parkpoom Wongpoom, who went on to become leading figures in the Thai horror scene with ghost story **Alone** (2007) and anthology movies **4bia** (2008) and its sequel **Phobia 2** (2009). After a hit-and-run, a photographer sees his pictures haunted by a long-haired apparition; jump scares ensue. Effective if hardly original, **Shutter** uses the concept of spirit photography as a springboard for the ghostly shenanigans typical of Asian horror of the time; amusingly, one of the set pieces involves a reverse of the **Rear Window**-inspired camera flash gag also seen the same year in **Saw**. The filmmakers were reportedly inspired by pictures of the 1973 Thai popular uprising, which resulted in seventy-seven deaths; amongst images of the day were several inexplicable shapes. Real-life spirit photographs appear in the movie itself. **Shutter**'s success popularized the genre in Thailand, launching a wave of supernatural flicks. The inescapable American remake starring Joshua Jackson came out in 2008, from Japanese director Masayuki Ochiai; like **The Grudge**, the story was this time set in Japan. **Shutter** was also reimagined twice for Indian audiences: in 2007 with Tamil horror **Sivi**, and in 2010 with Hindi flop **Click**.

## FRAGILE

Spain/UK, 2005
Director: Jaume Balagueró. Producer: Joan Ginard.
Screenplay: Jaume Balagueró, Jordi Galceran.
Music: Roque Baños. Cinematography: Xavi Giménez.
Cast: Calista Flockhart, Richard Roxburgh, Elena Anaya, Gemma Jones, Yasmin Murphy, Colin McFarlane.

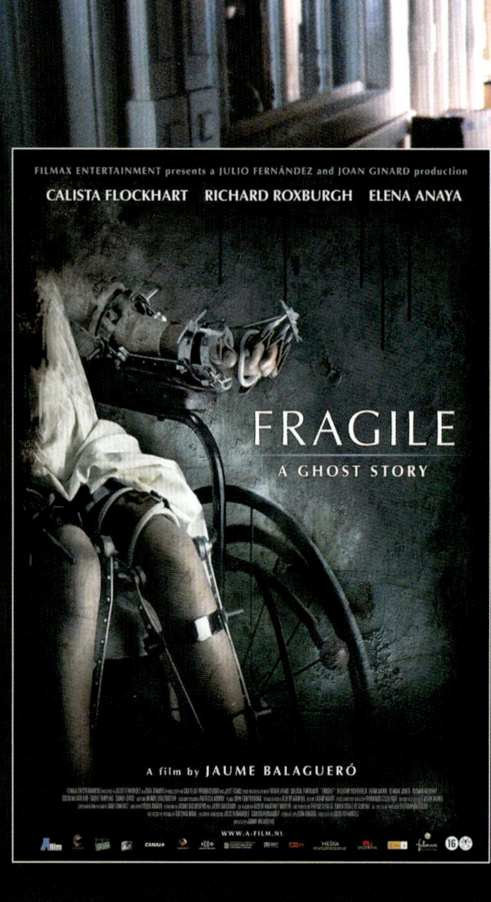

For his second English language movie (after 2002's **Darkness**), Spanish auteur Jaume Balagueró cast **Ally McBeal** star Calista Flockhart as the lead of this spooky UK-Spain co-production. Though this choice was criticized by many, Flockhart turns in a convincing performance as the caring, determined nurse who believes a spirit is hurting her young patients. Inspired by a series of old hospital photographs discovered in a friend's attic, **Fragile** is set in a rundown children's hospital on a rainy, remote island: a backdrop more in line with the Gothic tradition than the everyday, ordinary settings of the 2000s' new wave of ghost stories. The highlight of the movie is undoubtedly its villain. Revealed slowly, in close-ups or in shadows, 'the mechanical girl', as she is referred to by the children, is remarkably original in her design (although vaguely reminiscent of Marilyn Manson's old stage antics), with metal braces covering her body, her features stretched by a chin support. Despite a premiere at the prestigious Venice Film Festival, **Fragile** did not come out in the UK until 2007, and 2010 in the U.S. By then Balagueró had already risen to fame with found footage zombie movie **[REC]** (co-directed with Paco Plaza), whose success would almost single-handedly pull back production company Filmax (also involved in **Fragile**) from the brink of bankruptcy.

## THE MAID

Singapore, 2005
Director: Kelvin Tong. Producers: Pui Yin Chan, Titus Ho, Saw Yam Seah. Screenplay: Kelvin Tong.
Music: Joe Ng, Alex Oh. Cinematography: Lucas Jodogne.
Cast: Alessandra de Rossi, Huifang Hong, Benny Soh, Zhenwei Guan,
Mohd Haizad Bin Imram, Griffin Chan.

Eighteen-year-old Rosa (Alessandra de Rossi) moves from the Philippines to Singapore to work as a maid and lands on the first day of the Chinese Ghost Month (or Hungry Ghost Festival) during which, according to folklore, the lower realm opens and allows the dead to roam the earth. Unaware of the many unwritten customs that keep spooks at bay, she soon starts experiencing supernatural undergoings. Writer-director Kelvin Tong chose to film his second feature, possibly the first horror entirely made in Singapore, during the actual festivities; the crew made sure to light joss sticks and present offerings to ancestors on location as signs of respect for the spirits. Steeped in local culture and folklore, **The Maid** is pacey, relentlessly aims to scare, and clearly aims to compete with Western hits; Tong lists **The Exorcist** as an inspiration and a personal favourite. Half the movie is in English, the director's first language; the rest in Tagaloc and Chinese dialect Teochew. A massive hit in its homeland, **The Maid** won a number of festival awards worldwide. Tong further explored his home country's obsession with the supernatural in 2007 with spooky comedy **Men in White**, about a group of clueless ghosts haunting Singapore.

## P

UK/Thailand, 2005
Director: Paul Spurrier.
Producers: Narongsak Voraratchaikun, Panupong Dangdej.
Screenplay: Paul Spurrier. Music: Paul Spurrier.
Cinematography: Rich Moore, Paul Spurrier.
Cast: Suangporn Jaturaphut, Opal, Pisamai Pakdeevijit, Narisara Sairatanee, Amy Siriya, Paul Spurrier.

When British child actor turned filmmaker Paul Spurrier became the first Westerner to direct a movie entirely in Thailand, with a Thai crew, it was the crowning achievement of a long journey which started years prior, when he fell in love with the country. Entranced by its oddness, beliefs, customs, and contradictions, he started learning the language, working as a cinematographer on local productions while looking for investors for his project. **P** (also known as **The Possessed**) follows young orphan Dau (seventeen-year-old Suangporn Jaturaphut in her first ever role), who is forced to leave her village to work at a Bangkok go-go bar and uses her black magic powers to survive, but unwillingly unleashes something she cannot control. The title refers to *phii* (the Thai word for ghost, pronounced pee). Thai spirits come in many shapes and varieties; the one chosen here is a *phii bawb*, which possessed its victims and makes them yearn for raw flesh. Eager to be respectful of local traditions, Spurrier had the clapperboard, camera equipment, and cast and crew blessed a couple of days before the shoot. For all his efforts however, the movie was banned in Thailand, its subject matter clashing with the government's latest campaign to clean up the country's image.

## REINCARNATION

Japan, 2005
Director: Takashi Shimizu.
Producer: Takashige Ichise. Screenplay: Takashi Shimizu, Masaki Adachi. Music: Kenji Kawai.
Cinematography: Takahide Shibanushi.
Cast: Yûka, Karina, Kippei Shîna, Tetta Sugimoto, Shun Oguri, Marika Matsumoto.

Given how many film sets are reputedly haunted and how many deceased Hollywood celebrities have reportedly been sighted over the years, it is perhaps surprising that there aren't all that many ghost movies set around the motion picture industry. More intriguing yet is the fact that the rare examples (this feature, as well as Hideo Nakata's **Don't Look Up**) come from Japan.

Directed by no less than **Ju-on** filmmaker Takashi Shimizu, **Reincarnation** follows the crew of a movie re-enacting a mass murder in the very hotel it took place, thirty-five years after the events. Part of the *J-Horror Theater* series produced by **Ring** and **Ju-on** producer Takashige Ichise between 2004 and 2010, Shimizu's picture echoes the genre's thematic distrust of media and modern technology, but distinguishes itself by drawing inspiration from the likes of **The Shining**, and peppers the story with spooky gags such as the floating faces surrounding a car crash, or the distorted features of an apparition in the fish eye of a door peephole. Shimizu also turns the story into an interesting *mise en abyme*; on set, the crew resorted to various rituals, such as eating red rice, to protect the shoot and ward off spirits.

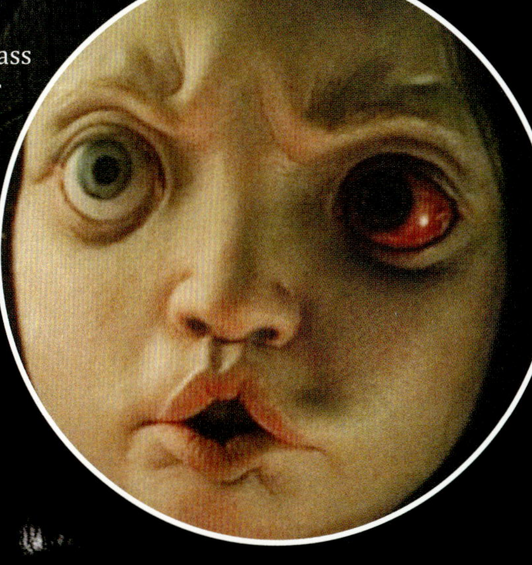

## WHITE NOISE

UK/Canada/USA, 2005
Director: Geoffrey Sax.
Producers: Paul Brooks, Shawn Williamson.
Screenplay: Niall Johnson. Music: Claude Foisy.
Cinematography: Chris Seager.
Cast: Michael Keaton, Chandra West, Deborah Kara Unger, Ian McNeice, Sarah Strange, Nicholas Elia.

The Japanese weren't the only ones to experience supernatural interferences with their technology at the start of the new millennium. **Ring** had its haunted videotape, **One Missed Call** its killer phones, and Michael Keaton heard the voices of the dead in audio recordings in this Universal production. Keaton plays Jonathan Rivers, an architect whose wife disappears overnight. He is contacted by Raymond Price (Ian McNeice), who tells him she has died and left him messages through electronic voice phenomena (EVP). Suspicious at first, Rivers soon grows obsessed with making contact, but discovers to his dismay that the souls who attempt to communicate are not all well-intentioned. More thriller than horror, with some very mild scares and a structure closer to a detective investigation than a ghost story, **White Noise** however highlights a phenomenon both fascinating and largely under explored in fiction: EVP, communication by spirits through tape recorders or other electronic devices, generally in ambient noise or static. British TV director Geoffrey Sax's movie may not make full use of EVP's potential for frights, yet it was enough of a box office hit, despite a January release (back then the traditional dumping ground for genre pictures studios didn't expect to see perform), to warrant an unrelated second chapter, **White Noise 2: The Light**, starring Nathan Fillion.

## THE BABY'S ROOM

Spain, 2006
Director: Álex de la Iglesia. Producer: Julio Fernández.
Screenplay: Jorge Guerricaechevarría, Álex de la Iglesia.
Music: Roque Baños. Cinematography: José L. Moreno.
Cast: Javier Gutiérrez, Leonor Watling, Sancho Gracia,
María Asquerino, Antonio Dechent, Terele Pávez.

Following the success of Mick Garris's *Masters of Horror* in the U.S., the *6 Films to Keep You Awake* (*Películas para no dormir*) television series offered Spanish viewers six episodes directed by some of the country's most successful and promising genre filmmakers, including Paco Plaza (the **[REC]** series), Jaume Balagueró (**Darkness**, **Fragile**), Narciso Ibáñez Serrador (**Who Can Kill a Child?**, 1976), and Enrique Urbizu (perhaps best known for penning the screenplay of Roman Polanski's 1999 **The Ninth Gate**). The full-length, unrelated tales followed the concept of *Stories to Keep You Awake (Historias para no dormir)*, which ran on TVE1 from 1966 to 1982 and saw, amongst others, adaptations of the works of Ray Bradbury and Edgar Allan Poe. A couple of stories from the 2006 series deal directly with our subject matter: **Spectre**, by Mateo Gil (writer of Alejandro Amenábar's **Open Your Eyes** and **The Sea Inside**), is a genre-bending supernatural romance where the ghosts may be manifestations of the protagonist's guilt and regrets; while Álex de la Iglesia (**The Day of the Beast**, **The Last Circus**) on the other hand terrifies his audience with **The Baby's Room**: a simple, effective haunted house story where a young father starts hearing odd noises through the baby monitor..

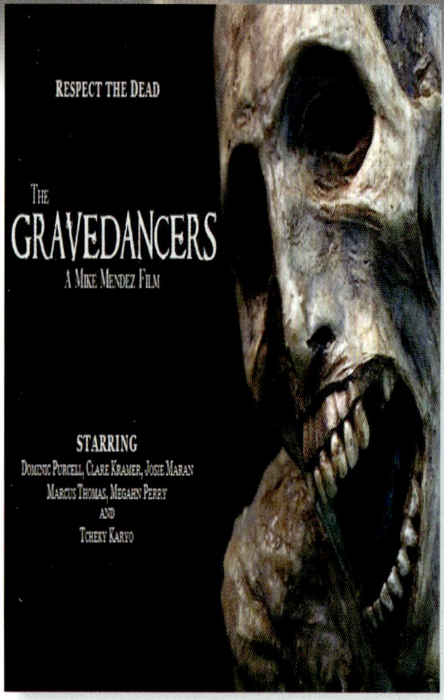

## THE GRAVEDANCERS

USA, 2006
Director: Mike Mendez. Producers: Al Corley, Lawrence Elmer Fuhrmann Jr., Bill McCutchen, Eugene Musso, Bart Rosenblatt.
Screenplay: Brad Keene, Chris Skinner.
Music: Joseph Bishara. Cinematography: David A. Armstrong.
Cast: Dominic Purcell, Josie Maran, Clare Kramer, Marcus Thomas, Tchéky Karyo, Megahn Perry.

Some unfortunate souls stumble into haunted houses, unaware; others bring their misfortune upon themselves through disregard for unwritten rules. Former college friends Harris (Dominic Purcell), Kira (Josie Maran) and Sid (Marcus Thomas) should have known better than to dance in a graveyard after a funeral, and are now persecuted by the spirits of a serial killer, an axe murderer and a pyromaniac. Director Mike Mendez is best known for his unique blend of humour and gore with movies such as **The Convent** (2000), **Big Ass Spider!** (2013) and **Don't Kill It** (2017); but **The Gravedancers**, his homage to **Poltergeist**, is an attempt at more mainstream, straight-faced horror. First envisioned at a time when evil, scary ghosts were few and far between, the movie took over five years to bring to the screen, only securing financing in the wake of the success of **The Grudge** (2004). It is perhaps most memorable for its fantastic, wide-grinned, Disney Haunted Mansion-inspired spooks, and its over-the-top finale. Joseph Bishara, who collaborated with Mendez on **The Convent**, would go on to collaborate with James Wan on the **Insidious** and **The Conjuring** franchises and become one of the genre's most in demand composers, as well as appearing in full prosthetic make-up as various demons in the movies.

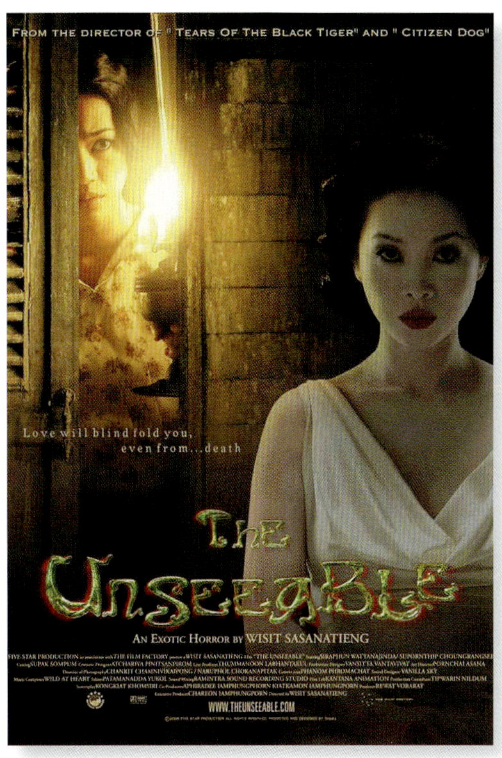

## THE UNSEEABLE

Thailand, 2006
Director: Wisit Sasanatieng.
Producers: Rewat Vorarat, Chareon Iamphungporn.
Screenplay: Kongkiat Khomsiri. Music: Wild at Heart.
Cinematography: Chankit Chanivikaipong.
Cast: Supornthip Choungrangsee, Siraphun Wattanajinda, Tassawan Seneewongse, Sombatsara Teerasaroch.

After a couple of highly colourful, genre-defying pictures (**Tears of the Black Tiger**, 2000, and **Citizen Dog**, 2004), acclaimed filmmaker Wisit Sasanatieng changed gears with pulpy ghost story **The Unseeable**, a work for hire he directed to keep himself occupied while waiting for more personal projects to come to fruition. In 1930s Siam, a pregnant country girl (Siraphun Wattanajinda) searching for her missing husband finds shelter in a mysterious suburban estate run by a domineering caretaker and a reclusive widow. Working on a much lower budget than he's accustomed to, Sasanatieng crafts a Gothic tale in the vein of Western classics such as **The Others** or **Wuthering Heights**, yet deeply rooted in local folklore and beliefs, like many Thai horrors, and playing on every ghostly cliché in the book. The Asian twist on a familiar storyline, along with its moody cinematography steeped in muted, earthy tones, truly elevate what could have otherwise been a fairly run of the mill entry. The look and atmosphere in fact pay homage to the works of Thai illustrator Hem Vejakorn (1904-1969), to the extent that the filmmaker ran afoul of the artist's copyright holders: a situation he solved by arguing his picture wasn't a direct adaptation of Vejakorn's tales.

## ALONE

Thailand, 2007
Directors: Banjong Pisanthanakun, Parkpoom Wongpoom.
Producers: Mingmonkul Sonakul,
Yodphet Sudsawad, Yongyoot Thongkongtoon.
Screenplay: Aummaraporn Phandintong, Banjong Pisanthanakun,
Sophon Sakdaphisit, Parkpoom Wongpoom.
Music: Chatchai Pongprapaphan. Cinematography: Niramon Ross.
Cast: Marsha Wattanapanich, Vittaya Wasukraipaisan,
Rachanu Boonchuduang, Hatairat Egereff, Rutairat Egereff,
Namo Tongkumnerd.

Guilt, grief and family are oft-explored themes in the horror genre, but rarely are they expressed in such extreme, literal ways as in this story of a former conjoined twin struggling to adjust to her new life after the operation which separated her from — and killed — her sister. Starring Thai-German pop singer Marsha Wattanapanich (who also sings the end credits), **Alone** (original title **Faet**, which translates as 'Twin') is reportedly derived from Agatha Christie's Hercule Poirot novel *Elephants Can Remember*, whose plot centres around a psychotic identical twin. Famous nineteenth century Siamese twins Chang and Eng Bunker are still a large part of Thai culture (the term 'Siamese' comes from Siam, the old name of Thailand), and also served as inspiration for the story. **Alone** marks the last directing effort as a duo of Thai horror sensations Banjong Pisanthanakun and Parkpoom Wongpoom (**Shutter**), who later directed separate segments of anthology movies **4bia** and **Phobia 2**, before Pisanthanakun went on to helm 2013's **Pee Mak**, as well as a couple of non-genre pictures, on his own. Like the filmmakers's previous horror hit **Shutter**, **Alone** got the remake treatment twice in India: **Chaarulatha** (2012) in Kannada and Tamil, and **Alone** (2015) in Hindi.

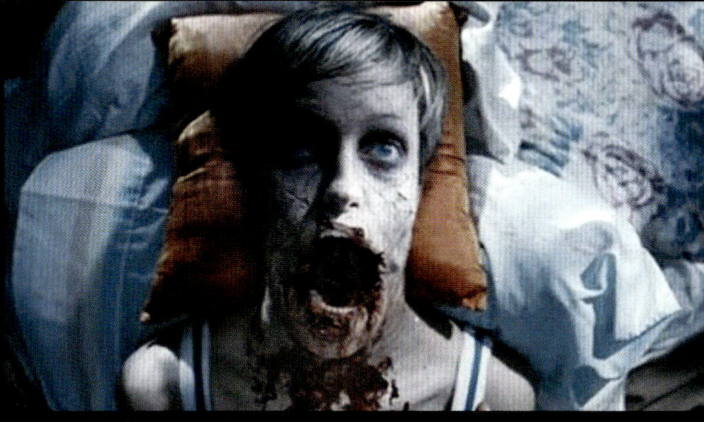

## DEAD SILENCE

USA, 2007
Director: James Wan.
Producers: Mark Burg, Gregg Hoffman, Oren Koules.
Screenplay: Leigh Whannell.
Music: Charlie Clouser.
Cinematography: John R. Leonetti.
Cast: Ryan Kwanten, Amber Valletta, Donnie Wahlberg, Michael Fairman, Joan Heney, Bob Gunton.

Australian writer-director James Wan and co-writer Leigh Whannell shifted gears after 2004's **Saw** with this old school, spooky throwback to Hammer films, **The Twilight Zone**, and **Poltergeist**. Born out of Wan's obsession with dolls (as a side note, his Twitter handle is @creepypuppet), and industry pressure to sign a new movie deal before the first **Saw** came out in theaters, this tale of a dummy possessed by the ghost of its ventriloquist (Judith Roberts as the chilling Mary Shaw) marked the duo's first big studio experience. Sadly, they found that larger budgets came with strings attached: reports of script doctoring and interference from Universal — the same company which would later cement Wan's A-list status with **Furious 7** — abound, confirmed by Whannell himself, who four years after its release called it 'the worst experience [he had] ever had'. Regardless, **Dead Silence** is filled with great imagery and effective set pieces, including a thrilling cat and mouse sequence in a crawlspace, and a blink-and-you'll-miss-it cameo from Billy, the puppet from **Saw**. Most fascinating perhaps today is seeing Wan develop many of the tricks and techniques he would later refine to great effect for the hugely successful **Insidious** and **Conjuring** franchises.

## GHOST SON

Italy/South Africa/Spain/UK, 2007
Director: Lamberto Bava. Producers: Pino Gargiulo, Enzo Giulioli, Marco Guidone.
Screenplay: Silvia Ranfagni, Lamberto Bava. Music: Paolo Vivaldi. Cinematography: Giovanni Canevari.
Cast: Laura Harring, John Hannah, Pete Postlethwaite, Coralina Cataldi-Tassoni,
Mosa Kaiser, Laura Susanne Ruedeberg.

Lamberto Bava (**Demons**) has made himself scarce on the big screen since the early nineties, working primarily in Italian television, but briefly came out of semi-retirement in the mid-2000s for gory, aptly titled shocker **The Torturer** (2005), and **Ghost Son**, an Italian-British-Spanish-South African co-production which the filmmaker described primarily as a fantasy and a love story. The plot is reminiscent of **Shock** (1977), a movie he'd written for his illustrious father and helped direct. After losing her husband Mark (John Hannah) under tragic circumstances, Stacey (Laura Harring) finds out she's pregnant, is plagued by visions of Mark encouraging her to kill herself, and eventually gives birth to a baby boy, only to grow increasingly convinced that the child is possessed by her late husband's spirit. Yet for the main part, the tone is more akin to melodrama than horror, the emphasis on Stacey's state of mind rather than stylistic flourishes; before veering into Grand Guignol once she starts getting bitten by her son while breast-feeding and poked by baby boners in the shower. Harring gives the role her all, and the South African setting, then in the midst of an international production boom, lends the picture a unique flavour.

## THE ORPHANAGE

Spain, 2007
Director: J.A. Bayona. Producers: Álvaro Augustin, Joaquín Padró, Mar Targarona.
Screenplay: Sergio G. Sánchez. Music: Fernando Velázquez. Cinematography: Oscar Faura.
Cast: Belén Rueda, Fernando Cayo, Roger Príncep, Mabel Rivera, Montserrat Carulla, Andrés Gertrúdix.

Spanish director Juan Antonio Bayona was only eighteen when, working as a freelance reporter, he interviewed Guillermo del Toro at the Sitges Film Festival and saw him as a mentor, remaining in touch with him throughout the years. He went on to direct music videos, until the script for **The Orphanage**, written by Sergio G. Sánchez, landed on his lap. This gothic tale of Laura, a mother (Belén Rueda) whose child mysteriously disappears from the old mansion they recently moved into was bound to appeal to del Toro, and the Mexican filmmaker agreed to help produce the picture, whose themes of childhood, innocence lost, and grief echo those of his works. His involvement allowed Bayona to raise a higher budget and film for ten weeks, a significant length for a first picture, on location in Northern Spain and on a soundstage in Barcelona. Largely inspired by Jack Clayton's **The Innocents** and Henry James's *The Turn of the Screw*, **The Orphanage**, in the great tradition of 1960s/1970s ghost stories, purposefully remains ambiguous as to whether the house is haunted or Laura's sanity is to blame. The second highest opening in Spain's history and winner of seven Goya awards, **The Orphanage** launched its director onto the international scene. An American remake was naturally announced upon U.S. release, with Mark Pellington and Larry Fessenden attached to helm at various points, but at time of writing the project appears to have stalled.

## PARANORMAL ACTIVITY

USA, 2007
Director: Oren Peli. Producers: Jason Blum, Oren Peli.
Screenplay: Oren Peli. Cinematography: Oren Peli.
Cast: Katie Featherston, Micah Sloat, Mark Fredrichs,
Amber Armstrong, Ashley Palmer,
Crystal Cartwright [uncredited].

The franchise that nearly never was, **Paranormal Activity** had the most humble beginnings of any in this book. First-time director Oren Peli filmed this story of a couple (played by Katie Featherston and Micah Sloat) experiencing demonic disturbances, over the course of seven days and nights, on a video camera operated for the most part by Sloat himself. A few festival screenings built strong word of mouth before Jason Blum and DreamWorks, impressed by Peli's resourcefulness, acquired the picture with the intention to remake it on a larger budget. A couple of test screenings, which saw terrified viewers leave the room in droves, convinced the producers to release the original instead. Peli's $15,000 picture was given a proper budget to enhance sound and visual effects, and film a new ending. The result, distributed in 2009 by parent company Paramount, is a case study in ingenuity and barebone scares: the camera is for the most part stationary, the framing wide and the sound diegetic, maximizing realism. The franchise now includes prequels (**Paranormal Activity 2**, 2010; **Paranormal Activity 3**, 2011), sequels (**Paranormal Activity 4**, 2012, and **Paranormal Activity: The Ghost Dimension**, 2015), and spin-offs (**Paranormal Activity: The Marked Ones**, 2014).

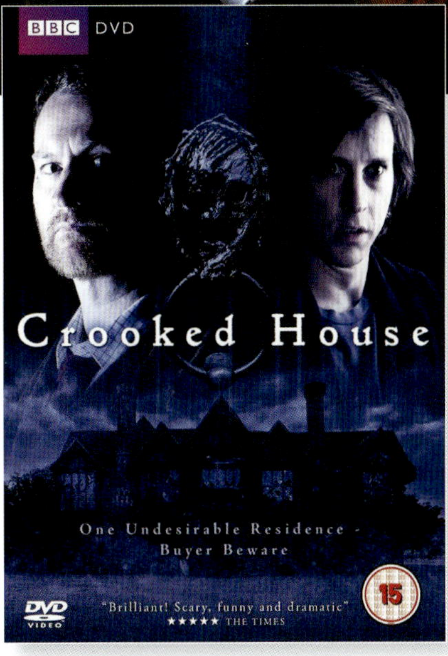

## CROOKED HOUSE

UK, 2008
Director: Damon Thomas.
Producers: Paul Frift, Mark Gatiss. Screenplay: Mark Gatiss.
Music: David Arnold, Michael Price. Cinematography: Ian Moss.
Cast: Lee Ingleby, Mark Gatiss, Derren Brown, Beth Goddard, Vanessa Havell, Philip Jackson.

Inspired by the works of M.R. James and the BBC tradition of Christmas ghost stories, **Crooked House**, an anthology movie aired in three parts on BBC Four in December 2008, is by nature meant for a much broader audience than the vast majority of features reviewed in these pages. Suspense is therefore mild and gore kept to a minimum, yet writer-producer Mark Gatiss (**Sherlock**) playfully manipulates clichés and expectations with these stories centered on the tragic events which have unfolded at the fictional Geap Manor throughout the last 300 years, and the house's influence to this day. 'The Wainscoting', set in the 18th century, introduces the original owner as his discovers that the timbers of the building are made of wood from the notorious Tyburn hanging tree. 'Something Old', about a couple announcing their engagement, to his family's dismay, during a party at the house in the 1920s, is the most overtly ghostly and arguably the most fun, with spectral brides, old curses, and a hint of repressed homosexuality. Starring the fantastic Jean Marsh (**Upstairs Downstairs**), it also makes the most out of its stunning location, Dorney Court, a Tudor house on the outskirts of London. Finally, 'The Knocker' brings the action into present day, and neatly wraps up the story with one last surprise.

## LAKE MUNGO

Australia, 2008
Director: Joel Anderson.
Producers: Georgie Nevile, David Rapsey.
Screenplay: Joel Anderson. Music: David Paterson.
Cinematography: John Brawley.
Cast: Rosie Traynor, David Pledger, Martin Sharpe, Talia Zucker, Tania Lentini, Cameron Strachan.

A perfect example of ideas making up for lack of budget, **Lake Mungo** was Australian first timer Joel Anderson's gear change after years unsuccessfully gathering financing for a more ambitious project. Filmed documentary style using a variety of formats (16mm, 35mm and Super 8 film; phone cameras; beta cam; VHS), and largely improvised, it opens with images of nineteenth century spirit photography, immediately grounding the story in a long history of ghostly media manipulation. We then follow the Palmers from Ararat, Victoria, who, after the accidental drowning of 16-year-old sister/daughter Alice (Talia Zucker), see her appear on photographs and videos recorded after her death. While the ghostly nature of these images is debated, Alice's personality is seen under a new light, as details of her secret life emerges... **Lake Mungo** lends itself to interpretation and reveals its layers slowly, subtly adding depth with each plot twist. At its core the study of a family dealing with loss, it looks at the stages of grief each member goes through in their own way, while touching upon the souvenirs we keep, how they affect our recollections, and how we choose to remember loved ones. No cheap scares to be found here; only an atmosphere of creeping dread and pervasive sadness, and a sense that things are never as they seem.

## THE ECLIPSE

Ireland, 2009
Director: Conor McPherson. Producer: Robert Walpole.
Screenplay: Conor McPherson, Billy Roche.
Music: Fionnuala Ní Chiosáin. Cinematography: Ivan McCullough.
Cast: Billy Roche, Eanna Hardwicke, Hannah Lynch,
Ciarán Hinds, Avian Egan, Aidan Quinn.

Ghost stories have always offered fitting metaphors for grief, but Irish playwright Conor McPherson's character drama **The Eclipse** takes the concept to another level. Widowed father of two Michael Farr (Ciarán Hinds) starts feeling a presence in his house at night. He volunteers at a local literary festival, where he's assigned to guide Lena Morelle (Iben Hjejle), a writer of supernatural novels, around town. They talk about ghosts, life, and lost ones, and soon develop feelings for each other, but she is entangled in a relationship with married bestselling author Nicholas Holden (Aidan Quinn), also a guest of the festival. A movie about ghosts more than a ghost movie, **The Eclipse**, shot in Cobh, near Cork, for a budget of 2 million euros, is a subtle, low-key, beautifully photographed story about a couple of grown-ups haunted by little more than the memories of the past. This slow-burn approach makes its few jump scares all the more startling, if rather incongruous. Based on a short story by fellow playwright Billy Roche, who also appears in a small role, the film, despite introducing a supernatural element and being reportedly inspired by the likes of Friedkin and Polanski, is never as powerful as when it lets its character drama play out, culminating in a simple yet devastating climax scene, in which Michael finally finds some closure for his loss.

## THE LOVELY BONES

USA/UK/New Zealand, 2009
Director: Peter Jackson. Producers: Carolynne Cunningham, Peter Jackson, Aimée Peyronnet, Fran Walsh. Screenplay: Fran Walsh, Philippa Boyens, Peter Jackson. Music: Brian Eno. Cinematography: Andrew Lesnie. Cast: Mark Wahlberg, Rachel Weisz, Susan Sarandon, Stanley Tucci, Michael Imperioli, Saoirse Ronan.

After his initial eight-year-long Middle Earth battle and the epics of **King Kong** (2005), Peter Jackson turned his attention to a smaller-scale, more intimate drama with **The Lovely Bones**, adapted from a 2002 best-selling novel by Alice Sebold. Following Susie, a raped and murdered teenage girl watching from limbo the events unfolding after her death, the story appealed to the filmmaker through its optimistic tone, in strong contrast with its difficult, sad subject matter, and struck him as an opportunity to step away from blockbusters and go back to the type of emotional fare he'd explored with great success in **Heavenly Creatures** (1994). Luc Besson (**Leon: The Professional**) and Lynne Ramsay (**We Need to Talk About Kevin**) had both been previously attached to direct; after Ramsay's exit and Jackson's attachment, major studios competed to finance the project, with DreamWorks eventually buying the rights. Amongst the main elements the movie changed, the afterlife – described as mundane on the page – became surreal and fantastical, adapting to Susie's changing moods. Co-starring Mark Wahlberg, Rachel Weisz, Susan Sarandon and Stanley Tucci, **The Lovely Bones** failed to impress critics or make its mark at the box office, but offered a break-out role to its young star, then fifteen-year-old Irish actor Saoirse Ronan.

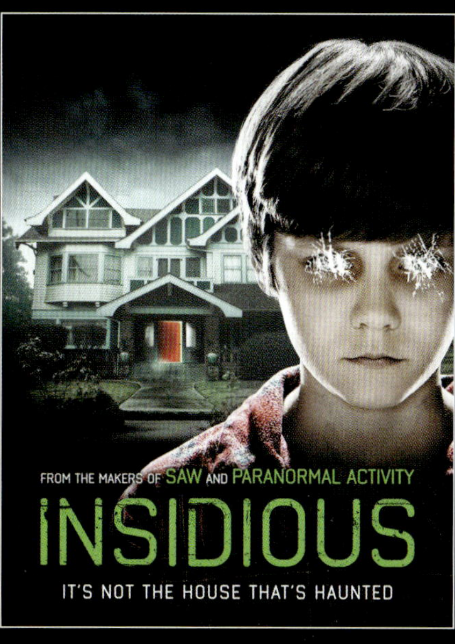

## INSIDIOUS

USA/Canada/UK, 2010
Director: James Wan.
Producers: Jason Blum, Oren Peli, Steven Schneider.
Screenplay: Leigh Whannell. Music: Joseph Bishara.
Cinematography: David M. Brewer, John R. Leonetti.
Cast: Patrick Wilson, Rose Byrne, Ty Simpkins,
Lin Shaye, Leigh Whannell, Angus Sampson.

'It's not the house that's haunted.' This logline, at the center of **Insidious**'s clever marketing campaign, hints at the twist: Patrick Wilson and Rose Byrne's son Dalton (Ty Simpkins) can project into an astral dimension called the Further, from which he unwittingly brings back souls of the dead. A major gamble and return to indie roots for **Saw** director James Wan and screenwriter-star Leigh Whannell after the consecutive box office disappointments of studio pictures **Dead Silence** and **Death Sentence**, **Insidious** placed the Australian duo back at the top of the horror firmament. Produced by the team behind **Paranormal Activity**, it also sealed Jason Blum's reputation as one of the most powerful genre producers of the decade, thanks to the simple but remarkably efficient model it pioneered: offering an experienced filmmaker full control and high back-end on a small budget, with distribution provided through a studio (in this case Sony Pictures). Shot in Los Angeles over the course of three weeks, **Insidious** eschews the graphic violence of Wan and Whannell's previous indie hit, in favour of atmosphere and effective jump scares, with a strident, terrifying score by Joseph Bishara (Mike Mendez's **The Convent**, 2000, and **The Gravedancers**, 2006), who also appears as the main demon. The movie also surprisingly crowned Farrelly Brothers favourite Lin Shaye, starring as demonologist Elise, as the new reigning Queen of Horror. Three sequels to date (**Insidious: Chapter 2**, 2013; **Insidious: Chapter 3**, 2015, directed by Whannell; and **Insidious: The Last Key**, 2018, directed by Adam Robitel) have explored the Further.

## THE SILENT HOUSE

Uruguay, 2010
Director: Gustavo Hernández. Producer: Gustavo Rojo.
Screenplay: Oscar Estévez. Music: Hernán González.
Cinematography: Pedro Luque.
Cast: Florencia Colucci, Abel Tripaldi,
Gustavo Alonso, María Salazar.

Uruguayan scarefest **The Silent House** (aka **La casa muda**) from first-time director Gustavo Hernández, is a case study in making the most out of limited resources. Shot over four days for a reported budget of $6,000, it follows Laura (Florencia Colucci) and her father Wilson (Gustavo Alonso) in real time as they explore, then find themselves locked into, a secluded cottage they intend to repair. The film is presented as one continuous set-up, a gimmick pioneered by Alfred Hitchcock's 1948 thriller **Rope**, and which helps keep the pace up and the action tense and contained. Part home invasion, part psychological thriller, **The Silent House** uses classic haunted house tropes, from bumps in the night to ghostly little girls. In one of its most effective and oft-copied scares, Laura uses the flash of a Polaroid camera to see her attacker in complete darkness; an idea likely inspired by **Rear Window**, and first used in **Saw** (2004), then in **Mama** (2013). Yet the finale twists the story into a different direction altogether, which, although not entirely satisfying in its logic, is certainly refreshing. Screened in Cannes as part of the Directors' Fortnight, then in festivals and theatres around the world, **The Silent House** received the inevitable remake in 2012, starring Elizabeth Olsen.

## THE AWAKENING

UK, 2011
Director: Nick Murphy.
Producers: Sarah Curtis, Julia Stannard, David M. Thompson.
Screenplay: Stephen Volk, Nick Murphy.
Music: Daniel Pemberton. Cinematography: Eduard Grau.
Cast: Rebecca Hall, Dominic West, Imelda Staunton, Isaac Hempstead Wright, Shaun Dooley, Joseph Mawle.

Despite its long tradition of ghost stories in literature and on screen, the United Kingdom had been conspicuously absent from the new wave of haunted houses and vengeful spirits — until 2011's **The Awakening**. Set in the aftermath of the First World War — 'a time for ghosts', as the introduction crawl reminds us — this old-fashioned tale of a woman with a dark past attempting to debunk a haunting at a boarding school boasts an excellent pedigree: written by Stephen Volk of **Ghostwatch** fame, directed by BAFTA winner Nick Murphy (who also wrote a draft of the script, adding the doll house scenes and the red ball bouncing down the stairs), and starring Rebecca Hall, Dominic West and Imelda Staunton. James Watkins (**Eden Lake**) was initially attached to direct, but then left to focus on Hammer's adaptation of **The Woman in Black**. Developed over fifteen years under various titles, Volk's screenplay started its life as a sequel to 1961's **The Innocents**, following a grown-up Flora coming to terms with the events of her childhood. Originated in the late nineties, and revived in the next decade thanks to Britain's horror resurgence, the project was eventually picked up by BBC Films, who requested Volk severed all ties with *The Turn of the Screw*, which they feared viewers may not be familiar with.

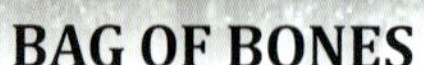

## BAG OF BONES

USA, 2011
Director: Mick Garris. Producer: Michael Mahoney.
Screenplay: Stephen King, Matt Venne.
Music: Nicholas Pike. Cinematography: Barry Donlevy.
Cast: Pierce Brosnan, Melissa George, Annabeth Gish,
Anika Noni Rose, Matt Frewer, Jason Priestley.

Another entry based on the works of Stephen King, this A&E two-part mini-series stars Pierce Brosnan as best-selling author Mike Noonan who grieves the death of his wife, and is haunted by visions of the dead while working on a new book at the couple's lakeside retreat. Set in Maine, like most of King's output, but shot in Nova Scotia, **Bag of Bones** was a passion project for Garris, who initially pushed to adapt the 1998 novel, which had first been optioned by Bruce Willis, as a feature. But studio horror at the time was, according to the filmmaker, very much based around teenagers, which made this grown-up tale particularly challenging to finance. Luckily the longer running time of a two-parter better suited this emotionally complex story which touches upon ideas of loss, racism and social justice.

Filled with references to King's universe, **Bag of Bones** is typically psychological and character-based, with a delicate turn from Brosnan, whose personal experience in some ways mirrors Noonan's, and appearances by Melissa George, Jason Priestley and Matt Frewer. Best known for his King adaptations (including 1992's **Sleepwalkers** and 1994's **The Stand**), director Mick Garris previously ventured into haunted territory with 1997 three-part miniseries **The Shining** and 2004's **Riding the Bullet**, both of which were based on King's works.

## HAUNTED 3D

India, 2011
Director: Vikram Bhatt. Producers: Vikram Bhatt, Arun Rangachari. Screenplay: Amin Hajee.
Music: Chirantan Bhatt. Cinematography: Pravin Bhatt.
Cast: Tia Bajpai, Krishna Bhatt, Mimoh Chakraborty, Nikita Janjani, Mohan Kapoor, Achint Kaur.

**Haunted 3D**, about a real estate agent (Mimoh Chakraborty) who falls for the beautiful spirit (Tia Bajpai) haunting the mansion he is about to sell, and travels back in time to save her, broke box office records for Hindi horror. Marketed as India's first 3D horror release, a claim which conveniently leaves aside 1984 Malayalam witchcraft pic **My Dear Kuttichathan**, and 1985 Bollywood chiller **3D Saamri**, **Haunted 3D** is the brainchild of director Vikram Bhatt (the **Raaz** and **1920** franchises, as well as several unofficial remakes of American hits), who conceived it after seeing **Avatar** in 2009. The gimmick, which was developed using the latest digital technology, presented unique challenges and ended up costing a third of the rather movie's impressive budget. Shooting on location in Ooty, a hill station in Southern India, meant that any damaged cable or camera accessory to repair would require a seven hour drive to Bangalore, the nearest metropolis; the filmmaker confessed being close to giving up and going back to 2D on several occasions. Nonetheless, Bhatt stuck to the winning formula for his next spook shows — black magic thriller **Raaz 3D** (2012) and monster pic **Creature 3D** (2014) — but failed to recapture the success of his ghost story.

## THE INNKEEPERS

USA, 2011
Director: Ti West. Producers: Derek Curl, Larry Fessenden, Peter Phok, Ti West.
Screenplay: Ti West. Music: Jeff Grace.
Cinematography: Eliot Rockett.
Cast: Sara Paxton, Pat Healy, Alison Bartlett, Jake Ryan, Kelly McGillis, Lena Dunham.

While filming 2009 indie hit **The House of the Devil**, writer-director Ti West and his crew spent a few nights at the Yankee Pedlar Inn in Torrington, Connecticut. Initially unaware of the hotel's reputation as a hotspot for paranormal activity, West quickly grew conscious of the building's unusual energy, and realized its employees believed it to be haunted. The seed for **The Innkeepers** — a character-driven story following the two employees (Sara Paxton and Pat Healy, both highly likable and amusing) left to man the front desk on the last weekend before the hotel closes — was planted into his brain. Haunted hotels are not only popular spots for real-life ghost hunters, but also a staple of genre literature, from Wilkie Collins's 1878 *The Haunted Hotel*, to Stephen King's *The Shining* and *1408*, and their screen adaptations. Known for his stylized slow-burn horrors, West gives the classic ghost story a twist by inserting very modern protagonists, nerdy minimum wage slackers searching for spirits to entertain themselves on the job. Cast and crew stayed on location during the shoot and naturally, reported a number of unexplainable incidents, from phones ringing with no one on the line, to lights switching on and off by themselves. Keep eyes peeled on the last shot of the movie, which very subtly hints at a different interpretation of its events.

## BHOOTER BHABISHYAT

India, 2012
Director: Anik Datta. Producer: Joy Ganguly.
Screenplay: Anik Datta, Deb Roy.
Music: Raja Narayan Deb.
Cinematography: Avik Mukhopadhyay.
Cast: Swastika Mukherjee, Parambrata Chatterjee, Sabyasachi Chakraborty, Samadarshi Dutta, Mumtaz Sorcar, Paran Banerjee.

Displaced ghosts who gathered inside Chowdhun House, an abandoned palace in Calcutta, now used as a film location, warn a filmmaker (Parambrata Chatterjee) of their plight when the place is set to be demolished and replaced with a shopping mall. Indian Bengali ghost comedy **Bhooter Bhabishyat** (which translates as **The Future of the Past**, or **The Future of the Ghost**) has strong social satire aspirations, as much of its humour is provided by the contrast between the spirits of various time periods and classes, from the Muslim cook, the refugee and the 1940s movie star, to the rock musician and the British officer. The story is largely told through flashbacks and, naturally, musical numbers, and characters at times speak in rhymes, in a style reminiscent of one of the movie's main inspirations, 1969 supernatural comedy **Goopy Gyne Bagha Byne**. **Bhooter Bhabishyat** marked the debut feature of Bengali commercial director Anik Dutta, who also penned the script and lyrics, and would go on to direct 2013 fantasy **Astonishing Lamp**, and 2017 thriller **The Mystery of the Murder of Meghnad**. A rare example of an ambitious supernatural adventure from Tollywood (Bengali cinema), it was remade in Bollywood (Hindi cinema) by Satish Kaushik under the title **Gang of Ghosts** in 2014.

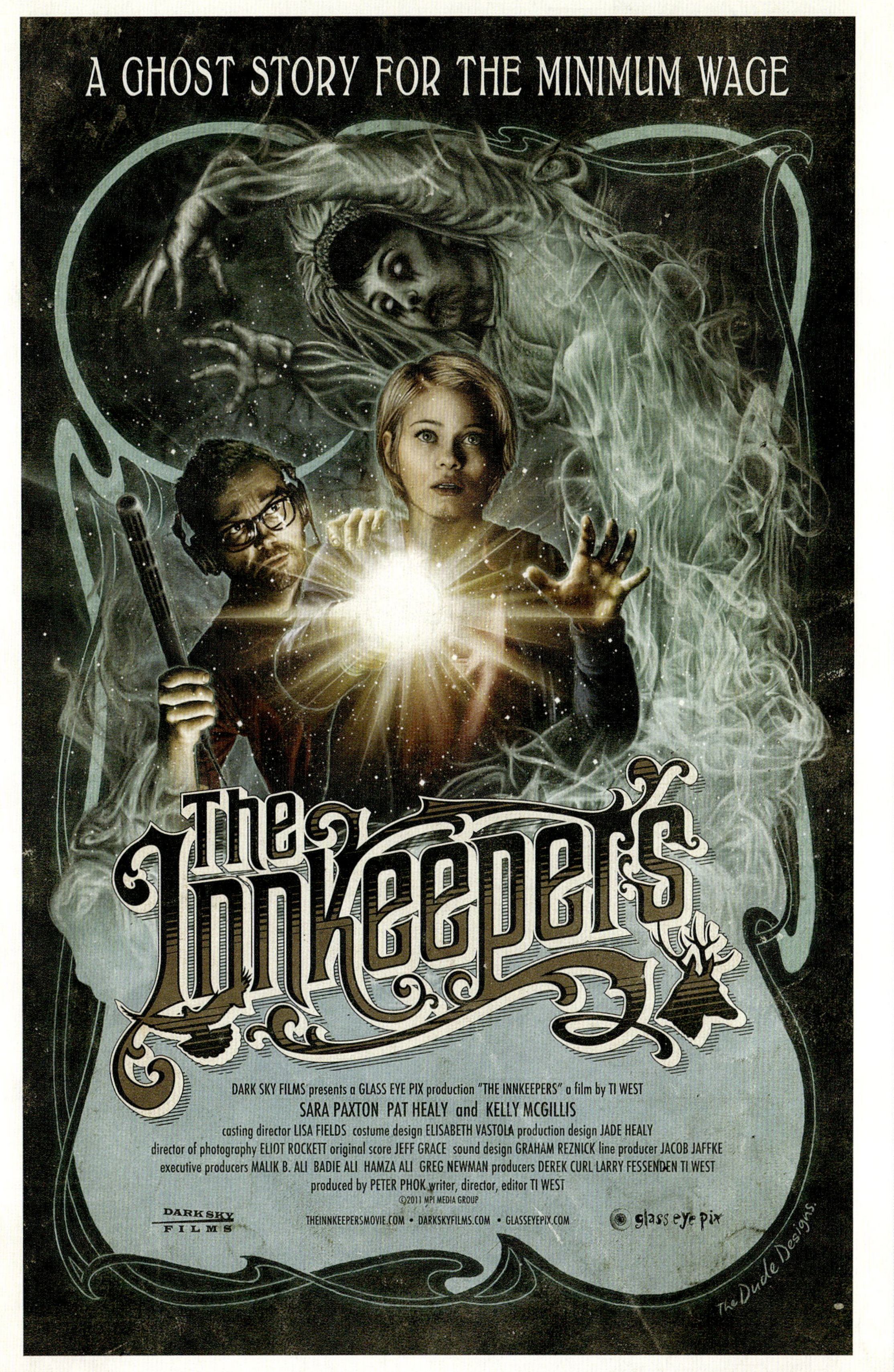
A GHOST STORY FOR THE MINIMUM WAGE
The Innkeepers
DARK SKY FILMS presents a GLASS EYE PIX production "THE INNKEEPERS" a film by TI WEST
SARA PAXTON PAT HEALY and KELLY MCGILLIS
casting director LISA FIELDS costume design ELISABETH VASTOLA production design JADE HEALY
director of photography ELIOT ROCKETT original score JEFF GRACE sound design GRAHAM REZNICK line producer JACOB JAFFKE
executive producers MALIK B. ALI BADIE ALI HAMZA ALI GREG NEWMAN producers DEREK CURL LARRY FESSENDEN TI WEST
produced by PETER PHOK writer, director, editor TI WEST
©2011 MPI MEDIA GROUP
DARK SKY FILMS
THEINNKEEPERSMOVIE.COM • DARKSKYFILMS.COM • GLASSEYEPIX.COM
glass eye pix
The Dude Designs.

## GHOST GRADUATION

Spain, 2012
Director: Javier Ruiz Caldera. Producers: Fernando Bovaira, Simón de Santiago, Sandra Hermida, Eneko Lizarraga, Edmon Roch, Francisco Sánchez Ortiz.
Screenplay: Cristóbal Garrido, Adolfo Valor.
Music: Javier Rodero. Cinematography: Arnau Valls Colomer.
Cast: Raúl Arévalo, Alexandra Jiménez, Javier Bódalo, Anna Castillo, Andrea Duro, Aura Garrido.

**The Breakfast Club** meets **The Sixth Sense** in this light and hilarious Spanish production about a teacher (Raúl Arévalo) who takes it upon himself to help the spirits of five 1980s high school kids — a jock, a pregnant girl, a bad boy, etc. — condemned to haunt the halls of their alma mater until they graduate. Filmed in a Madrid school over the summer holidays, **Ghost Graduation** (aka **Promoción fantasma**) is a joyous breath of fresh air, enhanced by an upbeat soundtrack, poking fun at the staples of the genre (possession, ghosts with unfinished business, flying objects manipulated by ghosts…) and referencing classics of both haunted house pictures and 80s teen comedies, while never going too broad or getting bogged down by its tributes. This comedic approach, beautifully executed by editor-turned-director Javier Ruiz Caldera, is radically different from Spain's traditional genre output, dominated by earnest, dramatic Gothic hauntings (**The Devil's Backbone**, **The Orphanage**, **Fragile**…) Caldera's previous release, 2009 parody **Spanish Movie**, revolved around spoofing movies ranging from **The Others** to **Pan's Labyrinth**. A minor hit in its homeland, **Ghost Graduation** premiered at the Toronto Film Festival and went on to gather festival awards around the world. An American remake produced by Will Smith's company is reportedly in the works.

## PARANORMAN

USA, 2012
Directors: Chris Butler, Sam Fell. Producers: Travis Knight, Arianne Sutner. Screenplay: Chris Butler. Music: Jon Brion. Cinematography: Tristan Oliver. Cast: Kodi Smit-McPhee (voice), Tucker Albrizzi (voice), Anna Kendrick (voice), Casey Affleck (voice), Christopher Mintz-Plasse (voice), Leslie Mann (voice).

Norman (voiced by Kodi Smit-McPhee), a lonely eleven-year-old boy with the ability to see ghosts, is all that stands between his hometown and a zombie army raised by a centuries-old witch, in this stop-motion 3D movie from Portland-based studio Laika (**Coraline**, 2009). Continuing animation's long-standing love affair with dark subject matters, **ParaNorman**, helmed by Sam Fell (**The Tale of Despereaux**, 2008) and screenwriter and first-time director Chris Butler, originated from Butler's desire to tell a zombie story for kids, inspired by *Scooby-Doo*, the films of John Carpenter, and the Amblin classics he grew up with. The first movie of its kind to make use of full-colour 3D printers, this visual effects-heavy feature pushes the boundaries of the number of locations for an animated film and the amount of characters appearing in crowd scenes, mimicking the feel of the live-action works it draws from. Like all good zombie movies, **ParaNorman** is ripe with social commentary — outsiders, fear of difference, fitting in: complex yet important topics to tackle for younger viewers — but also bursts with homages to the likes of **Halloween**, **The Evil Dead** and **Friday the 13th**, aiming to please an audience of grown-up genre fans and children alike.

## PIZZA

India, 2012
Director: Karthik Subbaraj.
Producer: C.V. Kumar.
Screenplay: Karthik Subbaraj, Prasath Ramar.
Music: Santhosh Narayanan.
Cinematography: Gopi Amarnath.
Cast: Vijay Sethupathi, Ramya Nambeeshan, Aadukalam Naren, Karunakaran, Jayakumar, Bobby Simha.

After an altercation with his ghost story-obsessed girlfriend, pizza boy Michael (Vijay Sethupathi) gets trapped in a haunted house while attempting a delivery in **Pizza**, a huge surprise hit from Tamil first-time filmmaker Karthik Subbaraj. With nods to classics such as **The Shining**, yet tonally veering more towards the likes of M. Night Shyamalan, **Silent House**, or **Paranormal Activity**, **Pizza** uses every spooky trick in the book in its first half, with eerie noises, disappearing bodies and dead cell phones as the hero fumbles his way through the darkened house; then switches gear for a murder mystery where the narrator becomes unreliable and the very existence of ghosts is questioned. Critically acclaimed and a commercial hit, the movie was remade in the Kannada language under the title **Whistle** (2013), in Hindi, starring former Miss India Parvathy Omanakuttan (2014), and in Bengali as **Golpo Holeo Shotti** (2014). It was also given a 2013 sequel, **Pizza II: Villa**, in which a different young couple face the supernatural in another house. This follow-up was written and directed by Deepan Chakravarthy, an amateur filmmaker who took it upon himself to pen a script after watching the original, and presented it to the producers in the hopes of turning **Pizza** into a franchise.

## SINISTER

USA/UK, 2012
Director: Scott Derrickson.
Producers: Jason Blum, Brian Kavanaugh-Jones.
Screenplay: Scott Derrickson, C. Robert Cargill.
Music: Christopher Young. Cinematography: Chris Norr.
Cast: Ethan Hawke, Juliet Rylance, Fred Dalton Thompson,
James Ransone, Michael Hall D'Addario, Clare Foley.

Producer Jason Blum (**Paranormal Activity**, **Insidious**) strikes gold again with **Sinister**, the terrifying story of Ellison Oswalt, a true crime writer (Ethan Hawke) who inadvertently puts his and his family's lives in danger when he opens a box of Super 8 films in the attic of the murder house they just moved in. Novelist and former Ain't It Cool News critic C. Robert Cargill pitched the concept, which came to him through a nightmare he had after watching Verbinski's 2002 **The Ring**, to director Scott Derrickson (**The Exorcism of Emily Rose**, 2005), who immediately sparked to the idea of making a classically-shot movie about a man who finds lost footage — rather than a found footage movie. The pair then brought it to Blum, who approved it immediately. Built around the incredibly chilling Super 8 movies Oswalt uncovers one at a time (the films were shot first, to set the tone for the rest of the picture), **Sinister** also features a new boogeyman, Bughuul, with his own mythology. The filmmakers drew inspiration from urban legends, as well as from the likes of Kubrick's **The Shining**, De Palma's **Blow Out**, and Mann's **Manhunter**. **Sinister 2**, from Irish director Ciarán Foy (**Citadel**, 2012) followed in 2015. Derrickson and Cargill joined forces again for 2016's **Doctor Strange**.

## THE WOMAN IN BLACK

UK/Canada/Sweden, 2012
Director: James Watkins. Producers: Richard Jackson, Simon Oakes, Brian Oliver.
Screenplay: Jane Goldman.
Music: Marco Beltrami.
Cinematography: Tim Maurice-Jones.
Cast: Emma Shorey, Molly Harmon, Ellisa Walker-Reid, Sophie Stuckey, Daniel Radcliffe, Misha Handley.

How fitting that the greatest success to date of the revived British horror label Hammer Films, known for its Gothic, period scares, would come in the form of a big-budget adaptation of Susan Hill's quintessentially English ghost story. Recently widowed lawyer Arthur Kipps (Daniel Radcliffe) travels from London to the village of Crythin Gifford to prepare the sale of Eel Marsh House, whose owner Alice Drablow just passed away. Some expressed doubt upon 21-year-old Radcliffe's casting as Kipps, his first role after the **Harry Potter** series, but the actor delivers a subtle, moody performance; his pale make-up, heavy sideburns and haggard look aging him appropriately. Atmospheric and lavishly produced, with Eel Marsh House interiors built at Pinewood and exteriors filmed all over England, **The Woman in Black** is a worthy heir to the Hammer tradition. Unlike the 1989 TV version, which revealed its titular character in broad daylight, director James Watkins (**Eden Lake**) keeps his ghost hidden for the better part of the picture, offering only glimpses in windows and glass reflections, saving her full appearance for the second half, when Kipps is stuck overnight in her house. Screenwriter Jane Goldman (**Kick-Ass**) may have taken more liberties with the source material than her TV predecessor, yet Hill this time declared herself satisfied, calling it 'a screen interpretation which remains faithful to the spirit of the book but, like the play, is true to its own medium'. A story of grief, in which every character mourns the loss of a loved one, **The Woman in Black** preserves the gloomy ending of the original story, yet infuses it with a welcome touch of hope. A sequel, **The Woman in Black 2: Angel of Death**, came out in 2014, without the involvement of Radcliffe, Goldman or Watkins.

## THE CONJURING

USA, 2013
Director: James Wan.
Producers: Rob Cowan, Tony DeRosa-Grund, Peter Safran.
Screenplay: Chad Hayes, Carey W. Hayes.
Music: Joseph Bishara. Cinematography: John R. Leonetti.
Cast: Vera Farmiga, Patrick Wilson, Lili Taylor, Ron Livingston, Shanley Caswell, Hayley McFarland.

Fresh off the success of supernatural indie **Insidious**, director James Wan, intrigued by the real-life aspect of the story and by its sequels potential, launched his third horror franchise with **The Conjuring**, a haunting tale based on a case file of controversial demonologists Ed and Lorraine Warren (played here by Patrick Wilson and Vera Farmiga). So keen was Wan to stay close to the facts that he invited Lorraine (Ed died in 2006) to act as a consultant, and the Perron family to visit the set. With over 10,000 cases investigated, the Warren files are fertile ground for horror adaptations, yet it is Ed himself who, nearly twenty years before cameras rolled on the first film, had insisted on bringing this specific story to the screen first. Playing on genre tropes, with a succession of effective, scary set pieces, **The Conjuring** is the direct descendent of haunted house classics: Wan freely admits the influence of **The Haunting** or **The Sixth Sense** on the movie's tone and pacing, and of **The Amityville Horror** (incidentally a real-life case the Warrens looked into), most notably for the score. The ball gag from **The Changeling** is also referenced. So successful was the movie that it became the object of a lawsuit, in which the current owners of the actual house claimed it brought unwanted attention to the property. A 2016 follow-up, **The Conjuring 2**, relocated to London to focus on the infamous Enfield poltergeist (though interior scenes were filmed on a Los Angeles soundstage), and launched two spin-offs: **The Nun**, and **The Crooked Man**, both in the works at the time of writing. A spin-off of the first movie, haunted doll movie **Annabelle** (2014), received its own sequel in 2017.

## HAUNTER

Canada/France, 2013
Director: Vincenzo Natali. Producer: Steven Hoban.
Screenplay: Brian King. Music: Alex Khaskin.
Cinematography: Jon Joffin.
Cast: Abigail Breslin, Peter Outerbridge, Michelle Nolden, Stephen McHattie, Peter DaCunha, Samantha Weinstein.

Vincenzo Natali is an oddity in the genre. Best known for his stunning debut **Cube** (1997), the Guillermo del Toro-produced **Splice** (2010), and contributions to many popular television series, the Canadian filmmaker has authored a series of truly original, personal, yet wildly different movies, on a variety of budgets, for which he always retained final cut. By all accounts his most accessible film to date, **Haunter**, starring Abigail Breslin (**Little Miss Sunshine**), is a classical take on the ghost story, with a twist: the haunting is told from the point of view of the spirit. Described by its director as the love child of Ingmar Bergman and John Hughes, **Haunter**, which Natali admits embarking on because it would be easier to set up than his long-delayed projects, takes a leaf from **Groundhog Day**, as its lead character is condemned to relive the same Sunday with her family over and over again. Shot in 25 days on a tight budget, and minimalistic in its approach, the movie relies on ideas and smart re-imaginings of ghost story tropes, rather than special effects or scares. This approach proved difficult to sell on the heels of **The Woman in Black** and **Insidious: Chapter 2**, yet makes for an intriguing, refreshing watch for fans of the sub-genre.

## MAMA

Canada/Spain, 2013
Director: Andy Muschietti.
Producers: J. Miles Dale, Barbara Muschietti.
Screenplay: Neil Cross, Andy Muschietti, Barbara Muschietti.
Music: Fernando Velázquez. Cinematography: Antonio Riestra.
Cast: Jessica Chastain, Nikolaj Coster-Waldau,
Megan Charpentier, Isabelle Nélisse, Daniel Kash, Javier Botet.

Childhood staples — dolls, clowns, cribs — subverted into night-time terrors make up a sub-genre of their own, and writer-director Andy Muschietti, along with producer and co-writer Barbara Muschietti, tackled the mother of them all with **Mama**, a variation of sorts on Mexico's Llorona. Jessica Chastain plays Annabel, a free spirit with little maternal instinct, who finds herself having to care for her boyfriend's nieces after their father's dramatic demise. To complicate matters, the girls are quasi-feral due to a long stay alone in the woods, during which their only companion was an imaginary mother figure. This ghostly mummy appears to have followed them to their new home, and grows increasingly possessive as Annabel's bond with her charges deepens. Based on Muschietti's fantastic 2008 homonymous short, which caught the eye of feature executive producer Guillermo del Toro, **Mama** is at its best when playing on the inherent creepiness of its subject matter and keeping its ghost hidden in shadows, or merely hinted at. Muschietti's deft use of wide frames and long tracking shots makes for its most striking moments, such as when Annabel walks down the hallway while Mama, just out of sight, plays with the girls in the room next door. A look at the original short is highly recommended, as well as mesmerizing test footage of actor Javier Botet rehearsing Mama's jerky, disjointed movements.

## OCULUS

USA, 2013
Director: Mike Flanagan.
Producers: Marc D. Evans, Trevor Macy.
Screenplay: Mike Flanagan, Jeff Howard.
Music: The Newton Brothers. Cinematography: Michael Fimognari.
Cast: Karen Gillan, Brenton Thwaites, Katee Sackhoff, Rory Cochrane, Annalise Basso, Garrett Ryan.

**Absentia** director Mike Flanagan hit the mainstream and started a fruitful collaboration with frequent partners Intrepid Pictures and Blumhouse (which would continue through **Hush** and **Ouija: Origin of Evil**) on **Oculus**, a haunted mirror story starring Karen Gillan, Brenton Thwaites and Katee Sackhoff. Flanagan developed the story from a 2005 short he wrote and directed. Expanding into a feature this tale of one man standing in a room in front of a piece of glass turned out to be a challenge; initial ideas included an anthology of stories featuring the cursed mirror, which the filmmaker described as a 'portable Overlook', after the hotel from **The Shining**. The few first companies approached tried to convince him to use found footage, the popular trend in the wake of **Paranormal Activity**, but he wasn't convinced. The key to cracking the story ultimately came from the idea of making the protagonists siblings who disagree on the mirror's evil powers, then jumping between two different timelines, events from the past slowly informing what happens in the present. Learning lessons from **The Exorcist** and the works of Stephen King, the movie takes its time introducing these characters before delving into the supernatural. **Oculus** was remade in Bollywood in 2017 under the title **Dobaara: See Your Evil**.

## PEE MAK

Thailand, 2013
Director: Banjong Pisanthanakun. Producers: Jira Maligool, Chenchonnee Suntonsaratoon, Suwimon Techasupinun, Pran Thadaweerawutar, Vanridee Pongsittisak. Screenplay: Nontra Khumvong, Banjong Pisanthanakun, Chantavit Dhanasevi. Music: Chatchai Pongpraphaphan, Hualampong Riddim. Cinematography: Narupon Sohkkanapituk. Cast: Mario Maurer, Davika Hoorne, Kantapat Permpoonpatcharasuk, Nuttapong Chartpong, Wiwat Kongrasri, Pongsathorn Jongwilas.

The legend of Mae Nak, who died in childbirth and came back as a spirit to wait for her husband's return from war, is said to have been adapted for the small screen, big screen, stage and radio over a hundred times, including recent hits **Nang Nak** (1999) and **Ghost of Mae Nak** (2005). The vast majority of these versions have focused on the tragic figure of the woman; **Pee Mak**, however, blends laughs and scares as it follows the husband (Mario Maurer), unaware that his wife (Davika Hoorne) is a ghost. Writer-director Banjong Pisanthanakun (**Shutter**, **4bia**) sets his story in the 19th century, yet modernizes it with pop culture references and contemporary language. One of the main challenges of the script was to remain faithful and respectful of the legend (so popular it has a dedicated shrine), while altering the ending, adding characters (the unlucky husband's four goofy best friends), and balancing humour and light scares. **Pee Mak** became the highest-grossing film of all time in Thailand, thanks in no small part to word of mouth, and an effective social media campaign that included themed Harlem Shake and dance routine videos. For its Halloween festivities, Singapore's Sentosa theme park created an attraction based on the movie.

## RIGOR MORTIS

Hong Kong, 2013
Director: Juno Mak. Producers: Juno Mak, Takashi Shimizu.
Screenplay: Philip Yung, Jill Leung, Juno Mak.
Music: Nate Connelly. Cinematography: Ng Man-ching.
Cast: Chin Siu-ho, Anthony Chan, Kara Hui, Chung Fat,
Lo Hoi-pang, Richard Ng.

Musicians and thespians stepping behind the camera for vanity projects are a familiar phenomenon, but Hong Kong pop star Juno Mak's first foray into directing, **Rigor Mortis**, is of a different nature: a love letter to 1980s hopping-vampire (or *geung-si*, the original title of this movie) saga **Mr. Vampire**. Starring **Mr. Vampire** co-lead Chin Siu-ho as a fictional version of himself, the film focuses on a down-on-his-luck actor who moves into a rundown building after his wife leaves him, and is saved from suicide by neighbour and retired vampire hunter Yau (Anthony Chan). But his attempt has caught the attention of twin ghosts who haunt the building... If the plot isn't always easy to follow (or summarize), and the mythology may seem complex to anyone unfamiliar with Asian cinema, **Rigor Mortis** is however a visual feast, with stunning long-haired ghosts (likely inspired by producer Takashi Shimizu's **Ju-on** series), reanimated corpses, and buckets of blood. A slew of well-known character actors, including Chung Fat (**Mr. Vampire II**, **Encounters of the Spooky Kind**) and Richard Ng (**Mr. Vampire III**, **Detective Dee and the Mystery of the Phantom Flame**), bring life and dimension to the supporting roles. Less comedic than the movies it pays homage to, **Rigor Mortis** mixes themes of loss and regrets, and ends in a touching finale which shows what would have happened without the intervention of the supernatural.

## SOULMATE

UK, 2013
Director: Axelle Carolyn. Producer: Claire Otway.
Screenplay: Axelle Carolyn. Music: Christian Henson.
Cinematography: Sara Deane.
Cast: Anna Walton, Tom Wisdom, Tanya Myers, Nick Brimble, Emma Cleasby, Guy Armitage.

This author's first feature film as writer-director, gothic romance **Soulmate** was an attempted return to the old-fashioned British ghost story, with a twist on the traditional narrative. The story of Audrey (Anna Walton, **Hellboy II**), a widow who moves to the country only to discover the cottage she occupies is haunted, it stemmed from the question: What if you decided to stay in a haunted house and engage with its ghost? Shot in a holiday rental in the Brecon Beacons, Wales, **Soulmate** was inspired by quaint, isolated villages visited on a trip to the countryside, as well as by classics such as **The Ghost and Mrs. Muir** (1947). Most of the micro-budget was allocated to the shooting schedule, making sure the cast — Walton, Tom Wisdom (**Dominion**), Nick Brimble (**Robin Hood: Prince of Thieves**), Tanya Myers (**Control**) and canine star Anubis — had time to focus on their performances. In the UK, the movie fell afoul of the BBFC for its graphic depiction of a suicide attempt. After the ratings board required 16 seconds of cuts, which made the scene clumsy and, in this writer's eyes, glamorized self-harm by hiding its most painful consequences, the opening scene was removed altogether for the British release, which was then given a 15 certificate for 'strong violence and gore', despite the movie's very mild, psychological content.

## THE BABADOOK

Australia, 2014
Director: Jennifer Kent.
Producers: Kristina Ceyton, Kristian Moliere.
Screenplay: Jennifer Kent. Music: Jed Kurzel.
Cinematography: Radek Ladczuk.
Cast: Essie Davis, Noah Wiseman, Hayley McElhinney,
Daniel Henshall, Barbara West, Benjamin Winspear.

Australian actress-turned-writer-director Jennifer Kent pulled no punches with her first feature, supernatural sleeper hit **The Babadook**, which was lauded as 'terrifying' and 'disturbing' by the likes of William Friedkin and Stephen King. Everything, from the sharp editing and precise colour palette to the performances, comes together beautifully for this story of a mother (Essie Davis) and her six-year-old son (Noah Wiseman) fighting the Babadook, a creature mysteriously come to life from a children's book. **The Babadook** isn't shy about its metaphor: the supernatural monster threatening the protagonists' home is a clear reflection of the mother's breaking psyche. One of the rare movies, along with Lynne Ramsay's 2011 **We Need to Talk About Kevin**, to broach the taboo topic of a mother struggling to bond with her child, the tale was reportedly inspired by a friend of Kent's whose son was convinced he was being threatened by an invisible monster, and who would ask his mother to speak to the creature each night to placate it. The idea made its way into a 2005 short, **Monster**, which later grew into **The Babadook** (the name is derived from the Serb word for boogeyman). Played by art department assistant Tim Purcell, who scored the part after standing in for a camera test, the titular monster has since become an unlikely LGBTQ icon, used as a symbol for the 2016 Gay Pride month.

## THE CANAL

Ireland/UK, 2014
Director: Ivan Kavanagh.
Producer: AnneMarie Naughton.
Screenplay: Ivan Kavanagh.
Music: Ceiri Torjussen.
Cinematography: Piers McGrail.
Cast: Rupert Evans, Antonia Campbell-Hughes, Hannah Hoekstra, Kelly Byrne, Steve Oram, Calum Heath.

A cinema archivist (Rupert Evans) moves with his family to an old house near a canal, and starts obsessing over the possibility of his wife cheating on him. In parallel, he discovers 1902 crime scene footage showing a murder that took place in his home. **The Canal** may share tonal and story similarities with Scott Derrickson's 2012 **Sinister**, but explores the dark side of its lead character's psyche, and his descent into madness. Irish writer and director Ivan Kavanagh, whose first horror movie, **Tin Can Man** (2008), was made for under 1,000 euros, gathered financing for this picture through the Irish Film Board and Ireland's tax incentive program. Exploring various film formats — the old footage is recreated using a 1915 hand-cranked Universal camera with black and white 35mm film — and playing with horror tropes, he found inspiration in movies such as **Suspiria** (1977), **Don't Look Now** (1973) and **Eyes Wide Shut** (1999), as well as the works of early pioneers of the medium. The result is a visual feast filled with creepy imagery, complemented by elaborate sound design — all sound effects were recorded specifically for the movie (rather than the typical low-budget approach of relying on a library).

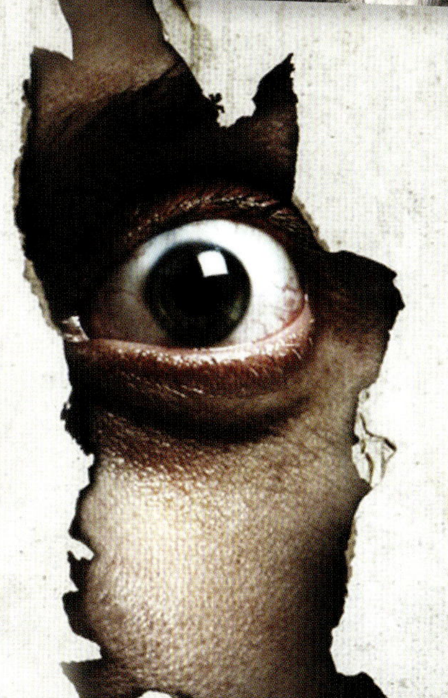

## HOUSEBOUND

New Zealand, 2014
Director: Gerard Johnstone. Producer: Luke Sharpe. Screenplay: Gerard Johnstone. Music: Mahuia Bridgman-Cooper. Cinematography: Simon Riera. Cast: Morgana O'Reilly, Rima Te Wiata, Glen-Paul Waru, Ross Harper, Cameron Rhodes, Ryan Lampp.

A haunted house mystery brings a family together in **Housebound**, the story of Kylie (Morgana O'Reilly), who gets sentenced to house arrest in the home where she grew up, with her mother (Rima Te Wiata) and stepfather (Ross Harper), and starts investigating various occurrences hinting at possible paranormal activity. Writer, director and editor of this dark comedy, newcomer Gerard Johnstone (twice winner of the New Zealand 48 Hours film competition, and co-creator of comedy series **The Jaquie Brown Diaries**, 2008) intended the movie to be amongst the few local productions to be commercially profitable, and had the idea come to him after watching an episode of the BBC's *Ghost Hunters*. Further inspiration came from classics such as **The Legend of Hell House**, **The Changeling**, or **The Haunting**, as well as **Clue**, **The Frighteners** and *Scooby-Doo*, yet the movie has its own unique tone and takes unexpected twists. The filmmaker extensively reworked and partly reshot the middle section after the initial cut left him unsatisfied. Much like **What We Do in the Shadows**, another acclaimed comedy horror from New Zealand released the same year, **Housebound**, although less goofy, relies heavily on its character dynamics and its knowing dissection of the sub genre.

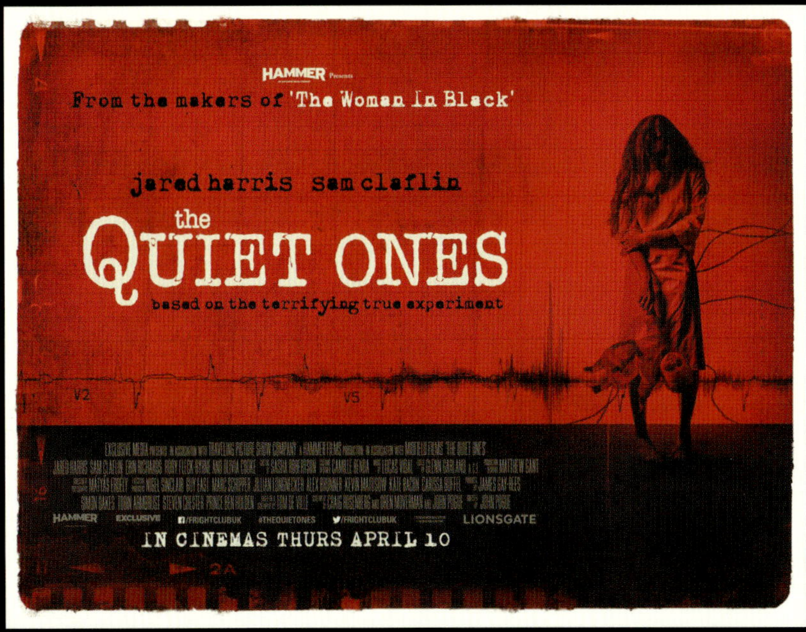


## THE QUIET ONES

USA/UK, 2014
Director: John Pogue.
Producers: Tobin Armbrust, James Gay-Rees, Ben Holden, Steven Chester Prince, Simon Oakes.
Screenplay: Craig Rosenberg, Oren Moverman, John Pogue.
Music: Lucas Vidal.
Cinematography: Mátyás Erdély.
Cast: Jared Harris, Sam Claflin, Erin Richards, Olivia Cooke, Laurie Calvert, Rory Fleck Byrne.

Following a major box office hit is no easy task, and after **The Woman in Black**, Hammer Film Productions decided to bet on another ghost story, this time inspired by actual events. Conducted in Toronto in 1972, the Philip Experiment, as it is known, saw a group of scientists attempt to conjure a poltergeist from Philip Aylesford, a character they created, in order to prove that the supernatural is no more than a manifestation of the human mind. In **The Quiet Ones**, a college professor (Jared Harris) studies a young girl (Olivia Cooke) haunted by a malevolent spirit, hoping to show that the ghost is created by her own negative energy. Yet beyond the fundamentals of the experiment, details of this Nigel Kneale-influenced story are entirely fictional; even the photographs shown in the end credits are fake, enacted by actors. While initial drafts centered on the team creating a ghost, director John Pogue, who wrote 2002's **Ghost Ship** and helmed 2011's **Quarantine 2: Terminal**, shifted the focus to the relationship between Harris and Cooke's characters, and the unusual methods through which the scientist plans to cure his test subject. Lensed in Oxford over the summer of 2012, **The Quiet Ones** was a commercial disappointment for Hammer, who would then turn their attention to the sequel to **The Woman in Black**.

## CRIMSON PEAK

USA/Canada, 2015
Director: Guillermo del Toro. Producers: Guillermo del Toro, Callum Greene, Jon Jashni, Thomas Tull.
Screenplay: Guillermo del Toro, Matthew Robbins.
Music: Fernando Velázquez. Cinematography: Dan Laustsen.
Cast: Mia Wasikowska, Jessica Chastain, Tom Hiddleston, Charlie Hunnam, Jim Beaver, Burn Gorman.

'It's not a ghost story, it's a story with ghosts in it', says Mia Wasikowska's character of her writing, incidentally encapsulating what Guillermo del Toro set out to achieve with **Crimson Peak**. Reviving the old-fashioned Gothic romance, with its crumbling ruins, ancient curses, and heroines in distress, while also paying homage to classic ghost stories (**The Innocents**, **The Changeling**, the works of M.R. James), del Toro focuses on Edith (Wasikowska), a headstrong American novelist who falls for mysterious British aristocrat Sir Thomas Sharpe (Tom Hiddleston). As Sharpe brings his young bride back to his English mansion, a house that bleeds red clay, he grows distant, focusing his time on his business and his intimidating sister (Jessica Chastain); while Edith discovers that the ghosts trapped inside Crimson Peak aren't the house's greatest danger. Steeped in bright colours, in subtle reference to Argento and Bava, **Crimson Peak** is a visual feast. Much of its blockbuster budget was allocated to its incredibly ornate production design, including the construction in intricate detail of all three stories of the titular house at Pinewood Toronto Studios. The ghosts themselves, computer-enhanced yet played by frequent del Toro collaborators Doug Jones and Javier Botet, look impressive, especially an ethereal apparition made of floating dust in sunlight.

## TALES OF HALLOWEEN

USA, 2015
Directors: Darren Lynn Bousman, Axelle Carolyn, Adam Gierasch, Andrew Kasch & John Skipp, Neil Marshall, Lucky McKee, Mike Mendez, Dave Parker Ryan Schifrin, Paul Solet.
Producers: Axelle Carolyn, Mike Mendez, Shaked Berenson, Patrick Ewald.
Segment 'Grim Grinning Ghost': Screenplay: Axelle Carolyn.
Music: Christian Henson. Cast: Alex Essoe, Lin Shaye, Liesel Hanson, V Nixie, Barbara Crampton, Lisa Marie.

A collection of ten stories from eleven directors, set in the same town on Halloween night, **Tales of Halloween**, created by this author, who co-produced with director Mike Mendez (**The Gravedancers**) and Epic Pictures, was born from a desire to celebrate the large community of filmmakers and fans who are bound by a common love for the horror genre and the Halloween season. The tone, therefore, errs more towards spooky fun than dark, serious scares. Produced like a feature, with all shorts filmed back-to-back over the course of six weeks in Los Angeles (as opposed to letting separate teams shoot independently and on their own schedule, as per **The ABCs of Death** or the **V/H/S** series), the movie was a labour of love for all involved, developed collectively by the filmmakers, who helped and advised each other whenever needed. This writer's segment — **Grim Grinning Ghost**, starring Alex Essoe (**Starry Eyes**) and Lin Shaye (**Insidious**), with cameos from Stuart Gordon, Mick Garris, Lisa Marie, Barbara Crampton, and canine thespian Anubis — tells a quick ghost story ending in a jump scare, inspired by the hitchhiking ghosts of the Disneyland Haunted Mansion, and by Disney's **The Legend of Sleepy Hollow** (1949).

## WE ARE STILL HERE

USA, 2015
Director: Ted Geoghegan. Producer: Travis Stevens.
Screenplay: Ted Geoghegan. Music: Wojciech Golczewski.
Cinematography: Karim Hussain.
Cast: Barbara Crampton, Andrew Sensenig, Lisa Marie, Larry Fessenden, Monte Markham, Susan Gibney.

After the loss of their son Bobby, Anne and Paul Sacchetti (Barbara Crampton and Andrew Sensenig) move to a house in the New England countryside, where she starts feeling Bobby's presence. Silhouettes are seen in the basement, which is inexplicably hot and smells of smoke. The house has a dark history, and when the locals tell them it needs a family, it sounds less like a welcome than a threat... As the synopsis may suggest, writer and publicist Ted Geoghegan's feature-length directorial debut **We Are Still Here** is a throwback to seventies horror, wearing its influences — **The Changeling**, the works of Lucio Fulci — on its blood-stained sleeves. On this rather simple premise, Geoghegan builds a rich mythology for his ghostly family, providing ample room for twists and revelations, and hosts a group of relatable, grown-up characters (Larry Fessenden and **Ed Wood**'s Lisa Marie round up the cast). The production design, tone and pace all channel the seventies, and the movie relies heavily on atmosphere and practical effects; the scene in which the men attempt a séance and end up possessed by one of the house's spirits, for example, is surprisingly effective despite being set in daylight, with minimal music, and entirely performance-based.

## BACKTRACK

Australia/UK/United Arab Emirates, 2016
Director: Michael Petroni.
Producers: Antonia Barnard, Jamie Hilton, Michael Petroni.
Screenplay: Michael Petroni. Music: Dale Cornelius.
Cinematography: Stefan Duscio.
Cast: Adrien Brody, Jenni Baird, Bruce Spence,
Greg Poppleton, Barbara Gouskos, Jill McKay.

Adrien Brody sees dead people in this rare Australian contribution to the genre. After the death of his daughter, a psychiatrist is plagued by nightmares and apparitions, leaving him clues to a mystery seemingly linked to past events of his childhood and to the train tracks near his home town. Shifting from psychological drama to supernatural investigation, **Backtrack** is an exploration of Brody's character as he deals with grief, guilt, and repressed memories. Perfectly pleasant if rather derivative — **The Sixth Sense** is first to come to mind, but familiar situations abound — writer-director Michael Petroni's mystery offers a fair share of spookiness, with some effective scares (the woman at the train station, the leaning ghost), moody photography, and an intrigue which keeps one guessing until its somewhat implausible but nonetheless satisfying resolution. Brody is his usual brooding self, while Sam Neill, playing his mentor, oozes creepiness. Strangely enough given the movie's gloomy tone, Petroni, whose writing credits include **Queen of the Damned**, a **Narnia** sequel and the adaptation of **The Book Thief**, had his first break in stand-up comedy. His real-life wife, Australian actress Jenni Baird (**The 4400**, **A Place to Call Home**), appears as Brody's on-screen spouse.

## DEAREST SISTER

Laos/Estonia/France, 2016
Director: Mattie Do.
Producers: Mattie Do, Christopher Larsen, Helen Lohmus, Annick Mahnert, Sten Saluveer, Douangmany Soliphanh.
Screenplay: Christopher Larsen. Music: Sten Sheripov.
Cinematography: Mart Ratassepp.
Cast: Amphaiphun Phommapunya, Vilouna Phetmany, Tambet Tuisk, Manivanh Boulom, Yannawoutthi Chanthalungsy, Maluly Chanthalangsy.

Laos' first ever submission to the Academy Awards in the foreign language category, **Dearest Sister** is the second feature from local filmmaker Mattie Do after **Chanthaly** (2013), which had the distinction of not only being the country's first female-helmed picture, but also its first horror movie. **Dearest Sister** tells the story of a young girl who travels from her village to the city to help out her cousin, who seems to have suddenly gained the ability to communicate with the dead while her sight mysteriously declined. Besides its supernatural aspects, the movie makes a point of depicting life in Laos, particularly from the point of view of women. The look of the blackened, ashy spirits haunting the protagonists was derived from the fact that the prevalent custom for funerals in the country is cremation. Do, a Los Angeles native who worked in the U.S. and Europe before moving to Vientiane, found the industry and infrastructure non-existent in Laos. Without any formal filmmaking training, she had to figure out every aspect of the process. With funding obtained in Cannes and through crowd-funding, and co-production help from France and Estonia, this micro-budget effort premiered at Austin's Fantastic Fest before spreading the word of Lao horror around the world.

## LIGHTS OUT

USA, 2016
Director: David F. Sandberg. Producers: Lawrence Grey, Eric Heisserer, James Wan. Screenplay: Eric Heisserer. Music: Benjamin Wallfisch. Cinematography: Marc Spicer. Cast: Teresa Palmer, Gabriel Bateman, Alexander DiPersia, Billy Burke, Maria Bello, Alicia Vela-Bailey.

Swedish director David F. Sandberg genuinely lived the Hollywood dream when in 2013, **Lights Out**, a two-minute short he had made with his wife Lotta Losten for a short film contest suddenly went viral, attracting the interest of every producer in Los Angeles. One of these turned out to be horror meister James Wan with his new company Atomic Monster, who offered to develop a feature version of the story, propelling Sandberg overnight from zero-budget, no-crew shorts, to a $5 million movie released on 2,835 screens throughout the U.S. The short film introduced the world to a creature only visible in the shadows, and disappearing in the light. Developing a 90-page story on such a slim basis required the addition of a backstory for the monster — now known as the ghost of a woman called Diana — strong rules for the supernatural, and themes of family and mental illness. Losten, who starred in the original, appears in the movie's opening sequence. **Lights Out** originally ended with the classic suggestion that evil may not have died, but the scene was cut following a test screening where the audience argued that it rendered useless the sacrifice of a major character.

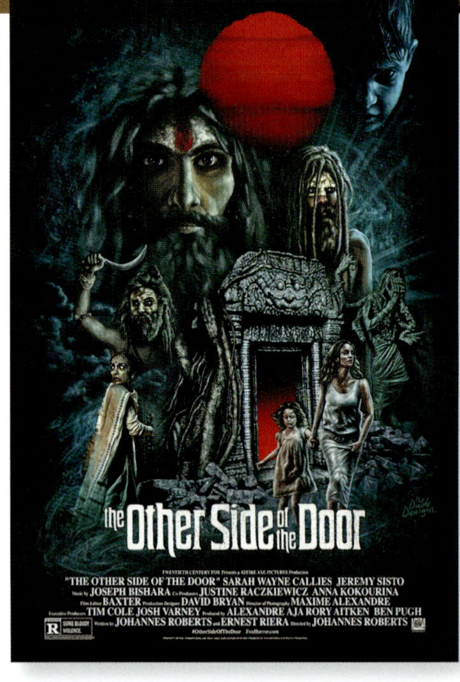


## THE OTHER SIDE OF THE DOOR

UK/Germany/USA, 2016
Director: Johannes Roberts.
Producers: Rory Aitken, Alexandre Aja, Ben Pugh.
Screenplay: Johannes Roberts, Ernest Riera.
Music: Joseph Bishara. Cinematography: Maxime Alexandre.
Cast: Sarah Wayne Callies, Jeremy Sisto, Sofia Rosinsky,
Logan Creran, Suchitra Pillai, Javier Botet.

Whenever a Western picture is shot in India, the culture shock felt by the characters on screen is experienced to some degree by the cast and crew. The same can be said of **The Other Side of the Door**, an American-British co-production, the story of grieving parents (Sarah Wayne Callies and Jeremy Sisto) who unleash evil when they break a crucial rule upon being offered the chance to say one last goodbye to their dead son. Filmed in Mumbai (including at Rudyard Kipling's former house), this Indian **Pet Sematary**, directed by Johannes Roberts (**47 Meters Down**, 2017; **The Strangers: Prey at Night**, 2018), who co-wrote with frequent collaborator Ernest Riera, captures the alienating, mad and frantic beauty of its location, giving this ghost story a unique flavor. Roberts and producer Alexandre Aja (**The Hills Have Eyes**, 2006) made sure depictions of beliefs and traditions remained faithful, while avoiding naming deities or customs which may have offended or otherwise worried the locals. The Aghori — or death cult — for instance are based on an existing population who live in burial grounds and ritualistically cover themselves with ashes, but are played by actors, as approaching the real-life cult members would have made the Indian crew uneasy. Also of note is the soundtrack from horror composer Joseph Bishara (**Insidious**).

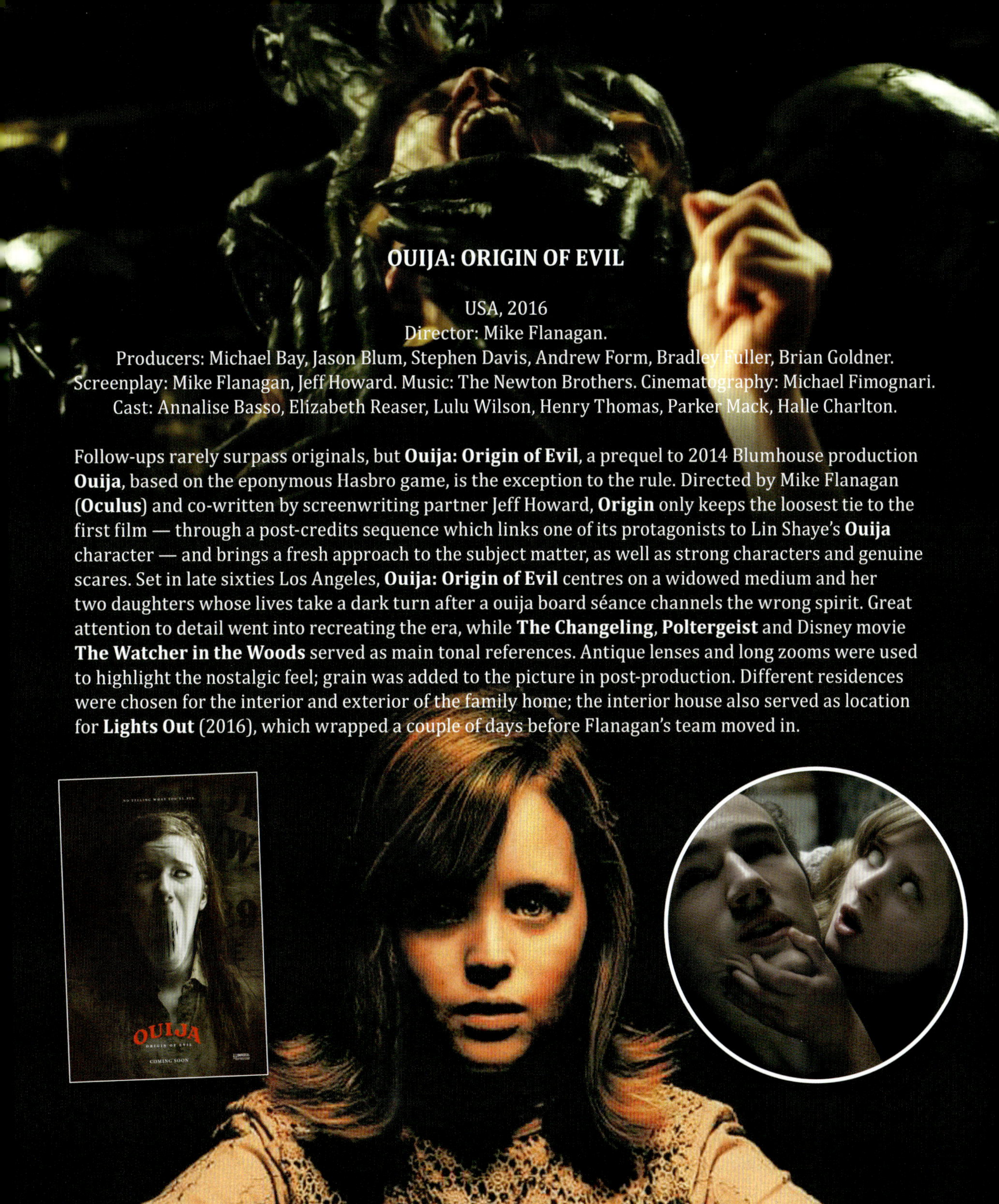

## OUIJA: ORIGIN OF EVIL

USA, 2016
Director: Mike Flanagan.
Producers: Michael Bay, Jason Blum, Stephen Davis, Andrew Form, Bradley Fuller, Brian Goldner.
Screenplay: Mike Flanagan, Jeff Howard. Music: The Newton Brothers. Cinematography: Michael Fimognari.
Cast: Annalise Basso, Elizabeth Reaser, Lulu Wilson, Henry Thomas, Parker Mack, Halle Charlton.

Follow-ups rarely surpass originals, but **Ouija: Origin of Evil**, a prequel to 2014 Blumhouse production **Ouija**, based on the eponymous Hasbro game, is the exception to the rule. Directed by Mike Flanagan (**Oculus**) and co-written by screenwriting partner Jeff Howard, **Origin** only keeps the loosest tie to the first film — through a post-credits sequence which links one of its protagonists to Lin Shaye's **Ouija** character — and brings a fresh approach to the subject matter, as well as strong characters and genuine scares. Set in late sixties Los Angeles, **Ouija: Origin of Evil** centres on a widowed medium and her two daughters whose lives take a dark turn after a ouija board séance channels the wrong spirit. Great attention to detail went into recreating the era, while **The Changeling**, **Poltergeist** and Disney movie **The Watcher in the Woods** served as main tonal references. Antique lenses and long zooms were used to highlight the nostalgic feel; grain was added to the picture in post-production. Different residences were chosen for the interior and exterior of the family home; the interior house also served as location for **Lights Out** (2016), which wrapped a couple of days before Flanagan's team moved in.

## PHANTOM OF THE THEATRE

China, 2016
Director: Raymond Yip.
Producers: Manfred Wong, Ruby Lin, Jay Wei, Jeffrey Chan.
Screenplay: Manfred Wong, Yang Mei Yuan, Li Jing Ling.
Music: Yu Peng. Cinematography: Michael Tsui.
Cast: Ruby Lin, Tony Yang, Simon Yam, Jing Gangshan,
Huang Hung, Lin Jiang Guo.

Raymond Yip's **Phantom of the Theatre** is something of an aberration in the Chinese film landscape. Censorship laws dictate that movies promoting 'cults or superstitions' be prohibited, a measure carried out with more or less severity over the last few decades, leading to movies as diverse as **Crimson Peak** or the **Ghostbusters** remake to be banned on the territory. It is remarkable then that a big budget, lavish production would tell this Gaston Leroux-inspired story set in 1930s Shanghai, in which a filmmaker (Tony Yang) decides to shoot a movie in an old theatre reputedly haunted by the vengeful souls of performers who died thirteen years before in a suspicious fire. The movie spirals into an improbable tale of romance and intrigue, but supernatural elements — moonlit see-through apparitions, spontaneous combustion — abound in the first half. Some turn out to be dreams, or have semi-rational explanations (as did Yip's not-so-haunted house in **The House That Never Dies**, 2014); others are clearly otherworldly and carefully surrounded by dialogue lines such as, 'There's no such things as ghosts', or the more puzzling, 'Only the guilty are afraid of ghosts'. An exercise in side-stepping the law, **Phantom of the Theatre** is hardly subtle or frightening, yet worth a watch for its lush production design and exotic setting.

## SADAKO VS KAYAKO

Japan, 2016
Director: Kôji Shiraishi. Producers: Reiko Imayasu, Toshinori Yamaguchi, Mikihiko Hirata.
Screenplay: Kôji Shiraishi. Music: Kôji Endô.
Cinematography: Hidetoshi Shinomiya.
Cast: Mizuki Yamamoto, Tina Tamashiro, Aimi Satsukawa, Misato Tanaka, Masahiro Kômoto, Masanobu Andô.

What's better than one legendary long-haired, creepy vengeful ghost? Sadako (Elly Nanami, seventh actress in the part) from the **Ring** saga faces off against **The Grudge**'s Kayako (Runa Endo) when a girl (Aimi Satsukawa) accidentally watches the doomed videotape and figures the only way to break the curse is to pit one *yurei* against another. In the great tradition of horror villain crossovers (**Freddy Vs Jason**, **King Kong Vs Godzilla**, **Frankenstein Meets the Wolf Man**...), **Sadako Vs Kayako** writer and director Kōji Shiraishi (**Noroi: The Curse**, 2005) brings a much-needed level of self-awareness and humour — the characters study urban legends, ghosts and cursed tapes at university — to the paper-thin plot, which started out as a 2015 April Fool's joke announcement. Fans reacted to the concept with such enthusiasm that the studios owning the properties, Kadokawa and NBC Universal, banded together and green lit the picture in December of the same year. Released within months of **Rings**, the second sequel to Gore Verbinski's **The Ring**, **Sadako Vs Kayako** is certainly the fan favourite of the two, and was promoted with the appropriate tongue in cheek quality, with Sadako throwing the first pitch at a baseball game, and beauty masks with the ghosts' faces as part of the merchandising.

## GHOST STORIES

UK, 2017
Directors: Jeremy Dyson, Andy Nyman.
Producers: Robin Gutch, Claire Jones.
Screenplay: Jeremy Dyson, Andy Nyman.
Music: Haim Frank Ilfman.
Cinematography: Ole Bratt Birkeland.
Cast: Andy Nyman, Martin Freeman, Paul Whitehouse, Alex Lawther, Paul Warren, Kobna Holdbrook-Smith.

Adapted from their Olivier-nominated stage play, which premiered in 2010 in Liverpool before sold-out performances in the London West End, Toronto and Australia, actor-writer Andy Nyman and *League of Gentlemen* alum Jeremy Dyson's **Ghost Stories** turns the anthology format of the play into a coherent feature, with equally terrifying results. Adding in an entirely new wraparound story following a paranormal debunker (Nyman) investigating three previously unsolved cases (revolving around a night watchman, a teenage driver and a businessman whose wife is pregnant — and for which the movie sticks fairly close to the original material), the movie gains emotional and philosophical depth, exploring matters of faith, hope and mental health. The most striking line of the film, 'the brain sees what it wants to see' — particularly relevant given Nyman's background as a magician and mentalist — leads to an unexpectedly bleak ending. Unlike other contemporary haunted house movies (**The Conjuring** series, **The Woman in Black**), **Ghost Stories** steers clear of Gothic trappings, instead opting for a grittier look reminiscent of British seventies horror. Clearly inspired by Amicus, Tigon, or the works of Nigel Kneale, it wears its influences on its sleeve, with subtle nods to classics betraying its creators' passion for the genre.

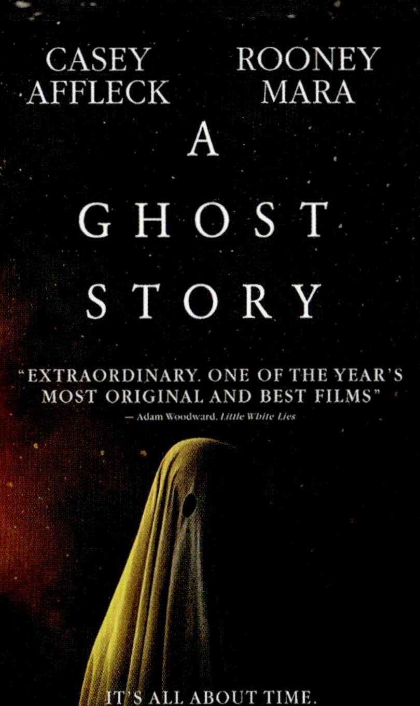

## A GHOST STORY

USA, 2017
Director: David Lowery.
Producers: Adam Donaghey, Toby Halbrooks, James M. Johnston.
Screenplay: David Lowery. Music: Daniel Hart.
Cinematography: Andrew Droz Palermo.
Cast: Casey Affleck, Rooney Mara, McColm Cephas Jr., Kenneisha Thompson, Grover Coulson, Liz Cardenas.

Casey Affleck wears a Charlie Brown-style white sheet to portray a melancholy ghost in **A Ghost Story**, writer-director David Lowery's meditation on grief, belonging, and the meaninglessness of existence. Filming in Texas in the summer of 2016, days after wrapping production on Disney tentpole **Pete's Dragon**, with **Ain't Them Bodies Saint** co-stars Affleck and Rooney Mara and minimal crew, Lowery kept his self-funded, experimental project on the lowdown to give himself the chance to fail, should the concept — a white-clad ghost silently watches his wife grieve his death — prove too abstract to work on screen. And indeed, **A Ghost Story** has divided audiences with its bold and earnest choices and its succession of long, mostly static, beautifully lit Polaroid-framed shots; a scene in which Mara angrily devours a pie over five long minutes has in turn been described as heartbreaking or interminable. The ghost, his sheet shaped by a hoop skirt and petticoats and weighted to remain in place, moves eerily slowly; a decision forced by the dramatic emphasis the outfit gave to each of Affleck's gestures. With the exception of a few pick-up shots, the actor insisted on playing the character himself in each scene, despite being covered head to toe.

## THE LODGERS

Ireland, 2017
Director: Brian O'Malley.
Producers: Julianne Forde, Ruth Treacy. Screenplay: David Turpin.
Music: Kevin Murphy, Stephen Shannon, David Turpin.
Cinematography: Richard Kendrick.
Cast: Charlotte Vega, David Bradley, Moe Dunford,
Bill Milner, Eugene Simon, Deirdre O'Kane.

Irish literature professor and composer turned screenwriter David Turpin (also scoring the picture) sees his first script produced with this tale of twins Rachel and Edward (Charlotte Vega and Bill Milner), who hide a terrible family secret in their dilapidated mansion on the outskirts of a small Irish village. Directed by Brian O'Malley (**Let Us Prey**), **The Lodgers** was filmed on location at Loftus Hall, a 700-year-old mansion in South East Ireland, known for its history of supernatural happenings. The stunning setting, crucial to the atmosphere and themes of the piece — the idea of the past infringing on the present — had to be dressed with props, but otherwise offered the perfect backdrop with its faded wallpapers, cracked windows and peeling paint; although it presented its own challenges, as the filmmaking crew were aware any walls or ceilings could collapse at any moment if leaned against or prodded, and only one person at a time would be allowed upstairs. Tragic and elegant, and deliberately steering clear of gory excesses and jump scares, **The Lodgers** is closer to **The Innocents** or **The Duke of Burgundy**, O'Malley's chief inspirations, than to recent hits such as **The Conjuring** or **The Woman in Black**.

## WINCHESTER

Australia/USA, 2018
Directors: The Spierig Brothers [Michael Spierig, Peter Spierig].
Producers: Tim McGahan, Brett Tomberlin.
Screenplay: Tom Vaughan, The Spierig Brothers [Michael Spierig, Peter Spierig].
Music: Peter Spierig. Cinematography: Ben Nott.
Cast: Helen Mirren, Sarah Snook, Finn Scicluna-O'Prey,
Jason Clarke, Angus Sampson, Laura Brent.

Originally developed by Hammer Films, American-Australian production **Winchester: The House That Ghosts Built** follows psychologist Eric Price (Jason Clarke), dispatched by the famed rifle company's board of directors to evaluate the mental health of Sarah Winchester, heiress to the company fortune, who believes her home to be haunted. Soon enough, things — and special effects — go bump in the night. Directed by Australian brothers Michael and Peter Spierig (**Undead**, 2003; **Jigsaw**, 2017), **Winchester** is mainly remarkable for the feat of drawing Academy Award winner Helen Mirren to a horror movie, and for being set and partially shot at the sprawling, fantastical Winchester House, in San Jose, California; a building Sarah Winchester expanded non-stop night and day for thirty-eight years, reportedly in the hopes of appeasing the spirits of those killed by the weapons sold by her late husband's company. The abode, known today as the Winchester Mystery House, boasts roughly 161 rooms, 17 chimneys, 47 fireplaces, two basements, three elevators, and thousands of windows, some of which in ceilings or opening onto walls. So complicated is its layout that each production unit was assigned a tour guide, to make sure no one got lost; though most of the filming took place in painstakingly recreated sets on a Melbourne soundstage. The mansion also inspired Stephen King's 2002 ABC miniseries **Rose Red**, though it was filmed on location in the Seattle area.

# INDEX OF FILM TITLES

Page references in **bold** refer exclusively to illustrations.